A Love for Learning: Motivation and the Gifted Child

Carol Strip Whitney, Ph.D.
with Gretchen Hirsch

Great Potential Press™

Copy editing: Jennifer Ault
Interior design: The Printed Page
Cover design:

Published by Great Potential Press, Inc.
P.O. Box 5057
Scottsdale, AZ 85261
Printed on recycled paper
© 2007 by Great Potential Press

11 10 09 08 07   5 4 3 2 1

Library of Congress Cataloging-in-Publication Data

Whitney, Carol Strip, 1945-
  A love for learning : motivation and the gifted child / Carol Strip Whitney
with Gretchen Hirsch.
      p. cm.
  Includes bibliographical references and index.
  ISBN-13: 978-0-910707-80-0 (pbk.)
  ISBN-10: 0-910707-80-4 (pbk.)
  1. Gifted children—Education (Elementary) 2. Education, Elementary—
Parent participation. I. Hirsch, Gretchen. II. Title.
  LC3993.22.W48 2007
  371.95—dc22
                          2007001832

Dedication

This book is dedicated to the memory of my beloved parents,
Harold and Marion Gillespie,
who motivated me to be all that I am today,
and to my many students,
who help keep that motivation alive every day.

Acknowledgments

Carol Strip Whitney, Ph.D., would like to acknowledge:

My husband, Richard Whitney, M.D., for the encouragement and everyday support of this book. My brother and sister-in-law, Dr. Gary and Elaine Gillespie, and their children, Brian, Julie, and Angie, gave sincere support. My daughter, Julie, her husband Mike, and their three beautiful daughters became an inspiration for nurturing the next generation to its fullest degree.

Kim Henderson, my principal and colleague, is the model administrator in the Classroom that Works. I know that her support for our program makes a difference every day. My gifted coordinator, Nancy Pusateri, has encouraged me, along with my wonderful staff of teachers. Sincere thanks to Suzanne Van Schaik and her gifted son, Michael, for their Story of Hope as a light to others. All of my graduate teachers from The Ohio State University continue to instill in me new knowledge and wisdom. And finally, my students are everyday inspirations for doing all that is good. Our future lies in their hands.

My heartfelt appreciation also to a woman of stature, knowledge, and wisdom, Dr. Joanne Rand Whitmore Schwartz, who so unselfishly served as a "silent partner" throughout the labors of this book.

Gretchen Hirsch would like to thank:

Literary agents Sheree Bykofsky and Janet Rosen, for their encouragement and assistance.

Jim Webb and Janet Gore and all the staff at Great Potential Press for their expertise and insistence that each book be the best it can be.

Sheila Lewis, for her always-on-target and very practical contributions.

My family—Tony, Stew and Lisa, Tobey and Scott—for listening and supporting me throughout this project.

Tom, Tyler, Trevor, and Amanda Hirsch and Ryan Huntley for their guidance through the world of smart children today.

Joanne Rand Whitmore Schwartz, Ph.D., for her kindness, insightful analysis, and never-failing good humor.

Contents

Foreword . . . . **xi**

Preface . . . . **xv**
    Positive trends xv
    New schools, new ideas xvi
    Grouping options xvii
    Summers off? No more xviii
    Follow the money xviii
    Value-added programs xix

Section I. The Seeds of Motivation 1

Chapter 1. The Turn-Off Effect **3**
    Losing Jane 3
    Who's gifted, and why does it matter? 4
    The issues facing schools and teachers 9
    State standards and *No Child Left Behind* 10
    What's so bad about elitism? 14
    Intelligences and giftedness 15
    Alternatives to demotivation 17
    The challenge 21
    In summary 22

Chapter 2. A 360-Degree Look at Motivation **23**
    What motivates a gifted student? 24
    Theories of motivation 25
    Intrinsic or extrinsic motivation: What works? 30
    Factors that impede intrinsic motivation 33
    Motivation-busters in our classrooms 35
    What lack of motivation looks like 37
    Is it underachievement? Or something else? 38
    An unexpected problem: Lack of learning skills 40
    Recovering motivation 42
    The gifted student's optimal classroom 43
    In summary 44

Section II. When Motivation Disappears:
Looking for Causes 47

Chapter 3. Physical Reasons for Loss of Motivation. . . 49
Vision problems 49
Hearing problems. 51
Learning disabilities: Visual and auditory processing disorders . 53
Reading disorders. 56
Case Study: Gareth 58
Attention Deficit Hyperactivity Disorder 60
Identification: Why does it matter? 63
Another viewpoint 65
Success factors 66
The enigma of identification 68
In summary 71

Chapter 4. Emotional Reasons for Loss of Motivation . 73
The consequences of fear 74
Depression 80
In summary 83

Chapter 5. Social Reasons for Loss of Motivation. . . . 85
Poverty 86
Complicated families 88
Friendships 92
In summary 95

Chapter 6. School Reasons for Loss of Motivation . . . 97
The old school 97
Differentiating instruction 100
The politics of giftedness. 105
The child and the teacher 108
In summary 110

Section III. Enhancing Motivation 111

Chapter 7. The Four C's in Action. 113
Sailing the C's. 113
Schools, teachers, and flow. 115
In summary 117

Chapter 8. Creating Challenge. 119
Let them be with others like them 119
Encourage them to excel, but not to be perfect 124
Encourage them to take risks and enjoy rewards 125
Build their resilience. 128

Provide them with mentors 130
In summary 132

Chapter 9. Creating Control. 133
A sound mind in a sound body. 135
Skills for living 138
The joys of solving problems. 145
In summary 146

Chapter 10. Creating Commitment 149
Tie investigations to real life and let students plunge in . . 149
Assess and grade fairly 151
Help children understand how grades relate to life goals . . 155
Modeling commitment 156
In summary 158

Chapter 11. Creating Compassion 159
Where are my friends?. 160
Issues with introverts 164
Dumbing down and fitting in 167
Dealing with taunting and bullying. 169
In summary 172

Section IV. Special Issues in Motivation 173

Chapter 12. The Classroom that Works. 175
Education for the future 175
An unexpected need. 181
Thoughts for teachers 182
...[S]he left her signature upon us... . . . . ***183***
In summary 183

Chapter 13. Motivating Every Student:
Who's in the Classroom? 185
The need for teacher diversity 186
Boys and girls together. 190
Boys and girls not together. 193
Who's in the home school classroom? 194
In summary 196

Chapter 14. Questions and Answers 197

Chapter 15. Parent to Parent: A Story of Hope 207
An easy start. 208
Off to school 209
A problem emerges 210
A roller coaster year 211

Uncertainty and a dip in motivation 212
Things get tougher... 212
...and tougher. 214
A disheartening change 214
An eye-opening conference 215
After advocacy 217
Some final words 217

Endnotes **221**

Additional Resources for Parents and Teachers **227**
Books. 227
Websites 228

References. **231**

Index **237**

About the Authors **241**

Foreword

Parenting can be surprisingly challenging, despite whatever instincts parents may have about how to be a child's first teacher and guide to optimal development. Likewise, teaching is always more challenging and complex than might be expected, as teachers face the wide diversity and complexity of individual students in each class. No job is more important than these two, because they contribute to the evolving futures of our society and world. Yet there are few resources available to guide parents on their journey, and teachers must search for resources to inform them about effective practices with exceptional students for whom they've had little or no preparation. Even though there has been substantial research conducted about developmental exceptionalities such as gifted students, most research results are reported in journals and books that are not typically referenced by parents and teachers in their efforts to find practical solutions to the problems they face.

This book is an outstanding resource for both parents and teachers that will empower them to enhance the motivation and academic achievement of gifted and talented students. Basing their work on solid research findings, the authors have translated a well-substantiated body of knowledge into practical ways of understanding and working with motivational issues that many intellectually gifted students experience. Most of us have general knowledge of what to expect of children at various ages and how to best guide their development, but information to help us understand those who deviate significantly from what is typical is often difficult to acquire. It seems that the educational needs of disabled students are more easily recognized and better served than those who are exceptional at the other end of the continuum of abilities—the gifted. And the gifted population presents more diversity and individuality than any other group, making it more challenging to gain the understanding essential to both effective parenting and teaching.

When parents and teachers share an accurate understanding of a child and commit to providing the most advantageous educational opportunities for him or her, the power of a partnership advocating for that child is released to make an optimal educational program possible. Such a partnership dramatically increases the possibility of making wise choices in the child's educational plan, program options, and selection of a school. Those decisions, now more available than ever to parents, have a profound impact on the motivation of gifted students to participate fully and to achieve academically.

Carol Strip Whitney is not only a scholar of the research literature, but a parent, grandparent, teacher, and leader in gifted education who writes from the practical base of experience. The children and adults who have contributed to her own growth in understanding the motivational issues of gifted students are reflected in her writing, and her examples add clarity to the content. She is not only an educator of gifted students, but a gifted educator. And Gretchen Hirsch, her writing partner, is also the parent and grandparent of gifted children, as well as a gifted writer who helps to make this book easy yet profound reading. Parents and teachers reading this book will gain insight into the motivational dynamics of students and themselves. They will finish the book knowing how to think about motivational issues and how to work on choosing the best educational opportunities for their gifted children. They will not only enjoy reading the book, but will feel more knowledgeable and competent as they meet the challenges of teaching and guiding the development of gifted youngsters.

I relate very personally to the authors' writing because of my own experience with children ages six, seven, and eight identified as highly gifted but failing in school. I learned my most important lessons about giftedness, motivation, and the teaching/learning dynamics from those children and their parents. It all revolved around expectations and gaining an accurate understanding of each child's giftedness and motivational makeup. I first learned that these children had been extremely accelerated in their intellectual development in the preschool years, usually becoming young experts on their favorite interests and thriving on self-directed learning with some parental support. However, the primary grades did not accommodate these students' advanced levels of learning nor allow their self-directed pattern of learning to occur in school. Their response was rebellion or withdrawal, in either case resulting in "school failure." The parents were befuddled by their children's radical change in personality and behavior, especially at school, and wondered what had happened. These children's teachers had intended to educate them well but had little understanding of their motivational characteristics and needs.

Faced with about two dozen of these "gifted underachievers" in my experimental special education class, I tried to restore the natural love of learning by incorporating their areas of interest and expertise into the standard curriculum. I did not rely on tests or measures to know each child's special needs but rather made each child a partner in the adventure of discovering what motivates, challenges, and rewards him or her. I learned about the fear of failure and the fear of success that young highly gifted children can feel. I found that the most powerful tactic in this partnership was giving the children the power of choosing and self-managing their learning paths with responsibility for evaluating the wisdom of the choices and management of time and behavior. It was more powerful than I ever imagined, even in such young children. And as time went on, we worked on self-discipline in areas of learning not so rewarding to the students, as well as on finding a healthy balance between the passions of each child and the need to develop basic knowledge and skills. I shared what I learned in my book *Giftedness, Conflict, and Underachievement* (1980), now out of print.

It was a treat for me to read the Whitney-Hirsch manuscript, which reflects so well my own learning experiences with motivational issues in gifted students. I urge you to read it carefully, ponder its profundity, and apply its teachings to your work with your gifted children. Remember that partnering to find solutions is key: parent-child, teacher-child, parent-teacher, parent-teacher-child, home-school. By incorporating the wisdom in this book into your partnerships, I am confident that you will be successful in your journey to guide the optimal development of your child. Thank you, Carol Strip Whitney and Gretchen Hirsch, for bringing to us such a wonderful resource for parents and teachers.

Joanne Rand Whitmore Schwartz, Ph.D.
Former Dean, College of Education
Kent State University
Kent, Ohio

Preface

Since the publication of our first book, *Helping Gifted Children Soar: A Practical Guide for Parents and Teachers*, in 2000, gifted education has undergone many changes. The passage of the *No Child Left Behind* Act has radically shifted the focus of American education to accountability—to making certain that students reach specific, quantifiable goals at specific, pre-determined intervals.

To ensure that their schools are performing adequately, states have instituted more frequent tests to measure students' proficiency against standards. Students, teachers, and parents are often consumed with worry about the outcome of the tests, and in some schools, instruction has become primarily a series of drills to make sure that students have the information they need to pass the tests. Emphasis is on raising the performance of the lower third of the class.

This kind of emphasis has significant implications for the education of gifted children, especially as it relates to motivation. Gifted children can and do learn everywhere; the trick is to maintain their motivation to *learn in school*. In far too many cases, these children *are* left behind, struggling to sustain their interest in schoolwork they mastered years ago. Without the learning challenges they require, their motivation to do scholastic work may wither and eventually die.

Positive trends

However, there are some lights at the end of the tunnel. Many public school educators who have wrestled with the concept of giftedness have begun to realize that our definitions of who is gifted may have been too narrow, excluding both racial and linguistic minorities. This new concern with inclusivity may be what saves the concept of gifted education altogether. The more that taxpayers consider gifted programming the purview of a very few white, privileged youngsters, the easier it is to take an ax to the instructional budget for these students.

Although we must be careful not to misidentify children just to meet a nebulous, artificial "diversity" goal, identifying every student who qualifies, regardless of race, sex, socioeconomic class, language preference, or living conditions, increases the number of gifted children served and makes school boards less likely to do away with programming.

We now know that while gifted students may achieve in every discipline, they usually have special aptitudes in only one or two areas: math and music, for example, or language arts and drama. Schools, therefore, have begun to provide more targeted opportunities for those with particular talents. Increasingly, accelerated classes in specific disciplines are replacing multidisciplinary classes that both educators and the public may perceive as extraneous to the school's educational mission. In these accelerated classes, the gifted resource teacher may become the teacher of record for the advanced students.

Because such classes are more equitable and also are embedded within the district curriculum, it is much more difficult to sweep them away if a levy or other school tax fails. A discrete "gifted program" that is or appears to be unrelated to the curriculum is much more easily eliminated. Grouping of gifted students in their strength areas has met with success, as it allows students to rise to the level of their ability and permits teachers to consistently challenge them.

New schools, new ideas

Some communities are experimenting with more extensive acceleration and specialization for students who are ready for it. Rigorous magnet schools, many of which have been in existence for decades, challenge students, regardless of race or income, in their talent areas, from the visual and performing arts to science and math to foreign languages.

New types of magnet schools—many funded at least in part by private dollars—are coming to the fore. In 2007 in Columbus, Ohio, a partnership among Battelle, The Ohio State University, and the Educational Council will open a new public high school that emphasizes math, science, and technology. Beginning with ninth graders, the school will eventually house no more than 400 students in grades 9-12 and be located on a research park adjacent to the university campus. As the school grows, eleventh and twelfth graders drawn from 16 different school districts will take part in hands-on, self-directed learning, such as independent research or group projects and community internships with the aid of teachers and expert mentors.

Schools such as these may offer great opportunities for the development and nurture of talented students in science and technology disciplines that the United States desperately needs. Although some suburban schools in the Columbus area feel that the new school isn't sufficiently different from their own programs to warrant their students' participation, students whose districts don't offer the depth of curriculum they require will benefit greatly from opportunities at the new Metro School.

In Wake County, North Carolina, The Wake Early College of Health and Sciences will open as a new high school in the Wake County Public School System in 2007, providing students the opportunity to earn free college credit while obtaining their high school diplomas. A partnership among the Wake County Public School System, Wake Technical Community College, and WakeMed Health & Hospitals is responsible for creation of the new school.

According to the school's website,[i] "Students enrolled in the school will follow an integrated curriculum of high school and college courses, allowing them to simultaneously fulfill the requirements for a high school diploma and a two-year associate degree...[and] accelerate their college careers." The school will have no more than 400 students, providing them with "a small school setting and a more personalized learning experience." For students who are gifted in these areas and wish to begin a career early, such a school might be a godsend.

Grouping options

Some schools offer ingenious grouping strategies that may be beneficial to gifted children. At the Key Learning Community, an Indianapolis Public School, students are "heterogeneously grouped in multiage classes where they work on projects and problem solving in the eight areas of intelligence: linguistic, musical, logical-mathematical, naturalistic, spatial, bodily kinesthetic, interpersonal, and intrapersonal. In addition to learning language arts, math, science, history, and geography, all students at the school learn to play a musical instrument, study a foreign language, engage in visual and performing arts, and practice physical education."[ii]

Obviously, in such an environment, it is not feasible to group children solely by age. Students progress at their own pace and, at the same time, learn to work cooperatively with others. The school also insists that students interact with the wider community, and it offers opportunities for apprenticeships and projects that benefit the city.

Although this learning community's philosophy is based on Howard Gardner's theory of multiple intelligences[iii] and is not a school specifically for intellectually advanced children, its personalized, relevant, self-paced learning and focus on altruism are attributes particularly suited to gifted students' intellectual, social, and emotional growth. These factors could be adapted by others who are interested in exemplary programming for gifted and talented children.

Summers off? No more

Year-round schooling is gaining currency in many states. The old reasons for the long summer vacation, primarily that children were needed to handle farm chores, are no longer valid. Year-round schools that offer shorter blocks of vacation time throughout the year can be advantageous to gifted students.

Because teachers must use virtually the entire first month of school for re-teaching what students have "lost" over the extended summer break, gifted students suffer most. Bored and distracted, they are especially underserved during this "wasted" period. These students are ready and eager to plunge back into academic work. To ask them to wait is like holding a thoroughbred horse in the gate for a month. When the gate finally opens, the horse isn't going to break smartly and rush to the head of the pack. He's more likely to amble and wander off the track, aimless and undirected. And so might gifted students. Although the year-round option often makes scheduling family vacations difficult for working parents, full-time school is an interesting concept for gifted students.

Follow the money

Some districts in California, Ohio, Texas, Minnesota, Washington, other states have instituted a philosophy of allowing education tax dollars to follow the student to whatever school he wishes to attend. This option can be of great benefit to a gifted student who needs to be in a higher-performing school to receive an appropriate education. It also encourages competition among schools and appears to lead to higher performance for all.

Other districts now allow school-based budgeting, which gives principals and teachers far greater input into deciding where education dollars will be allocated in their particular schools. These decisions formerly have been made at the central office level, but studies find that allowing budgeting decisions to be made by individual schools results in funds being spent more effectively.

Not all students need the same things; a school with a large population of minority English Language Learners may require a totally different emphasis from a school in which most of the students are white and native speakers of English. School-based budgeting allows those who are intimately involved in the education of their students to design programs that work for their schools.

Value-added programs

The concept of value-added instruction is sweeping the country in response to the shortcomings of one-time-yearly proficiency testing. Value-added analysis of student scores on standardized tests is longitudinal and measures how a student is progressing from year to year. It recognizes the fact that not all children come to school with the same knowledge base and the same ability to learn, which complicates the issue of accountability that new legislation demands.

Value-added analysis, which involves multiple types of data collection over a long period of time, makes it easy to see if a student is progressing, even if she has not yet reached proficiency. Progress measurements combined with achievement tests can give a relatively complete picture of the student's performance and can aid educators in deciding how to intervene to help her make progress and meet the standards.

It may seem as though value-added analysis is of importance only for children who have not reached minimum proficiency, but it may be useful for gifted students as well. Achievement test scores alone, especially if the student far surpasses the state's standards for proficiency, tell parents, teachers, and administrators very little about the student's growth and progress. Many gifted students enter school near or even above that level of achievement. They may always do well on the tests, or even obtain the highest scores the tests will allow (called the "ceiling effect"); thus, these tests are unable to adequately reflect the students' potential. Unless there are value-added assessments, these students may not make the progress of which they're capable.

However, the real benefit is that value-added assessment measures students' progress against scaled standardized tests, *not* against their achievement of a particular performance standard, which they may have left behind years before. For these students, progress against the tests is a more accurate, objective measure than progress against state-mandated minimums.[iv]

So in spite of the fact that many may decry the state of American public education today, there *are* concerned school boards, administrators, teachers, and parents who, with persistence and perseverance, are attempting to bring about the changes that will guarantee an appropriate education for every child, including the gifted student. There are innovative partnerships among business, industry, schools, and research institutions that may result in an overhaul of the types of programs to which gifted students will have access.

Everyone who has an interest in keeping gifted learners motivated should follow the issues related to their education and lend support to innovative programs that offer a way out of stultifying curricula, age-based advancement, and other roadblocks that these children face every day. It may be a long road, but the goal is worth the effort.

Section I

The Seeds of Motivation

Chapter 1
The Turn-Off Effect

Losing Jane

"I'll never forget her first day of kindergarten," says Leigh Ann,[1] mother of seven-year-old Jane. "She was so excited she was almost vibrating. She couldn't wait to get in the schoolhouse door. I was eager to have her go to school, because frankly, she was wearing me out.

"Jane was a whirlwind of energy who never stopped talking or questioning. No matter when I put her to bed, she couldn't fall asleep until 10 P.M. There was so much going on in that little brain. Because she couldn't write, she dictated her first story to me when she was four years old. At that time, she also had an imaginary playmate whose name was Billy Brickers. I had to set a place at the table for Billy every night, and she held elaborate conversations with him, some of which she asked me to write down.

"Jane was a bit younger than some of the other kindergartners, but she was given early entrance because she'd been reading since she was three years old and was capable of completing the kindergarten curriculum. She sailed through the screening.

"Kindergarten met our expectations. The teacher, Ms. Robbins, was warm and encouraging, and the classroom was a child's dream. Books, animals, learning stations, and students roaming from activity to activity. Although the room was often rather noisy, it wasn't chaotic. There was a rhythm to it. Jane was engaged nearly every moment, and her teacher never tired of answering her questions.

"Her teacher did say that Jane had a little trouble at reading time because she was already reading, and in some cases, she'd memorized the books Ms. Robbins chose to read to the class. Jane often blurted out what was coming next or how the story ended. We finally decided that the best thing to do was to give Jane a single-subject acceleration—to send her to one of the second-grade rooms for their reading program. It gave the other kindergartners a chance to enjoy the books and allowed Jane access to literature and teaching that more closely matched her ability.

"In first grade, all of that flexibility pretty much disappeared. There was a sort of down-to-business attitude. Jane's learning became much more routine. She usually understood the concepts being introduced on the first or second try, but then she was stuck in a holding pattern, waiting for the others to catch up. She started to become distractible and restless because so much of her time was spent waiting as the teacher explained things over and over to other students.

"I set up a conference to speak with Jane's teacher. She was very kind and said she could differentiate to some degree, but realistically, she couldn't make all of the accommodations that Jane might need because of the complexities and demands of her teaching schedule and the other children in the class. Jane was still being single-subject accelerated, and the teacher hoped that the higher-level reading would be enough, but in this case, it wasn't.

"Today, I feel as if the school has almost lost Jane. Second grade seems to be just like last year. There's some new subject matter, but the idea seems to be to get the students ready for testing that won't even begin until next year.

"My eager little girl has lost much of her initial enthusiasm and excitement about school. She's still curious and interested in things outside the classroom. She has a passion for ballet, and she knows a great deal about marsupials. But instead of helping develop her skills and talents, her school experience is primarily teaching her to take tests. She's not engaged because there's no time to investigate her passions. She spends so much time relearning what she already knows that she's beginning to have disciplinary issues. I certainly never expected that, and I'm so disheartened.

"My once-joyful child is often sad, frustrated, even angry. She has less and less in common with her schoolmates, so she has fewer friends than she once did. I think if there were a gifted program in our schools, it might help, but we don't have one, and I don't know where to turn."

Who's gifted, and why does it matter?

There are approximately three million children in America who, like Jane, can be classified as gifted. In recent years, the definition of a gifted learner has been expanded. According to the National Association for Gifted Children, gifted children may exhibit not only specific academic abilities or general intellectual prowess, but also creativity, leadership, and exceptional talent in the visual or performing arts.[2]

Gifted children are found in every socioeconomic class and racial group. Many children with physical handicaps and learning disabilities also are gifted. Some gifted children may be highly able in one area of specialization, such as science or literature, and quite average in their other scholastic subjects. Others seem to be gifted in every curricular domain, as well as in leadership and creative endeavors.

Some children are prodigies in music, art, or even in business, and these are the children who show up on television and are lauded for their exceptional talent. Not every talented child is profoundly gifted, however. Some are mildly to moderately gifted, achieving at one to three grade levels beyond their age peers. In fact, moderately gifted students may be more different from the profoundly gifted than they are from their non-gifted peers. Some gifted children are very shy and introverted, while others are outgoing. Whatever their degree of giftedness, gifted children may exhibit one or a combination of the following traits:[3]

- *General intellectual ability or talent*

  The child probably:

  —Is intensely curious and drawn to complexity in learning.

  —Has a larger vocabulary than other children and uses it appropriately.

  —Likes to explore new ideas, formulate hypotheses, synthesize, and analyze.

- Specific academic abilities in domains such as reading, mathematics, science, or language arts

  The student may demonstrate:

  —Overwhelming enthusiasm for learning in the area of giftedness; the child's eagerness to learn is greater in kind and degree than other students' enjoyment of favorite subjects.

  —Great success in the special-interest domain—for example, completing Algebra 1 in sixth grade.

  —Aptitude for and rapid mastery of classroom skills such as comprehension and memorization. These children may be as much as three to four years beyond age mates in their ability to perform educational tasks, especially in their talent areas.

- Creativity in thinking

  The child often has the ability to:

  —Originate and express complex original ideas, both orally and in writing.

  —Think independently and be comfortable with being "different."

  —Tolerate ambiguity and take risks.

- Creativity in the visual or performing arts

  The student may:

  —Show a desire to produce original creative works.

  —Demonstrate exceptional observational skills and understanding of spatial relationships.

  —Be skilled in the ability to share feelings through music, drama, or other creative outlets.

- Leadership

  Children who have leadership abilities may:

  —Be self-confident, well-organized, fluent, and able to solve problems.

  —Demonstrate good judgment and understand the short- and long-term implications and consequences of decisions.

  —Set high expectations for themselves and others while still maintaining the respect and affection of other students.

Many of these traits are measured on some type of standardized achievement instrument, such as the *TerraNova Test*, the *Iowa Test of Basic Skills*, or the *Stanford Achievement Test*. Ability is measured by the *Wechsler Intelligence Scale for Children*, the *Cognitive Abilities Test* (CogAT), the *Stanford-Binet Intelligence Test*, or the *Otis-Lennon School Ability Test*, among others.

Some school districts also use the *Torrance Tests of Creative Thinking*, *Creative Products Scales*, the *Leadership Skills Inventory*, and the *Fundamental Interpersonal Relations Orientation Behavior* (FIRO-B) instrument to measure other types of gifts, such as creativity, artistry, and leadership ability. Students may also build a portfolio of creative work or present a creative performance.

A Quick Look: About Identification

Not every child exhibits every characteristic of giftedness, but if your child possesses several of these traits, there is at least a potential for giftedness and a need for further observation.

Gifted children often:

- Speak early, although some very bright children are late talkers.

- Use an advanced vocabulary and complex sentence structure.

- Understand wordplay and puns.

- Have a highly developed sense of humor. They "get" jokes at a very early age.

- Remember everything. Tell them something once, and they'll recall it months later. And they'll also remember where you said it, what you were wearing, and that it was raining at the time!

- Think very quickly, answering questions almost before they're asked.

- Demonstrate exceptional powers of concentration, especially in subjects they are passionate about.

- Are logical and may debate you into the ground, pointing out inconsistencies and flaws in your argument.

- Display a high level of intuition and flexibility in thinking. They often understand concepts after only one exposure, but they may not be able to tell you how they arrived at that understanding.

- Demonstrate originality in thinking, art projects, stories, drama, and make-believe.

- Are curious about many things and may be voracious in their quest for knowledge about areas in which they're interested, which can run the gamut from Anabaptists to zithers.

- Are highly energetic. They may travel only at warp speed.

- Require less or more sleep than other children of the same age. Some cannot turn off their brains and therefore sleep little. Others are so exhausted by what's going on in their minds and bodies that they sleep a great deal.

- Are intense and driven in their learning and their relationships. They invest heavily in both.

- Are sensitive and may be easily crushed by events that seem trivial to onlookers.

- May be concerned about moral questions such as homelessness, poverty, hunger, and genocide and often feel impelled to try to help resolve highly complex social issues.

The point of identifying gifted learners is to ensure that they receive the most appropriate education—that is, to provide them with the same types of accommodations that other special needs children require. If we ask a child who is slow to learn to master a curriculum that is too difficult, he may give up in frustration. The same is true at the other end of the spectrum. If we provide able learners with a curriculum too easily mastered, we run the risk of undermining and demotivating them, setting the stage for boredom, disappointment, and underachievement. We also rob society of the opportunity to profit from what these creative, innovative, clear-thinking children could accomplish if we set their minds free.

Because school budgets are squeezed tight, many districts drop services for gifted students because there are relatively few of them. Experts estimate that only 3-5% of children are intellectually gifted, and administrators may feel that they can get more for their money by allocating scarce dollars to programs that benefit a larger population of students.

In spite of the obvious benefits that accrue to society if its finest minds are honed by high expectations and rigorous study, gifted children and their parents and teachers continue to fight an uphill battle to gain access to the curricular options and differentiated instruction that these students require.

The issues facing schools and teachers

The public school population is more varied and diverse than ever before. In some urban school districts, more than 100 languages are represented in the student body. Waves of immigration from Latin America, Africa, and Asia mean that for many students, English is a second language. Mainstreaming has placed more students with physical disabilities in regular classrooms. With the availability of more precise diagnostic tools, physicians and psychologists are able to identify students with learning disabilities, and these children are also found in public school settings.

There is a continual flow of children in and out of the mainstream classroom to receive special tutoring, reading support, and various types of therapies. The inclusion of all of these children within the regular classroom promotes many positive social and educational goals, but it puts a stress on teachers, who must manage myriad schedules and interventions while they attempt to keep each student up to speed with the subject matter.

It's small wonder that some teachers find it difficult to give their gifted students the attention they'd like to. "We hope that these students learn without as much direction as others," says one elementary educator. "My classroom has 25 students. Three are English Language Learners, three are special needs students, and one is gifted. I'm pulled in lots of different ways trying to teach and assess all of them appropriately. And there are 18 more students—good, average-ability little kids—who are equally deserving of my attention. What about them?"

Many classrooms contain teachers who do not fully understand the nature of giftedness. Unfortunately, most teacher training courses give scant attention to gifted and talented education, so many teachers are less prepared than they should be to deal with these special children. These teachers might not be aware that a messy, disorganized student with horrible handwriting can be more intellectually capable than a high-achieving, compliant student with good study habits. These well-meaning educators may be outstanding teachers for the majority of children, but without training, they will have some difficulty recognizing or understanding the characteristics and needs of gifted students.

Most teachers want support and education in how to differentiate and extend existing curriculum for all students every day, but they are daunted by the idea of trying to provide an individualized program for every student.

State standards and No Child Left Behind

Teachers also must deal with the specter of annual testing in various subject areas. With the advent of state proficiency tests and the *No Child Left Behind* Act, teachers and schools are now judged not on how well their students think and learn, but on how well they perform on specific tests on specific dates.

Tonya, who teaches fourth grade in a large urban school district, elaborates. "It's very difficult. According to current educational policy, I alone am completely responsible for how my students do on proficiency exams. I have so many wonderful students in my class, and they have motivated, dedicated parents. But I also have students with alcoholic or absent parents. Their lives are chaotic, and the fact that they even make it to school every day is a triumph. I'm proud of them for wanting to learn when they could so easily give up.

"I have students who've witnessed murder, domestic violence, and drug dealing and are so traumatized that they're afraid speak in class. I have students who spend hours watching violent television programs and act that out in the classroom. Sometimes I feel more like a ring-master than a teacher. But when test time comes around, the kids are expected to get it together.

"Some students, even those from impoverished, disadvantaged backgrounds, do very well on the tests, but some are simply unable to pass them, at least the first time around. They may be tired or sick or anxious on test day. Maybe a family member is having surgery. Maybe the child was hassled and bullied on the way to school. Maybe the bus broke down or the family's breaking up. These are not optimal testing conditions. But if the children fail, the finger points at me, not at all the circumstances that are conspiring against the students.

"I'm not turning out widgets here; I'm trying to teach children, who aren't interchangeable units in some factory."

The pressure on students to achieve particular state standards affects both them and their teachers. Even dedicated, creative teachers who find their jobs hanging in the balance may end up teaching to the test—that is, preparing students for success on a standardized instrument, rather than providing them with opportunities for analysis, application of concepts, and creative as well as critical thinking.

To ensure that their students' heads are filled with the information asked for on the tests, teachers may feel forced to adopt instructional methods that are less effective for gifted students. They may be required to teach both content and test-taking skills by controlling, correcting, and lecturing rather than by guiding and exploring.[4] These one-size-fits-all methods choke off depth and breadth of instruction, and it's precisely that depth and breadth that gifted students need to reach their potential.

The retreat from individualized education bothers both parents and teachers and can create significant problems for students. "I want my gifted child to be taught in the public schools," says the father of a gifted third grader, "but I wonder how teachers can possibly meet his special needs when they have to adhere to such a rigid state-mandated curriculum. How does my child get any kind of meaningful learning under those circumstances?"

"The testing is really hard on sensitive children," adds one teacher. "Some of my gifted students assume that they must answer every question correctly to meet their own standards of performance. They agonize and suffer. Many of them are in tears during the test. How can this possibly be good for them?"

Many parents may not know that there's a new national standard that states that all teachers now must be HQT, which means "highly qualified teachers." Certainly, most people can see the benefit of ensuring that students are taught by competent, educated teachers. However, to comply with the new standards, some teachers have to go back to school or take state competency examinations in their subject areas, and of course, they have to be fully licensed or certified by the state. So while teachers are getting kids ready for the tests, they're also preparing themselves for the same kinds of pressure. Schools can be very high-stress environments these days.

Ironically, after all of the test preparation, gifted children may not test well because their brains have been anesthetized by mind-numbing drill and repetition of sample test items. They stop listening and they stop learning. When the test comes, they aren't ready because they tuned out weeks or even months ago. And even if they pass the test, their score is likely to reflect only the most superficial snapshot of their real capabilities.

In addition, studies are proving that students who are frequently subjected to high-stakes exams can exist in a nearly constant state of test anxiety. In Perrysburg, Ohio, for example, a study showed that two-thirds of elementary students and three-quarters of secondary students said that the state tests cause "excess stress," and the higher the grade level, the more anxious the students became. Interestingly, higher-level students experienced great frustration because they "felt cheated out of demonstrating deeper levels of knowledge and understanding on the math, science, reading, writing, and citizenship tests."[5] If average-ability students suffer this sort of frustration, gifted students undoubtedly feel even more cheated because their knowledge is even deeper and broader than that of their peers.

Since the passage of *No Child Left Behind*, greater emphasis is placed on students who drag down the average than on those who lift it. While school districts concern themselves with community report cards and possible Draconian measures if their schools do not achieve appropriate yearly progress, they may be forced to pay less attention to students who can—and should—work beyond grade level.

Carol Tomlinson, Ed.D., president of the National Association for Gifted Children, observes, "This federal legislation is a laudable advance toward equity. Its impetus to ensure that all children achieve proficiency in the foundational skills of learning is clear.... [However], at present, [the NCLB Act] aims the nation's attention and resources at ensuring that non-proficient students move systematically toward proficiency. There is no incentive for schools to attend to the growth of students once they attain proficiency, or to spur students who are already proficient to greater achievement, and certainly not to inspire those who far exceed proficiency."[6]

The parent of a Texas third grader says, "Heather is off the chart in all of the language arts, but she does less well in math. There are concepts in math that she simply doesn't understand, and math will become harder and harder for her if she doesn't figure them out. I spoke to the teacher, and she said that because Heather is still above the proficiency level, she's doing fine and doesn't need any additional help. When I asked about challenging her in language arts, the teacher told me quite matter-of-factly that she had to teach to the average student and that any enrichment Heather needs will have to come from us. We're happy to do that, but isn't the role of the public school to meet the educational needs of *every* learner?"

However parents and teachers might dislike the current atmosphere of drill and test, test and drill, the fact is that testing is here to stay, at least for the foreseeable future. The federal government and the states have put their considerable weight—and budgetary influence—behind this educational style. The boat has sailed, and as adults, we can either sit in the deck chairs bemoaning the fate of education or we can begin to investigate the ship, finding new ways to engage and excite children about learning. Testing does not have to replace real education for our brightest students—or indeed for any student. We can use preparation for tests as an opportunity for creative teaching.

For example, perhaps the course of study for the year dictates that children will learn to calculate the area of a circle, square, triangle, and rectangle and convert English to metric measurements. Of course, some of the facts can be learned by rote, but one creative teacher had her gifted students apply these important measurement lessons by:

- Dreaming of a house they in which they'd like to live in the future.

- Drawing a rough diagram of their future house.

- Refining their plans on quarter-inch grid paper.

- Figuring the area of every room, hallway, or open space. No portion of the house could remain unmeasured, and each home had to contain circles, squares, rectangles, and triangles.

- Creating a roster of all the areas of the home and converting the measurements to their metric equivalents.

- Building the house to scale from wood, file folders, aquarium gravel, and a variety of other materials.

Each activity the children carried out was aligned with a specific learning goal prescribed by the district. When a district official made an unannounced visit to the class, the teacher was prepared to demonstrate what curricular goals were being addressed as the children worked.

These students were learning the district-mandated facts, but they were also studying measurement of areas in far greater depth and complexity than they would have if they'd simply completed worksheet after worksheet of geometric problems. They were relating the subject to real life, involving all of their senses, and using various learning styles. They were fully immersed and passionate about their constructions. Were they ready for standardized testing on measurement of area and metric conversion? Of course, and they performed admirably, helping the district raise its "report card" score.

Likewise, a study of the stock market or a module on personal finance can extend a unit on decimals, fractions, and graphs. As long as district goals are being met, there's no reason a gifted program cannot offer the challenge that the students require.

The key to using testing effectively and relieving students' test anxiety is to help them understand that each test is not a final evaluation, but simply a way to discover what the students know and what they need to learn. Tests identify areas of strength and pinpoint knowledge gaps that need to be filled so the student can advance to higher-level work. Test results guide teachers in how and when to present materials. More frequent testing also allows students to show what they know at regular intervals, so that the students' final grade doesn't depend to a great extent on the outcome of one cumulative test covering a full semester's work.

What's so bad about elitism?

There are some people who believe that "all children are gifted" and that no money should be spent on such an elitist enterprise as a gifted program. It's interesting to note that many school activities could fall under the elitist banner—if by elitist we mean that some children are included by reason of talent or aptitude and others are excluded. For example, the marching band is closed to students who can't march, read music, and play an instrument proficiently all at the same time. Although many young men and women would like to compete on a varsity soccer, baseball, basketball, football, or hockey team, the varsity is reserved for students who have shown unusual competence in the sport. Yet when we suggest that some students, because of their genetic endowment and talent, are more intellectually competent than their peers, elitism is trotted out as a reason to deny them the most appropriate education.

The facts, however, argue in favor of "elitism." We know that when we group talented musicians together in the school orchestra and allow them to attempt difficult compositions, they push one another to make more beautiful music. The sound becomes better and better as the students build relationships by studying and learning from each other and their teacher. When we put our most talented athletes on the field, they support and challenge each other, and they learn from one other's successes and failures. With good coaching, the team improves.

The same is true of grouping intellectually talented students together and providing them with the teachers and resources they need. According to Linda Kreger Silverman, Ph.D., of the Gifted Development Center in Denver, "If we really want to create a young man with elitist attitudes, all we have to do is place him in an unchallenging program for 12 years and allow him to be the smartest one in the class with no one in second place. Let him get by doing his homework in class, never taking home a book, and acing the tests without having to study. By the time he graduates, ...he will have a ballooned sense of his own importance and place in the universe."[7]

If we allow gifted students access to the peers and programs that test their limits, they are less likely to grow swelled heads. They meet others who are as capable or even more talented than they. The interaction among students of comparable intellectual ability has the same effect it does on the basketball court and in the orchestra pit. Relationships and teamwork are strengthened, competence is enhanced, and at the same time, students become more realistic about their place in the school and in society.

We speak comfortably about elite athletes in our schools. If the purpose of school is education, why are we so uncomfortable with the concept of elite students?

Intelligences and giftedness

All children *are* gifts, all children *have* talents, and the goal of education should be to pursue opportunity and equity for every student, as well as to demand excellence for—and from—all learners. It's been proven that when the bar is set higher for the entire class, all students, even the brightest, learn more. "Parents and schools must provide all students with equal opportunity but not with equal treatment," says David Sousa, Ed.D., author of *How the Gifted Brain Learns*. "Treating all students as if they learned the same way is folly."[8]

Howard Gardner posits eight intelligences—linguistic, logical-mathematical, spatial, bodily-kinesthetic, musical, interpersonal, intrapersonal, and naturalistic—that is, eight areas in which students process and acquire information and skills.[9] This has obvious implications for the ways in which they learn.

Some students have a clear preference for one type of learning—for example, the student who sings *Fifty Nifty United States* to recall the states in alphabetical order, or writes a musical composition about Roy G. Biv to remember the color spectrum. However, most students use a mixture of styles to learn, retain, manipulate, and analyze information, facts, and data.

Although Gardner has said that his work "was developed as a theory of the mind, not as an educational intervention,"[10] it has become just that. Most textbooks now contain margin notes that show teachers how to present the same subject matter in ways that appeal to the various learning styles.

So far, so good. There's nothing inherently wrong with modifying a teaching style to match a learning style; excellent teachers have been doing it for decades. But teaching to the student's style is not all there is to meeting the intellectual needs of the gifted child. The gifted learner needs much, much more.

For example, say a first-grade teacher is presenting a unit on simple addition. She imparts that information in several different ways to help all of the children understand the concepts. She uses lecture for children who learn best through hearing, manipulatives for tactile types, and pictures and graphs for students who are visually oriented. For the majority of the class, this kind of instruction may be adequate.

However, for the gifted first grader who can already add two columns in her head, the lesson lacks the complexity and intellectual stimulation necessary for the child to gain maximum benefit. It doesn't matter whether the student's learning style has been accommodated if she already knows what the lesson has to teach. No matter how effectively the material is presented, the student's time and brain power are being wasted. The gifted student requires that the *substance* of the lesson, not just the presentation, be differentiated. The student who is already far ahead of her classmates should be doing new and different work, not old work in a different way.

A student forced to relearn material that he has already mastered is like a chef in a fine restaurant who is not allowed to prepare anything but toast. Restaurant-goers are deprived of the chef's full repertoire of dishes, and the chef feels constricted, thwarted, and frustrated. The difference is that the chef can leave the kitchen, but the law requires students to remain in school.

No matter what their learning styles, gifted students learn differently, faster, and in greater depth than other students when they are sufficiently engaged in their area of interest. They require challenge, not rote learning, recitation, and repetition.

In a time of scarce resources, many educators have used Gardner's theory to buttress the idea of teaching gifted children in mixed-ability classrooms, and with proper differentiation of the curriculum and exceptional, masterful teaching, an inclusive classroom in which there are several gifted students can work well. In general, however, the instructional methods used in mixed-ability settings are aimed at average students who comprise the majority in the classroom. There is the potential for loss of motivation when typical instruction meets an atypical mind.

Alternatives to demotivation

When a gifted child's motivation to learn in school wavers and she shows signs of leveling out, reaching a plateau, or underachieving, parents and educators search for methods that will re-engage her and jump-start the impetus to learn. In the last few years, several trends have gained steam.

Acceleration

Of all the options available for motivating gifted students to learn and achieve, the one most thoroughly researched is acceleration—that is, "matching the level, complexity, and pace of the curriculum with the readiness and motivation of the student.... It does not mean pushing a child [or] forcing a child to learn advanced material or socialize with older students before he or she is ready. Acceleration is about letting students soar [and developing] a strategy that respects individual differences."[11]

Although there are many acceleration options, they fall into roughly two groups. One is acceleration of placement, which involves moving a student ahead one or more grade levels either by early enrollment in kindergarten or college or a whole-grade skip, or by moving the student ahead in one subject only (single-subject acceleration) to place him in a more advanced curriculum. The second is acceleration of the curriculum, which is done by moving a student through a subject more quickly, but does not involve a change in grade or class placement. In this kind of acceleration, material is covered in less time, often using self-paced learning.

Even with incontrovertible evidence that acceleration is beneficial to gifted students, many educators use it sparingly, if at all. The reasons for only tentative acceptance of acceleration are often related to factors that have nothing to do with intellectual ability. Myths abound, and the educational establishment has bought into them. Some of these myths include:[12]

- It's better to keep students with same-age classmates.
- Acceleration hurries children out of childhood.

- Acceleration hurts children socially.
- Acceleration is not fair to other students.
- Students will be offended if one of their classmates is accelerated.

None of these arguments is confirmed by research. Although acceleration should be carefully considered and the options selected should be congruent with the child's specific needs and social and emotional readiness, acceleration is an effective strategy that keeps motivation high and honors students' desire to learn.

Charter schools

Charter schools are publicly funded schools that receive some exemption from the rules and regulations of other public schools. Parents, teachers, or others may apply for a charter to open a school. Depending on where the school is located, the charter may be granted by the local school board, the state board of education, or a public institution of higher education. Charter schools can focus on particular domains such as math and science or performing arts, and they may be specifically oriented toward gifted students.

Advocates say that charter schools support educational innovation and student motivation by allowing alternatives to traditional schooling. Opponents respond that such schools divide students along racial and economic lines and undermine the concept of "common school" education.

Some charter schools have failed because those who were granted the charter took the money and provided little in the way of curriculum. Some charter school "educators" know little about school governance or pedagogy. These knowledge gaps may cause them to waste resources, design inappropriate course offerings, or concentrate on discipline and order to the exclusion of real learning.

A charter school that is well run, has a solid curriculum, and makes differentiated education of students its primary mission can be successful, and many are, but parents need to investigate a charter school thoroughly before enrolling their child.

Virtual schools

Virtual or online schools are also an option for some gifted students. Virtual schools range from specific real-time courses held at the student's school to virtual academies that allow gifted students to attend full-time from home and earn a diploma. Some schools are affiliated with a school district; students attend virtual classes, and the district grants the diploma. Other schools offer only a few extension opportunities and do not grant a diploma. These virtual schools are no more than an adjunct to the student's in-school education.

There are advantages to online schooling. The anonymity provided by the virtual school allows students to explore in depth without the peer pressure that often causes them to hide their intelligence and individuality. For students with some types of disabilities, attending online classes can provide a welcome relief from working around the disability in the public school setting.

Many online courses are self-paced so that students can move quickly through the material. In some schools, students may choose to take a survey course in a particular subject area or focus on one aspect of the subject for the entire term. This permits great depth of exploration and satisfies the student's curiosity. Because the Internet spans the world, virtual schools can include students from many countries. Exposed to other cultures and ideas, students develop a wider perspective on global issues. All of these benefits can unleash gifted children's innate motivation.

However, there can be a downside. Besides burnishing their intellectual skills, children need to learn to relate to people face to face, individually and in groups. For students who may already have difficulty with relationships, the computer can become an attractive substitute for human interaction. Communicating with a screen doesn't teach children empathy, compassion, and respect for others. When their schoolmates are faceless, students may say and do inappropriate things because their behavior is not mediated by the physical presence of others.

The virtual learner can become isolated and lonely. He may be slow to develop social skills and the ability to work with others, both of which will be necessary in the adult world. Part of schooling is learning to become a responsible citizen, and virtual schools do little, if anything, to encourage growth in this important area.

Home schooling

Parents choose home schooling for many reasons. Some want a religious foundation to scholastic endeavors. Others want to shield their children from bullying, materialism, and other attitudes they consider counterproductive to healthy development. Still others have legitimate concerns about their children's physical safety.

Some parents choose to home school because their gifted child has experienced a downward motivational spiral toward underachievement in school. In some cases, students themselves identify the motivational issue. They recognize that they are learning far more at home and in community settings than they are in school, and they may ask to be released from the day-in, day-out drudgery that they must put up with in their classes. It's not unusual for such children to beg their parents to take them out of that environment and teach them at home. Although their motivation to learn in traditional school has waned, they may exhibit exceptional motivation to learn at home, especially if the home school environment encourages self-efficacy, self-pacing, enjoyment of learning for its own sake, challenging explorations in the areas of strength, and consistent hard work in areas of weakness. Many students excel in home schools and are admitted to the nation's most prestigious universities, where they continue to set the pace for other students.

However, Michael Whitley, Ph.D., cautions that motivational challenges that show up in public school may also rear their heads in the home school setting. Because the parent is present in a way that a public school teacher cannot be, there is a danger that the child may learn to depend on the parent's pushing and supervision to accomplish academic tasks and therefore not develop the self-sufficiency to achieve on her own. "My goal for parents," Whitley says, "is to change the child, not just the geography."[13]

Talent searches

According to officials at the highly regarded Belin-Blank Institute for Gifted Education and Talent Development at The University of Iowa, home of the Belin-Blank Exceptional Student Talent Search (BESTS), "The goal of a talent search is to discover, via above-level testing, students who need further educational challenge to fully realize their academic talent. Above-level testing is an educational procedure in which a test developed for older students is administered to younger students. Students who do well on a grade-level test have correctly answered most of the questions on that test....The results of an above-level test [such as the *Explore* test for younger students and the SAT or ACT for middle schoolers] can tell us what students are ready to learn."[14]

Since the first talent search was instituted at Johns Hopkins University in the 1970s, the movement has burgeoned, growing from a few hundred students to tens of thousands in recent years. Clearly, there is a large pool of talented youngsters whose capabilities should be tapped for their own good and for the world's benefit.

The majority of students taking the tests report the experience to be fun and informative rather than intimidating, and the participants and their parents gain:

- An objective baseline that can be used to ensure the student's appropriate placement in school.

- An opportunity to participate in a wide range of enrichment activities, classes, and institutes provided by the sponsoring universities.
- A portal to important information regarding scholarship opportunities and other assistance.

Talent searches are currently conducted by the Johns Hopkins University Center for Talented Youth, the Duke University Talent Identification Program, Northwestern University's Midwest Talent Search, and the University of Denver's Rocky Mountain Talent Search.

Summer enrichment programs

Summer programs such as Camp Invention, Summer Institutes for the Gifted, ATLAS (Academically Talented Learners Achieving Success), or other specialty programs can add a special flavor to the overall motivation of gifted children by providing classes or other educational experiences in areas of specific interest. Additionally, these programs allow gifted children the opportunity to interact with other highly motivated learners.

The challenge

The motivation of gifted children is usually a multi-factored undertaking. Each child is unique, and a motivational strategy that is effective for one student may backfire with another, leaving the child undirected and rudderless. But with some basic knowledge of motivational theories and an understanding of what works, parents and teachers can help gifted learners motivate themselves to ever higher levels of satisfaction and achievement.

We must work together to make both our homes and our classrooms special places where gifted students can thrive. We must address the issues that surround testing demands and ask our constituents to open their hearts and minds to new ways to expand the learning of gifted children within the constraints that have been put in place. It's doable, and if our children are to reach their full potential, we must do it.

In summary

- Giftedness encompasses not only intellectual attainment, but also creativity in thinking and problem solving, exceptional talent in the fine or performing arts, and/or a well-developed ability to lead others.

- Gifted children are found in all races, ethnicities, and socioeconomic groups, so identification methods must be multi-factored, wide-ranging, and inclusive.

- Gifted students who are far beyond proficiency may have difficulty finding sufficient challenge in school, and without the challenges that make learning interesting, gifted children may become bored and disengaged. Their motivation may slide, and the students are at risk of becoming underachievers.

- Parents, teachers, and others involved in the education community have a variety of options that may ignite students' motivation. Two of the most promising are acceleration, which is a useful, cost-effective way for students to pace their own learning in their talent areas, and above-level testing to discover areas of talent.

Chapter 2
A 360-Degree Look at Motivation

Ms. Wilson teaches a group of elementary-age gifted students who are exceptional in reading. She works with this cross-grade group an hour each day. They qualified for the gifted reading program based on their scores on both ability and achievement tests.

As a relatively new teacher, Ms. Wilson has become more and more fascinated by her extremely able students and is particularly interested in what motivates them. When they come to her classroom, they are ready and eager to learn. They find their own materials, get down to work quickly, ask insightful questions, and often figure out their own problem-solving strategies with only minimal guidance.

Today, it's their turn to teach the teacher. "Boys and girls," she says, "I'm very interested in what keeps you wanting to learn. What turns your motor on? Why are you excited about some things and not about others?"

Almost before the words are out of her mouth, hands shoot up and answers pour out.·

"I like it when I've done a good job and I get to pick my own reward sticker," says Megan, who's in second grade and has already had a short poem published in the kids' page of her local newspaper.

"Last year, when I wrote that research report on the pyramids, you gave me a certificate of accomplishment. My mom framed it, and it's in my room. That was really special for me," says Juanita, who's in fourth grade.

"I don't need stickers and stuff," says Darius, a third grader whose favorite reading is *Lord of the Rings*. "I know when I've done a good job, and I like the way it makes me feel."

"Me too," echoes 10-year-old Jacob, an exceptional writer who's polishing his own collection of short stories. "Learning something new makes me feel pride in myself. I don't care too much about test scores if I'm really learning."

"I like having you for a teacher," says Serena, who's in fifth grade and enjoys reading Isaac Asimov. "We work so hard in here, but you make all this stuff interesting and fun. You make us understand how it fits into our real life, and you tell us you know we can do it. It's good that you believe in me when I don't think I can figure it out."

If you are the parent or teacher of a child like one of these, congratulations. You have a real advantage in the struggle against demotivation. Gifted children, by nature, are motivated to learn. Indeed, gifted students have such interest in and curiosity about things around them that it's nearly impossible for them not to learn. Therefore, we do not so much motivate gifted children as we encourage their inborn propensity and yearning to learn.

However, in spite of their innate thirst for knowledge, gifted learners, like other students, can develop motivational challenges in school. Their motivational deficit may manifest itself in a variety of ways, and their behaviors look like those of any other unmotivated student. They may procrastinate, forget to turn in assignments, or refuse to do their homework in spite of threats or punishments. Their attention may wander during lectures and explanations, and that behavior can lead to test failure. Or they may experience fear of letting down their teachers and parents if they don't consistently achieve at high levels, and this fear can be paralyzing. Many gifted children feel different from their classmates, so some of them "dumb down" to fit in better. This conscious effort to not do well in school can make them feel as though they are not true to themselves because they do not believe that others will accept them as they really are, and this may lead to depression. Sometimes gifted children become class clowns to cover up their differences from others. For all of these reasons, many of them suffer from underachievement.

What motivates a gifted student?

Although there is some discrepancy in wording among the various definitions of "motivation," what they have in common is the statement that *motivation is a desire for and movement toward a specific goal.* Motivation is more than a wish or a daydream; true motivation awakens and sustains actions that propel a person closer to a goal. At its base, motivation is also a search for personal meaning and a reflection of a person's deepest values.

The development of a student's values is an ongoing adventure, and parents and teachers are powerful influences along the way. They are the significant adults who can challenge gifted students to answer to the important question: How do you want to be great?[1]

Although by adolescence most children have developed some sort of ethical system, gifted children often organize and articulate their values at a younger age. Because they have a clear vision of what they believe to be important, gifted students can be very self-motivated. Parents and teachers may have to do little to light their fire and, in fact, may serve primarily as touchpoints and advisers as the children move along a self-determined course of action.

However, this is not always the case. Some gifted students are pulled and tugged in several directions. Their moral sense is often finely honed, and they see a multitude of issues that call out for attention. Because there is so much to do to right the world's wrongs, they have difficulty choosing a path to follow, and they may become overly discouraged and depressed. If they are unable to see the connection between their scholastic work and the real world, their motivation may ebb. It can be difficult to get them back on track.

In this situation, parents and teachers can be especially important in helping children to develop specific, meaningful goals. They can model how to focus and harness one's energy for the attainment of what matters most in one's life. Adults can also help children learn to be resilient—to bounce back from disappointment and frustration and to conquer anxiety and stress.

Theories of motivation

There are almost as many theories about what motivates people as there are theorists to think them up. There are behavioral, social, biological, and cognitive theories—and more. These theories state that people, including students, are motivated by a desire to:[2]

- Have a good relationship with significant others, such as parents or teachers.

- Achieve a pleasant consequence or avoid an undesired one, such as ridicule, embarrassment, or failure.

- Join a group, either socially or as part of a larger purpose.

- Increase physical or psychological comfort.

- Solve, or at least understand, a problem.

- Eliminate risk.

- Feel secure.

- Eliminate barriers to personal success and accomplishment.

- Take control of their own lives.

- Understand the purpose of their existence.

At various times, most people will be motivated by many such desires. Typical student goals include receiving a specific grade on a test, gaining entrance to an advanced class, or earning a scholarship. A student may be motivated by wanting to be viewed as the smartest in the group. Conversely, he may not care about others' perceptions of his intelligence, wanting only to learn as much about a subject as possible.

Other student motivators might be peer acceptance, a wish to be taken seriously as a member of the creative community, or a vision of becoming a CEO, a millionaire, or a professional athlete. A student may even be motivated to become a con artist and direct his behavior toward learning to scam others with flair and audacity. The goal is whatever the student chooses; the behavior is what helps her reach the goal.

The theories of motivation often discussed in relation to student achievement are Attribution Theory, Goal Theory, and Self-Determination Theory.

Attribution Theory

This theory of motivation proposes that students explain success or failure by attributing these outcomes either to internal or external factors that are, or are not, under the student's control. For example, if a student fails a test, he may attribute the failure to the fact that he didn't study, which is an internal factor under his control. However, he may say he failed because the teacher didn't give the class notice of the test or that she doesn't like him. Obviously, these are external factors over which the student feels he has little or no control.

It stands to reason that a student who thinks success is a result of effort and ability will not be afraid to approach tasks that are difficult. If she fails, she may still persist in the task because she believes that she can learn if she tries harder. Her motivation tends to remain high because her concentrated effort will likely bring about a satisfying conclusion.

A student who attributes outcomes to her own actions is said to have an *internal* locus of control. She believes that her daily decisions matter in the conduct of her life and that fate has little to do with what happens to her. She learns to take charge of her own actions and understands that she is responsible for her own success to failure.

Conversely, a student who believes that luck or some other outside factor determines his success will feel less satisfaction when he accomplishes a task. He is more likely to quit if he fails because, "There's nothing I can do about it anyway." He works with little enjoyment because he doesn't see the connection between his efforts and his accomplishments. He has an *external* locus of control. A child like this may not have much belief in the effect of his own decisions or, indeed, in himself.

For gifted children to exercise their talents and develop an internal locus of control, they need flexibility within limits. At home, the child makes choices among alternatives and within guidelines that the parents deem appropriate. The parents exercise consistent, appropriate discipline and help the child see the relationship between actions and consequences.

At school, teachers can enhance self-belief by offering options and choices within the strictures required by district courses of study. As students take some responsibility for their learning, they come to understand that their decisions and actions have a direct correlation with the rewards—or penalties—they receive.

For example, a Midwestern school district decided that all fifth-grade mathematics students who were participants in the gifted math class should be given the opportunity for pre-algebra in the sixth grade. They asked the gifted teachers to use the sixth-grade math workbook during the spring semester and to compact the curriculum (that is, teach the year's course of study in one semester) so that the students mastered the concepts and skills in the workbook in time to make the switch in the next academic year.

The gifted teachers discussed the situation with the students and discovered that the young people were concerned about so much drill and repetition without the excitement of the hands-on learning they were used to in their gifted math program. Although they liked the idea of pre-algebra at an earlier stage of their academic careers, they were strongly demotivated by the idea of filling out dozens of workbook pages to reach their goal.

"We talked with the students about it," says one of the teachers. "We made a plan that included their completing required problems on certain pages every day but also allowed for some hands-on options. The twist was that they had to explain to us how their project choices related to what they were learning in the workbook. Negotiating this compromise with the students met the district requirements, extended the curriculum, and helped the students tie their workbook learning to real-life projects that required critical thinking and analysis. Once they saw relevance, the students hopped on the bandwagon. The demotivation problem was solved because they were invested in making the compromise work. They had a degree of control, and they were happy to have some choice in how they learned. It put responsibility on the gifted students, and they seized the ball and ran with it."

That classroom is now a hotbed of self-directed learning. Their teacher reported, "The students sometimes work together and sometimes by themselves. In this class, cooperative learning is really cooperative. The brighter students don't end up doing all the teaching, as often happens in a mixed-ability cooperative learning group.

"Because I have only a few students in the class, I can be very attentive to those who have some emotional struggles brought on by self-imposed worries about perfect performance or differences in speed of learning. I serve much more as a coach than a taskmaster. I have time to know who they are and what turns them on, and I can hook their learning to their interests. For example, one child was having trouble with probability theory, but when I was able to show her some examples that were related to her adored Golden Retrievers, she caught on instantly, and I know she'll never forget those concepts.

"The students actually ask for homework and are eager for me to extend and extend—and extend—the lessons. It's exciting to watch their intellectual attainments, of course, but it's almost more thrilling to see their social and emotional growth. Because of their ability, these children sometimes feel lost and out of place in their regular classes. In this class, however, they've found a *real* peer group—other kids they can talk to and who understand them. They feel at home and confident, and they enjoy each other's company so much. And of course, they're friends outside the class, too, so they have people to pal around with at lunch and at recess. They aren't alone and isolated because they're smart. It's wonderful to see."

Goal Theory

While Attribution Theory focuses on students' self-explanations of success and failure, Goal Theory helps explain the reasons students achieve. It posulates that students view achievement in relationship to three types of goals:

- Task (or learning or mastery) goals, which focus on becoming competent in a discipline or set of skills.

- Image (or performance) goals, which are related to how the student wishes to be viewed by self and others.

- Social goals, which reflect the student's social reasons for achievement. Social goals may include peer approval, community or family approval, teacher approval, and others.

Goal Theory includes the concept that students are motivated either to avoid failure or to achieve success. Avoiding failure is usually associated with performance goals—that is, attempting to look good to others—while achieving success is more often related to mastery goals.

Students with a performance goal orientation tend to believe that the reason for achievement is to show one's ability, especially as compared to others. Those who are attempting to "look good" may select very easy tasks that they can accomplish with little effort, thus presenting a competent image. They may also choose very difficult tasks, which either allows them to "show off" when they achieve them or gives them a ready excuse if they fail.

Students with a mastery goal orientation focus on mastering skills and knowledge to gain understanding and to challenge their own abilities. They are less concerned with their ranking against others, preferring to compete against themselves. They usually select tasks they view as challenging yet possible. Mastery goals appear to be related to greater success in school and a more positive, stable self-image. Parents and teachers can stress the importance of learning and mastery goals by rewarding effort and improvement, as well as specific accomplishments and grades.

Inextricably intertwined with mastery and performance goals are social goals—a desire to demonstrate social responsibility, perhaps through community action, and to find a peer group in which to enjoy social relationships. Many schools today encourage social responsibility through group projects that allow students to interact and develop commonality of purpose around an issue of importance, but social interaction also can be fostered by allowing lots of time for class discussion of ideas and concepts. Students learn to listen to and be respectful of all viewpoints—even those with which they disagree—and to navigate through the social world.

Self-Determination Theory

Self-Determination Theory is promulgated primarily by Edward Deci and Richard Ryan of the University of Rochester. According to the Self-Determination Theory website, "…human beings have a set of basic psychological needs which are universal."[3] These needs include a sense of competence, a sense of relatedness to others, and a sense of autonomy. Competence is the student's ability to achieve desired outcomes. Relatedness is her ability to form connections to others within a social group. Autonomy describes her ability to initiate and regulate her own behavior.

According to the theory, motivation increases when students are asked to assume greater control over their lives and learning, and this viewpoint appears to be confirmed by higher graduation rates in schools that support greater student autonomy. These schools typically combine high expectations of student performance with an attitude of joint responsibility for learning by staff and students.

Students in such schools say they have a strong voice in policies and practices, considerable choice and control over important segments of their learning, and a great degree of support from their teachers and administrators, all of which allow the students to develop their own abilities to learn and study. Conversely, in schools and situations in which students have little voice, it appears to be more difficult for them to learn to set and achieve goals, take responsibility, and manage negative emotions.[4]

Even in a test-heavy environment, classroom instruction can foster motivation and provide gifted students with the growth and challenge they require. Gifted students' autonomy and competence can be awakened by giving them some options in what material they study and how they demonstrate their mastery. A classroom in which respect for all students is paramount leads to a sense of relatedness among the entire group, from the most able students to those who are struggling.

Intrinsic or extrinsic motivation: What works?

Whatever their differences, all major motivational theories share a belief in the existence of *intrinsic* and *extrinsic* motivation, which has to do with where motivation comes from. The source of motivation may arise from inside the student himself. He learns for the sake of learning and enjoys the quest for knowledge without the need for a reward. A student exhibiting this kind of behavior is said to be intrinsically motivated or inner-directed. The goal is knowledge for its own sake, and the corresponding behavior is study and learning.

Extrinsic (outer-directed) motivation arises from outside the person and is generally a means to an end, which is often some form of tangible reinforcement. Grades, paychecks, bonuses, and promotions are all extrinsic motivators. The goal may not be participation itself, but the reward that participation brings.

As they explore and learn, very young gifted children are the most nearly perfect examples of intrinsic motivation—the type of motivation that encourages them to ask and answer questions without worrying about the "One Right Answer"—and the kind of motivation that often goes to sleep when the thrill of learning is replaced with classroom regimentation and rote learning.

Gavin is a case in point. Gavin just turned four years old and goes to preschool. He hasn't been tested yet, but both of his older brothers have been identified as gifted learners, and he appears to be on the same path, with a highly advanced vocabulary and a great sense of humor unusual in one so young.

Gavin's current passion is Hot Wheels® cars. He plays with them like any other four-year-old boy, but he also sorts and classifies them by name, function, speed, and color. When presented with a carrying case of 50 of the tiny vehicles in which some spaces are empty, he knows precisely which cars are missing and where they belong. He asks his grandfather to read him stories about Hot Wheels cars, and he watches Hot Wheels videos. Although Gavin can't tell you precisely how the cars are made, he certainly knows a great deal about them. He has soaked up the information effortlessly, just because he has a strong internal drive to know.

An older gifted student may develop an intense interest in dinosaurs, Harry Potter®, robotics, English literature, cancer research, or any number of other topics. Once her intrinsic motivation is engaged, she indulges her thirst for knowledge, unimpeded by testing, evaluation, or a need to show her work.

On the other hand, in certain circumstances, a gifted student may be almost entirely extrinsically motivated. Although a student competing for an internship in a laboratory initially might be moved to action by a love of science and a passion for discovery, at the time of the competition, the motivator is no longer the enjoyment of pure research, but rather the reward of gaining the internship.

The interplay between external and internal motivation varies, and in most cases, the two coexist. Suppose, for example, that a talented yet disadvantaged high school student-athlete suffers multiple fractures of the leg. The accident takes him out of the season. The college athletic scholarship he counted on is now in jeopardy because scouts have no current statistics and are concerned about his ability to compete after recovery and rehabilitation.

This student wants to go to college. He now realizes that his only way into the college of his choice is an academic scholarship. He still wants to prove himself as an athlete, but now he will have to compete for a position as a walk-on. His desire for the academic scholarship is a potent extrinsic motivator; he begins to take more responsibility for his classroom work. He brings the focus and discipline he developed on the sports field to the classroom, becoming a far more autonomous learner. His grades jump.

During a history class, he becomes interested in the American Civil War. He attends a Civil War re-enactment with his parents, immersing himself in the battlefield strategies of Lee and Grant. He becomes an expert, which increases his feelings of academic competence. He also is fascinated with how battlefield strategies might be employed in sports and life. He meets other history buffs who provide validation for his interest, and he gains a powerful sense of relatedness.

In this particular area of study, intrinsic motivation has taken over. The student is free to learn whatever he wants and to study as deeply as he wishes, without pressure and without fear. He has not forgotten his outer-directed goal of getting to college, and he will continue to focus on grades and achievement to take him there, but he is also exercising another, deeply satisfying type of motivation.

Both intrinsic and extrinsic motivation are necessary for children to learn. Mihaly Csikszentmihalyi and his colleagues studied adolescents who were gifted in music, art, athletics, math, and science. Those who were artistically gifted were motivated to continue their participation for the intrinsic enjoyment of it. However, unless they also could see extrinsic value, such as the prospect of employment in their talent area, they eventually were inclined to give up the pursuit. Conversely, those who were talented in math and science felt that they could easily find employment in their fields, but their interest in their talent areas diminished unless they felt intrinsically rewarded as well.[5]

Motivations sometimes compete with one another. A gifted boy may relish taking care of young children; he does it for the enjoyment of watching them learn and grow. If he babysits, he may earn some money, but his primary motivation is the fun of being with the younger children. At the same time, he may strongly desire acceptance by a particularly macho peer group who considers caring for children a "girly" activity. One intrinsic motivation. One extrinsic motivation. How does he choose? Or can he find a way to successfully meld the two desires?

Factors that impede intrinsic motivation

Experts agree that while extrinsic motivation can be useful in initiating a learning task, particularly one that is time-limited, routine, and relatively unexciting, such as committing multiplication tables to memory, there are clear advantages to intrinsic motivation. It is intrinsic motivation that helps students make sustained progress toward significant goals, learn to take risks and explore, and develop their potential to the fullest. On the other hand, those who are primarily extrinsically motivated are likely to put forth the least effort necessary to obtain the reward rather than the amount of effort required to make progress in learning.[6]

There are educators who believe that extrinsic rewards have no place whatsoever in the classroom and that intrinsic motivation cannot be developed if rewards are used. This viewpoint is somewhat unrealistic because most children, even the most gifted, may need help in developing the discipline and persistence necessary for academic success. Classroom rewards can help children learn good study habits and the skills they need to move along the path toward independence.

In addition, children require consistent, relevant feedback from their teachers as they strive to learn. The feedback is an external motivator that encourages the student and propels her toward the love of learning itself. Thus, intrinsic motivation is strengthened by an extrinsic factor. Without the teacher's feedback, students might become confused and less able to differentiate between what they know and what they don't know. And confusion can short-circuit motivation.

External rewards are somewhat like training wheels on a bicycle. We don't expect children to jump onto a two-wheeler and pedal down the street without some practice and support. The wheels come off when the child is confident in her ability to ride, and the same is true of classroom rewards.

Rewards can be very powerful motivators when they are used to mark progress, not necessarily as prizes for perfect performance. For example, a shy child who gives an oral presentation can be given a reward for standing up and speaking in front of the class. A more outgoing child for whom oral reports are a breeze might be rewarded not for the actual presentation, but for exceptional research and organization. Rewards, like the curriculum itself, should be individualized. They are most effective when students help in identifying what their rewards should be and how they should be used to measure progress.

Unfortunately, in some American classrooms, intrinsic motivation may be almost completely blocked as teachers are forced to emphasize performance goals such as test scores rather than mastery goals that involve continual improvement and self-discovery. Because of the emphasis on students doing well on every proficiency and achievement test, teachers may fall into the trap of teaching primarily to a student's deficiencies—that is, if a verbally talented child has weaker math skills, a majority of the student's time may be devoted to improving the deficiency rather than developing the area of talent. Over time, the child may become more proficient in math, but his verbal skills may decline, and his motivation will likely take a downward plunge.

It doesn't have to be that way. Required objectives can be mastered by allowing students to reach learning goals by way of their particular interests and passions. Hooking into their interests greatly enhances intrinsic motivation. For instance, while a child completes the course of study required by the school district, she also may select from a list of extension activities that feed her passion and interest. A child who is fascinated by the Renaissance may use that period of history to learn about art, music, mathematics, literature, sociology, medicine, or any number of other subjects. And a child who is intrinsically motivated to learn will learn more and in more depth than one who is concerned only about a grade on a particular test.

A Quick Look: Intrinsic and Extrinsic Motivation in the Classroom

	Characteristics of the Classroom	Teaching Methods that Promote	Typical Rewards
Intrinsic Motivation	Students and teachers set learning goals together Enjoyment Challenge Mastery Empowerment	Choice Inquiry Independent study Skill development Hands-on activities Tied to real life Testing assesses learning, mastery of concepts, and self-improvement	Satisfaction Sustained drive toward further learning Confidence Competence, self-determination Teacher praise for interest, effort, and Improvement
Extrinsic Motivation	Teachers set performance goals Uncertainty Dependency Performance and test anxiety	Drill and repetition Memorization Prescribed outcomes Tests, quizzes Worksheets Testing assesses recall of facts	Grades Competitions Gold stars, stickers Honor rolls Teacher praise for performance Postcards to parents Social events

Motivation-busters in our classrooms

Stress and threat

Two of the most significant barriers to the exercise of intrinsic motivation are stress and threat, and some American schools serve up plenty of both. Students may be threatened in the classroom with detention, suspension, grade reduction, peer rejection, and teasing or bullying. In 22 states, they also may be threatened with corporal punishment—that is, being struck by a school authority with a hand or paddle. Since corporal punishment teaches children that hitting is an acceptable way to get what one wants, parents in many states have banded together to outlaw this type of behavior by school officials.[7]

Some students fail because they are so worried about the outcome of the tests that stress overcomes their ability to think. They freeze and do poorly. If they then go home and are further threatened with grounding, withdrawal of privileges, reduction in allowance, or other punishment, the stress continues.

Some students use stress as an impetus to improve performance. For others, especially those gifted children who are sensitive and intense, threats and punishment can be frightening and immobilizing.

However students appear to respond on the surface, there are bodily changes that accompany stress and real or perceived threats. The adrenal glands release a hormone called cortisol, which prepares the body to fight or flee. The student's muscles tense, his blood pressure increases, and his immune system is momentarily depressed. Levels of serotonin, which modulates emotion, may fall, and a decrease in serotonin may trigger impulsive, aggressive behavior.[8]

According to Eric Jensen, author of *Teaching with the Brain in Mind*, "It can't be repeated enough: Threats activate defense mechanisms and behaviors that are great for survival but lousy for learning.... Survival always overrides pattern-detection and complex problem solving. Students are less able to understand connections.... Learning narrows to memorization of isolated facts."[9] It should be expected, then, that the intrinsic motivation of a gifted student, whose emotions may be more fragile, will likely suffer in an atmosphere overloaded with performance goals and accompanying stress.

Competition

Although some gifted students enjoy competition, others may deliberately underachieve because they want to be liked and accepted by their peers. If they win every geography bee or get the highest grade on every test, potential friends may consider them show-offs and "brainiacs." These students mask their capabilities in order to fit in with their classmates. But covering up who they are is stressful, exhausting, and may start them down the road to depression.

For some gifted children, competition also may exacerbate tendencies toward perfectionism. If the child's self-expectations include perfect classroom performance, losing a competition, even if the child comes in second, may feel like abject failure.

The self-esteem movement

The self-esteem movement has done much to undermine intrinsic motivation because true self-esteem flourishes in an atmosphere of achievement. Says Martin E. P. Seligman, Ph.D., professor of psychology at Penn State University, "The feeling of self-esteem is a byproduct of doing well."[10]

Students feel good about themselves when they succeed at a task that includes some degree of challenge or risk. When adults pile on the plaudits for completing simple assignments, it doesn't heighten students' self-esteem. Lavish praise for tiny steps forward may very well tell children that the significant adults in their lives—their parents and teachers—don't believe that they are capable of much.

If gifted children receive gold stars, pizza parties, and applause for minimal accomplishment, they may wonder why everyone is making such a fuss. They know that their limits haven't been stretched, but because the attention is so pleasant, they may continue to seek the easy task just to bask in the glow of approval. They may come to believe that learning is a snap and that they will succeed at everything they do.

Although parents and educators should give children hope and help them create positive, healthy self-concepts, they also should insist that students grapple with difficult assignments that help them learn to connect hard work and success. Adult must lead children to a realistic assessment and acceptance of both their gifts and their areas of relative weakness. They should also instill the idea that mistakes, errors, and failures are an essential part of learning, not something to be feared and avoided.

Both success and failure can move a student toward achievement, and it's in rising up after being knocked down that a child learns resilience. Rather than rewarding students for success and penalizing failures, parents and teachers can help children focus on the lessons they learn from each outcome. When adults praise learning, even if it comes from failure, the child's self-concept is likely to improve.

If research proves that threats, stress, competition, lowered expectations, and a performance-based atmosphere can negatively affect the development of intrinsic motivation, why are they still so prevalent in our classrooms? Because they work. These motivation-sapping strategies are very effective in promoting students' quick recall of important facts over the short term, and in an era of testing, quick recall is the skill most necessary for success. Successful test scores make a school district look good and keep the money flowing.

Small wonder, then, that some classrooms are full of lethargic learners who master only what they must to get past the next test. Their motivation is anesthetized, and they really don't care about learning in school.

What lack of motivation looks like

Anesthetized motivation in a gifted child may manifest itself in a variety of ways, most of them frustrating and sometimes infuriating to parents and teachers who have such high hopes for the student.

Adults usually report that their first indication of a gifted child's lagging motivation is that her performance in class or on homework assignments and tests is not what one would expect from a child with a superior intellect. The student has scored high on ability tests, indicating giftedness, but her classroom work and test scores that measure achievement don't mirror her ability scores. The child may exhibit a variety of troubling behaviors that include:

- Laziness, i.e., the child doesn't participate fully in academic work and doesn't seem interested in much except lounging around the house watching TV, playing video games, or talking on the phone.

- Defiance, i.e., the child refuses to participate and challenges authority figures to make her do particular tasks.

- Distraction/Disengagement, i.e., the child may participate but complains that the work is irrelevant and performs inadequately.

- Procrastination, i.e., the child delays the work.

- Passive aggression, i.e., the child agrees to do the work but then reneges.

Is it underachievement? Or something else?

All of these behaviors may result in poor test scores, although some particularly bright students can pass tests on the strength of listening, even inattentively, to classroom lecture and discussion. Nevertheless, rarely turning in homework and exhibiting a lackadaisical attitude toward daily instruction will in time earn a student the title of underachiever.

However, when it comes to gifted students, the underachieving label may be misapplied because there is no universally agreed upon definition as to what constitutes underachievement. Is it poor grades? A refusal to complete assignments? An unpleasant classroom demeanor? And how long must a behavior last to be called underachievement? All of us have periods of time when we don't perform optimally, so where do parents and teachers draw the line and decide that underachievement has become chronic?

In addition, gifted children may bear a burden of expectation that other students don't. Once a child has been identified as gifted, parents and teachers often believe that the student will perform at a very high level across the entire curriculum. However, the majority of gifted students are not excellent in every domain. They have areas of specialization. Francine, 10, is brilliant in science but makes less than adequate grades in language arts. César, 11, is already a talented musician/composer who skates along the edge of failure in science. Could either of these students legitimately be called an underachiever?

Although it's certainly true that some gifted students do not perform at a level we expect of them, they may do so on grounds that have little to do with intellectual prowess. One of the chief reasons that motivation may lag is a significant mismatch between the required curriculum and the gifted child.

For example, Shaylah, a gifted ninth grader, is drifting through math, inattentive and careless. She's a quiet student who is never disruptive in the classroom, but her test scores are very low and her homework virtually nonexistent.

However, in the world outside of school, Shaylah is known as a tireless worker for ecological causes. She has spent hours creating a regional elementary education project that helps children understand the importance of keeping trash out of their community storm drains.

Although her daily math homework doesn't reflect her capabilities, Shaylah's calculations regarding the costs of treating polluted storm water and the percentages of pollutants that affect local water quality are correct, exacting, and demonstrate an advanced level of research skill. An underachiever? Not at all. Shaylah is just a child whose interests are not met by a standard curriculum.

Some gifted students may consciously refuse to complete what they consider meaningless homework assignments. Are they underachieving or "demonstrating integrity and courage when they choose not to do required work that is below their intellectual level"?[11] If the curriculum cannot keep up with the student, which one is underachieving?

In some cases, as parents and teachers examine the reasons for a motivational slump, they are chagrined to discover that virtually the *only* place that the student is unmotivated is at school. Such a situation needs to be addressed quickly to keep the student from turning away from academic pursuits altogether. His curriculum and classroom situation must be examined. Learning options that allow him to regain a passion for learning must be implemented. Differentiated instruction is essential; an intense desire to learn that is constantly thwarted by a one-size-fits-all curriculum may result in a tamping down of motivation and a stultifying boredom that can take years to correct.

Boredom that begins in the elementary classroom can become full-fledged underachievement by the time a child reaches middle and high school.[12] Parents of gifted children should listen carefully to continuing complaints of boredom, for research clearly shows that boredom is a close cousin of frustration. A child who is nearly desperate to learn and is given nothing but a standard curriculum will be frustrated, then bored, and then, depending on her personality, may become angry and defiant or anxious and depressed.

A bored child also may *submerge*—that is, cover, suppress, or hide his talents and blend into the classroom. Submersion is usually the result of witnessing or experiencing negative consequences for questioning the curriculum or the teacher. Teachers who must reach specific, state-prescribed learning targets may react negatively to a student who wants to go beyond the day-to-day lessons. If the child persists, a power struggle is likely; the student is suddenly a "behavior problem." Some children choose to avoid that designation by taking another route—the invisibility of submersion, an "emotional self-pres-ervation response to a repressive environment."[13]

Submerged students may do well enough to squeak by, and their teachers are probably never aware of their outstanding capabilities because the students have masked them so expertly. These children are rarely, if ever, challenged, and their talents are squandered as they mean-der through school, unengaged and uninterested.

An unexpected problem: Lack of learning skills

Surprisingly, there's another category of student who may have unsuspected motivational challenges: gifted achievers. In the early grades, many gifted students enjoy school and master every learning challenge quickly and easily. They do the work required, but the tasks are so far below their capabilities that they soar easily to the top of the class. Par-ents are delighted with their children's performance, and teachers applaud them. Their grades are excellent, and they receive honors and accolades for their achievements. Nonetheless, this situation may be a disaster waiting to happen.

For example, Mario, a gifted sixth grader, blasted his way through the curriculum in elementary school. He earned top marks without much effort. Suddenly, in the first semester of middle school, he became bewildered by more complex assignments. His homework was often incomplete, and his test scores plummeted in spite of his obvious ability.

Mario's once abundant self-confidence took a nosedive. He became listless and almost inert, befuddled by his unexpected freefall from the head of the class. His motivation stalled. The only way he could explain his lethargy was to say that he was bored, but that excuse didn't ring true with his parents or teachers. He wasn't bored. He was scared.

Mario's situation was in some ways predictable. Because he achieved without effort in elementary school, he never learned the relationship between work and accomplishment. He could usually complete his class assignments and homework in a few minutes, so he never developed regular study habits or time management skills. Rarely challenged by his scholastic endeavors, he gained little practice in setting goals and perse-vering to reach them. In middle school, he had his first challenging classes, and he abruptly discovered that even for gifted students, learning and feelings of self-worth are tied to overcoming challenges and contin-uing to persevere, even the face of discouragement and difficulty.

Fortunately, Mario's parents and his team of teachers intervened quickly to get him back on track. Mario was gifted in reading and writing, and he wanted to see his work in the school magazine. His teachers used that desire to reshape his attitude and upgrade his skills. They spoke with Mario as they would with a peer. They set high expectations and helped him see that a slapdash product would not be of sufficient quality to be published. They worked with him to establish a reasonable goal—that he would have one short story published in the magazine by the end of the school year.

The language arts teacher laid out the steps that Mario needed to accomplish before one of his pieces would be ready for publication. They included:

- Writing a certain number of words each day until the short story was finished.

- Editing the piece for style and readability.

- Re-editing for word usage, spelling, grammar, and punctuation.

- Submitting the story by the deadline.

These small interim goals broke the project into manageable chunks and allowed Mario to focus intensely in an area of interest to him. His teacher's obvious belief that Mario could write a high-quality story fired his creativity and relit his motivation to try.

His other teachers showed Mario that the technique of setting large goals and breaking them down into achievable steps was an effective way to eliminate some of the panic that caused him such distress in his other subjects as well. His parents provided a place for him to study and insisted that homework be completed before he participated in anything else. They also showed him some time management techniques that worked for them on their jobs. Most important, Mario's parents trusted him to assume responsibility for his own homework assignments. Although they were available for guidance and assistance, they expected him to handle this part of his life by himself.

Mario bloomed in the new environment. He knew that the significant adults in his life believed in him, and he proved that he was worthy of their belief. He began to understand the linkages between effort and achievement, which increased his feelings of self-efficacy and heightened his internal locus of control. His confidence was re-established, and this time, that confidence was not based not on the sand of test results, but on the bedrock of real learning.

Although there were occasional setbacks, Mario's work ethic improved. He met his obligations, and his inventive short story was published by the end of the year. It was also entered in a national contest for student writers and received an honorable mention.

Mario had always had the ability and intrinsic motivation to excel, but without the skills, he was intensely frustrated and in danger of not being able to express his unique talents. Today, Mario is studying creative writing at a major university. Although he'd like to make a living as a novelist, he's also interested in teaching.

Mary Elizabeth, the parent of fourth-grade twin girls, explains the skills issue this way: "The girls have completely different intellectual patterns. Kylie is gifted, and everything comes too easily. She doesn't have a clue about working hard. Kaylene doesn't have her sister's intellect, but their grades are identical because Kaylene is a bulldog. She never gives up on an assignment until she understands it. She works and works and envies her sister's quick mind. I have a hunch that in the future, though, it's Kylie who's going to turn to her sister to learn how to persevere when she doesn't fully understand a concept the first time around."

Children need opportunities to master tasks that become progressively more difficult and challenging. As one prominent educator noted, "We do not succeed in spite of our challenges and difficulties; we succeed precisely *because* of them."[14] Mastery of challenges develops resiliency and optimism for the next task.

Recovering motivation

Although motivational theories may differ in some aspects, most experts agree that certain factors are necessary to kick off, maintain, or recapture motivation.

- Motivation requires a meaningful goal and a reward that is commensurate with goal accomplishment. Such a reward may be tangible or intangible.

- The goal must be *challenging* but obtainable so that attaining it fosters a sense of competence and self-efficacy—that is, the student's positive belief in his ability to cope with situations and outcomes. The goal should test the student's capabilities but not overtax them.

- The goal must be important and valuable enough to inspire *commitment*. To be meaningful, motivation must be sustained, and only important goals will engage the student for the long term.

- The student must feel that she has some *control* in how she reaches the goal. If the child believes that goals are reached by chance or circumstances outside her ability to control, motivation wanes. Control also implies *choice*; the student is given considerable latitude in what and how she chooses to learn.

These three C's will go a long way toward instilling motivation, but especially for gifted children, a fourth C is essential: *compassion*. Although many gifted children are hardy souls who can roll with the punches, others are bundles of raw nerves, quick to be hurt, take offense, worry, misunderstand, and be misunderstood. They flourish in a place where they are not showered with false praise, but are treated with respect for their special talents and empathy for their special needs.

The gifted student's optimal classroom

The four C's are most often found in what is called a constructivist learning environment, and teachers from around the country agree that gifted students respond well to such an atmosphere. This environment focuses on the relevance of learning and includes an emphasis on real-world problem solving; a presentation of many perspectives, all of which may have some validity and may be combined to arrive at a more comprehensive "truth"; and the concept that the teacher is a coach and guide rather than a purveyor of facts. In constructivist classrooms, students don't sit passively soaking up data and theories. Instead, they breathe life into their own learning. They build on what they already know and create increasingly abstract concepts. Since each student's experience and degree of knowledge are different, each student's learning is different from every other student's, even if they are working on the same topic.

Although there are many opportunities for hands-on projects, there is also ample time for students to reflect on what they have learned. They learn in the context of real life, including social problems and moral issues, so that what they discover is relevant and meaningful in the context of daily activities. Constructivist teachers help students make connections and encourage them to analyze and synthesize information, which are activities that are particularly attractive to gifted learners.

Gifted children are more likely to motivate themselves when they feel safe and are able to trust those who influence them. They must understand the objectives of study and be given the tools and skills they need to set appropriate goals, as well as the support necessary to achieve them. They need honest feedback, high expectations, relevant experiences, lots of listening, and teachers and parents who believe in their abilities.

Adult belief in students' abilities is a powerful predictor of classroom success. In fact, it can become a self-fulfilling prophecy. Research, primarily by Harvard professor Robert Rosenthal, Ph.D., dramatically demonstrates that when teachers expect students to do well and grow intellectually, the students meet those expectations. Conversely, when teachers don't believe in the students' ability to grow, they don't.[15] And when gifted students are motivated by the high expectations of significant adults they trust, growth can be astonishing.

Motivation is not a constant. It is fluid, changeable, and can be greatly affected by physical, social, emotional, and scholastic issues. It also varies by context. A student may be unmotivated to complete a book report yet quite motivated to write his own futuristic novel.

Motivational options may vary by gender. Because of brain differences between boys and girls, motivation methods that work for one sex may be ineffective with the other. Motivation also changes with age. Strategies that effectively motivate younger students may fall flat with adolescents.

When a gifted child's motivation is shaky, she needs adults who can help her recapture the satisfaction of working to her capacities. Being one of those adults is an awesome responsibility, a sometimes perplexing challenge, and a source of great joy.

In summary

- The major motivation theories include Attribution Theory, Goal Theory, and Self-Determination Theory. Any or all of these theories can be at work in a student at any time.

- Extrinsic motivation is related to rewards, such as grades and recognition. Intrinsic motivation is related to work for its own sake. Intrinsic motivation results in more effective learning, but both types are frequently intertwined.

- The underachievement of gifted students is a complicated issue. A student may be highly motivated to learn, but he may find that the school doesn't meet his needs for intellectual stimulation and challenge.

- Underachievement is multifaceted and usually involves social and emotional dimensions, as well as low grades, limited participation in the classroom, and incomplete homework.

- To be motivated, a gifted child requires challenge, control, and commitment, as well as a compassionate environment.

Section II

When Motivation Disappears: Looking for Causes

Chapter 3
Physical Reasons for Loss of Motivation

Gifted children are often volatile, sensitive, intense, and prickly. Therefore, if their grades plummet or their motivation to learn in school diminishes, parents and teachers often look first for emotional causes. This may be a mistake. Although psychological issues may be a factor, the child may have a physical problem that results in a motivational slip. Conversely, a child may still be highly motivated but plagued by an undiagnosed special need.

Physical issues can range from simple vision and hearing deficits to complex learning disabilities that have gone unnoticed because of the child's exceptional intellect. Many of these physical conditions exhaust the child. Straining to see, hear, or understand what's happening in the classroom uses tremendous amounts of energy, and an overly fatigued gifted child may exhibit reactions ranging from excessive sleeping (which may be mistaken for depression) to lashing out inappropriately (which may be confused with a behavioral disorder). Parents suddenly hear, "I can't," "The work is too hard/boring/stupid," "I don't care," or "I don't understand." To figure out what's going on, it's oftentimes wise to start with the body.

Vision problems

Even a small change in vision may make it harder for any child, even the most gifted, to attend to schoolwork. If it's an effort for him to read a book or if he can't see figures and numbers on the board as well as he used to, he may become restless and inattentive, even if he'd rather participate and be part of the life of the classroom. Homework that involves reading or worksheets may become more difficult; he may make more mistakes, become discouraged, or stop turning in papers altogether. At that point, parents or teachers often lay down the law, revoking privileges and demanding that work be completed before the child is allowed to do anything else. It's a power struggle in the making, yet the reason for the struggle may remain hidden.

Children may not be able to articulate that they're having trouble with their vision, especially if the change is subtle and has come on slowly. Some signs are obvious and indicate that the child needs the attention of a vision specialist: crossed eyes; independent movement of one eye (amblyopia or lazy eye); itchy, red eyes; crusty eyelids; and tilting the head or closing one eye so that the "good" eye is used. Some students complain of headaches or nausea. Other children mention blurred or double vision.

Other cues are not so overt. Some behaviors that may suggest vision problems include:

- *Avoidance of close work.* The child may try to avoid tasks involving textbooks or worksheets with small print or complex figures at school or at home. This behavior may be mistaken for lack of motivation or even defiance.

- *Changes in attention span.* Because the child frequently looks away from her work or the chalkboard, she may appear to be daydreaming, when in fact she is seeking relief from eyestrain or discomfort. Some children may actually close their eyes in class, which the teacher may interpret as inattention or disrespectful behavior.

- *Frequent blinking, eye rubbing, or even shaking of the head* in an attempt to clear the vision. These behaviors may look like tics, which are habitual twitches, especially in the face, often associated with autism spectrum disorders or Tourette's syndrome.

- *Reading problems.* The child reverses letters, loses his place, or can't remember what he read. All of these issues can be traced to defects in visual functioning, but these traits may also make parents and teachers suspect dyslexia or other reading disorders. Dyslexia and vision deficits can coexist, but sometimes a simple correction can improve vision, change the child's performance, and re-ignite motivation.

- *Poor performance on timed tests.* The child's vision doesn't allow her to process the test as quickly as her peers, making her appear less able than she is.

Parents should remember that simple screening tests are not sufficient to diagnose all vision problems. A child may have excellent *sight*—that is, he can see clearly and accurately—but have significant *vision* problems because vision deals with the ability to use visual information to learn. School screening exams, for example, are designed to discover which students might need further examination or referral to their pediatricians or eye specialists. The tests deal primarily with visual acuity and clarity, but eye problems may also involve issues such as eye coordination, depth perception, peripheral vision, color vision, and astigmatism. Only a complete evaluation gives parents and teachers a comprehensive understanding of a student's vision challenges.

Jack was a child who needed vision help. As he grew through elementary school, he became less able to excel and a more disruptive class clown, even though he had begun with great promise. A family friend suggested a visit to an ophthalmologist, who discovered a variety of vision problems. Jack underwent eye surgery and was fitted with corrective lenses.

Once the glasses were on his face, Jack's first words to his physician were, "Doc, look! I always thought your desk was curved, but it has corners!" Although they'd been discussed in class, Jack had never seen a right angle and couldn't make sense of many forms and shapes. When his vision improved, he zoomed ahead. His class clown tendencies never abated, but he became the student he was capable of becoming. A gifted writer, he put his comic tendencies to work writing television scripts and has enjoyed a successful career.

Hearing problems

Like vision issues, hearing loss has a dramatic impact on the ability to learn, and if the loss is gradual, the child may be almost unaware of the deficit. However, diminished classroom performance, coupled with frustration, behavioral changes, and some specific, hearing-related clues, may suggest a hearing impairment. These include:

- *Speech that is louder or softer than that of the child's peers.* Some children are naturally soft-voiced or boisterous, but a child who shouts or whispers most of the time may not be able to appreciate the volume of her own voice because she can't hear it very well.

- *Slower vocabulary development than that of her peers.* Children learn to speak by overhearing—that is, listening to others speak. If overhearing is difficult, it's not surprising that vocabulary would then lag behind that of hearing children.

- *Frequent requests that you repeat what you said.* Yes, some children simply zone out when parents or teachers make requests or demands, but a child with a hearing deficit may be listening with all his might yet still be unable to understand what's asked of him.

- *A loud environment.* The child may want the television or video games tuned to frequencies that are painful for other members of the family. Children often like their music loud, sometimes with a booming bass line, but a child who requires that everything be turned up or can't easily hear ambient sounds such as a blender or doorbell is a candidate for an auditory evaluation.

- *Detachment.* The child may be unaware of things going on in her immediate environment and thus appear inattentive. She may ask "off the wall" questions that have little to do with the topic being discussed. The types of mistakes that the child makes often are related to her inability to hear. If she misunderstands basic concepts because she has not heard the full explanation, she will be less able build on those concepts and acquire more sophisticated understanding.

Although many identified deaf or hard of hearing children are gifted students and perform beautifully in the classroom, a gifted child with an unsuspected hearing loss may fall behind simply because he doesn't have access to the types of support that other hearing-impaired students receive. Under these circumstances, a motivational decline would be the norm rather than the exception.

As with vision screenings, a simple hearing test conducted by school personnel will not detect all hearing difficulties. If such a test indicates that the child has normal hearing but adults continue to notice behavior that might indicate a hearing deficit, more sophisticated testing should be carried out. The child's pediatrician can coordinate such testing, or parents themselves can make arrangements for it.

Of the many causes of hearing loss in children and young people, the most common are recurrent ear infections (*otitis media*) and loud noises. Experts estimate that a large majority of children will have at least one ear infection during childhood, and of those who do, half will have three or more before their fourth birthday.[1] Although most ear infections result in discomfort and a temporary hearing loss, they are generally treated and resolved. However, *otitis media* can occur without pain, and if there is fluid in the ear for an extended period of time, the child may be unable to hear specific speech sounds. She will have difficulty understanding what others say and will develop speech that is difficult to understand.

In older children, especially 'tweens and teens, hearing loss may be directly linked to noise. Everything from rock concerts to lawn mowing to "boom cars" can have long-term effects on hearing. Recent research shows that about 12.5% of children ages six to 19 in the United States have hearing loss as a result of noise.[2]

Sound pressure is measured in decibels (dB). Loud noise can ruin a child's hearing by damaging or destroying the hair cells in the inner ear that carry sound waves to the brain. Prolonged exposure to any noise above 90 decibels can cause gradual hearing loss. According to the Wise Ears!® program of the National Institute on Deafness and Other Communication Disorders, some typical school-age situations that can have an effect on a child's hearing include lawn mowing with a power mower (90 dB), shop classes (power tools and other noises can reach 100 dB), personal music devices that deliver sound directly into the ear (105 dB), and rock concerts (110dB).[3]

The National Institutes of Health caution that as noise levels rise, exposure time before hearing may be damaged is decreased. They state that for every three decibels over 85dB, the permissible exposure time is cut in half. Therefore, standard traffic noises (85dB) can begin to damage hearing in eight hours, but a power lawn mower can do the job in roughly two hours, unless adequate ear protection is used. A personal music player at 105 dB can cause hearing damage in less than 30 seconds, so you can imagine the effects of a rock concert. In fact, if you've ever chaperoned a school dance and left with ringing ears, your hearing was damaged, at least temporarily.[4] Our children lead noisy lives. As parents and teachers, we must help educate them in ways to mitigate their exposure to today's loud environments.

Learning disabilities: Visual and auditory processing disorders

Gifted children have exceptional cognitive and/or artistic powers. They also may be highly creative or great leaders. All of these attributes are related to the ways in which their brains function. Gifted students' brains frequently incorporate new learning quickly and "make the transition from novelty to routine in less time."[5] They may develop more efficient neural pathways that help them solve various types of problems with less effort than that required by average students. Their brains may mature more quickly than other students.' Some studies indicate that a certain type of brain wave activity in gifted adolescents more closely resembles that of college students than that of their average-ability peers.[6]

Generally, learning disabilities are also related to the way a child's brain functions, and having a gifted brain does not preclude having a learning disability. A child may have very efficient neural pathways and at the same time have a genetic defect or other brain-based issue that impairs her ability to read, write, or interpret information gained through the senses. This child is called "twice exceptional"—that is, gifted, but with a disability.

The combination of high ability and leaning problems can be difficult to understand and live with. Parents, teachers, and the children themselves are often frustrated and angry because the brain is in some ways at war with itself. In domains in which the brain is efficient, the child may learn almost effortlessly. In other areas, he may struggle, flounder, and even give up. Some of the most common issues include visual and auditory processing problems and trouble with reading and writing.

Problems with vision that are not related specifically to acuity or clarity are called visual processing problems, and they can have far-reaching effects. Visual processing has to do with the child's ability to use and interpret information that she gains visually. The eyes and brain are not working together in a synchronized fashion. Such a disability may have a huge impact on the child's ability to reach the potential afforded by her giftedness.

The child may have problems with spatial relationships—that is, knowing where objects are in space, either singly or in relationship to each other. Reading and math may be problematic because he has difficulty seeing how symbols, signs, letters, and numbers work together. For example, if a child can't perceive the relationship and spacing between two numbers and the symbol "÷," then he will have a hard time with division. If he can't see the difference between the letters *m* and *n*, reading will be a challenge.

Being unable to judge where objects are in space can also make the child appear clumsy. She may walk into things. Her supplies and projects might fall off her desk because she can't judge the width or depth of the desktop. On the playground, she may not be good at games such as kickball because she can't figure out where the ball is until it hits her. In class, her fine-motor skills may not allow her to replicate what she sees, which may make it nearly impossible for her to write within the margins of her paper or line up the numbers to solve even the simplest math problems.

Some children forget what objects and symbols look like. They are unable to hold the picture of the object in their minds or to call it up when necessary. How can a student read a story if he can't remember what the word "the" looks like from Friday to Monday or even from Monday to Tuesday?

Just as there are visual processing problems, children may have auditory processing issues, even if their hearing is perfect. Auditory processing refers to the ability of the brain to recognize, interpret, and use information gained through listening. Children with auditory processing disorders have difficulty with those functions. They may hear every word with crystal clarity but be unable to comprehend the meaning of what they've heard. Children with auditory processing problems may:

- *Be inattentive in class and not understand or remember oral instructions, especially those with multiple steps.* Imagine trying to hear a flute in an orchestra in which the rest of the instruments are tubas and bassoons. That's what it can be like for students with auditory problems who are trying to find meaning in the torrent of words that comprise a typical school day. The child may forget instructions immediately or be unable to recall them later. Exhausted and baffled, even the most gifted child may give up and simply occupy a seat.

- *Not be able to discriminate between similar-sounding words,* like *cat* or *bat, big* or *pig, hen* or *pen,* which makes reading, spelling, or other language tasks extremely difficult. The child also may not understand oral presentations or lectures because similar-sounding words may be confusing.

- *Seem to be daydreaming.* In fact, the child may listen very intently but struggle to understand what the teacher and other students are saying. The child is often off task, even if she's trying to do what the other students are doing. Sometimes, however, the child really is daydreaming because there's no other option available. She can't keep up, so she quits trying and retreats.

- *Be unable to participate well in classroom groups.* Children with auditory processing disorders may perform relatively well in one-to-one interactions with a teacher or another student but have a great deal of trouble with groups, simply because there are too many strands of conversation to follow. It's too noisy for the child to be able to concentrate and function.

- *Be disorganized and "spacey."* Because it's hard for these children to follow directions, maintain focus, pay attention, and listen, they may be less able to organize themselves, their space, and their work.

Since many of the symptoms overlap, children with auditory processing problems may be incorrectly diagnosed with Attention Deficit Hyperactivity Disorder (ADD/ADHD). Although a child may have both conditions, sometimes the issue is strictly one of auditory processing.

All of these processing issues make it very hard for a child, even the most gifted, to learn. Motivation requires a match between task difficulty and the student's abilities, and when those abilities are dulled by an unsuspected problem, the match is not achieved; motivation will probably dip. However, when the curriculum and instruction are modified to meet the needs of the child, his giftedness will likely spur him on to success.

Reading disorders

Dyslexia is the term applied to most reading disorders, and many people believe that dyslexia is simply the reversing of letters—*d* for *b*, for example. However, dyslexia is far more. According to the National Institutes of Health, it is "a specific learning disability that is neurological in origin. It is characterized by difficulties with accurate and/or fluent word recognition, and by poor spelling and decoding abilities."[7]

In other words, children with dyslexia have difficulty with reading and writing, no matter how hard they work to master the skills. On the other hand, they may be extremely gifted in areas that don't depend on language. Many visual and performing artists, scientists, and mathematicians have contended with dyslexia throughout their lives. Some of these notables include artist Pablo Picasso; General George Patton; actors Henry Winkler, Whoopi Goldberg, Tom Cruise, Danny Glover, and Patrick Dempsey; successful businessmen Sir Richard Branson and Charles Schwab; Olympic gold medalists Greg Louganis and Bruce

Jenner; designer Tommy Hilfiger; politician Nelson Rockefeller; and president Woodrow Wilson.

Dyslexics may but do not always have advanced visual and spatial skills. In the United Kingdom, the Arts Dyslexia Trust encourages research into the reasons for the connection between dyslexia and good visual-spatial faculties which can lead to exceptional ability and achievement in the arts and sciences.[8]

Dyslexia is not, then, a recipe for disaster, but an issue to be addressed. It requires modification of the curriculum and instruction, as well as coordination among parents, teachers, and others who may be involved in supporting the child's learning.

One of the most common learning disabilities, dyslexia is brain-based and often inherited. A study at the University of Washington showed that dyslexic children use nearly five times the brain area as normal children to complete a simple language task. Researchers concluded that there are chemical differences in the brain function of dyslexic and non-dyslexic children. "Their brains were working a lot harder and using more energy than the normal children," says Todd Richards, one of the investigators in the study.[9] And that study followed only one learning task. These children are often terribly weary after one day in a typical language-based schoolroom.

Many children with dyslexia have difficulty discriminating among the various sounds of spoken language, which makes it much harder for them to learn the relationships between letters and the sounds they represent in words. Therefore, these students find it hard to sound out words, and since they lack a basic awareness of the sounds of letters, phonics instruction can be meaningless to them. Dyslexic children may also have visual issues; letters may seem to shimmer, float, overlap one another, or blur.

Beyond the obvious reading difficulties, dyslexic students often have deficits in short-term memory. In a complicated set of oral instructions, they may forget all but the first step. When they finish that portion of the assignment, they may be surprised that other students are continuing to work. They wonder what's taking the others so long, and if they ask the teacher what to do next, they may be met by exasperation and a demand that they learn to pay attention. Paradoxically, these children may have exceptional long-term memory.

Dyslexic children may also find it difficult to name specific objects; however, they may come up with the name of an object in the same category. For instance, show them an apple, and they might call it a pear.

These children are frequently late for events and often behind when turning in assignments because both their perception of time and their ability to tell time are affected by their condition. They also may be slow-speaking, and they may stammer or mix up syllables because of delays between thought and action.

Discouraged by her inability to conquer the most basic of school tasks, a dyslexic child may become anxious, depressed, and enraged. As she sees first graders master skills that still elude her in the fifth grade, her self-image shrivels. It's easy for a child who struggles with reading to think of herself as "dumb," even if she's highly gifted. It's common for students with language challenges to lose motivation to learn in an atmosphere that is heavily language-based, such as a subject-specific classroom. However, gifted students with dyslexia may still demonstrate considerable motivation in school settings such as the vocal music department, shop, drama, the media center, or the laboratory, and in locations beyond school walls, such as a dance academy, an art studio, or a science museum.

A student with a reading disorder may be able to hide his problem for many years, using his exceptional intelligence to work around the disability. By the time adults discover the issue, he may need extensive assistance in skill development and recovery of motivation.

Reading and writing deficits can be a bit of a puzzle. Many students who have trouble with reading and writing do not have dyslexia, and some students with dyslexia appear to have ADD/ADHD. Although a child can have both, professional testing is essential to discover precisely what issues need to be addressed. Treating a child for ADD/ADHD won't help a reading ability, and treatment for dyslexia doesn't ameliorate ADD/ADHD.

Case Study: Gareth

Artistic and creative, Gareth, age 12, was failing sixth grade, although he had excelled from kindergarten through fifth grade. He had a thorough physical and checked out perfectly. Gareth had always been slow in turning in written work and his homework was often messy, but nothing indicated a learning disability.

After careful questioning by an intervention specialist, Gareth finally opened up and admitted that he had rarely, if ever, read a book. When he had to give a book report, he found out what other students were reading and asked them about the plot and what they thought of the book. He then incorporated those opinions into brilliant oral reports that always received high grades.

Many teachers commented on Gareth's intense attention during instructional periods. One even mentioned that she felt as if she were under a microscope. What no one knew was that he was memorizing everything he heard in class because it was difficult for him to read the textbook. Although he could sight-read words he'd learned from observation and listening in the lower grades, he had great difficulty sounding out unfamiliar words and grasping concepts in text.

Depending on how much reading was required on a test, his grade could range from an A to an F, but he always had plausible excuses for a lower grade. Because Gareth possessed a keen intellect and a great deal of natural charm, he could often talk teachers into giving him an oral test—and he excelled on this type of assessment.

The intervention specialist was impressed with Gareth's unusual learning strategies and inventive workarounds and recommended that he be tested further for both giftedness and disability. On ability tests, he scored in the highly gifted range, but he suffered from dyslexia. His brilliant mind had allowed him to accommodate his disability, but as schoolwork became harder, his compensation methods began to break down. He could no longer maintain the façade, and he was worn out and discouraged. His motivation, except in art class, had virtually disappeared. With assistance, Gareth's reading issues were addressed, and he continued his interest in art.

Today, Gareth is a junior in a magnet school for visual and performing arts and is widely known for his work in both two and three dimensions. Although some special training has helped him increase his fluency in reading, it remains a struggle. Although he will probably never make the letter grades that he would be capable of if he were not burdened by his reading problems, his parents and teachers have encouraged him to pursue his art studies and to think about career choices that will allow him to use these special gifts. Neither his teachers nor his parents consider Gareth an underachiever because his motivation and work ethic in his area of expertise are exemplary.

Gareth is fortunate that the adults in his life do not define him by his disability or dwell on what he cannot do well. Although they have devoted time and effort to improving his reading, their major focus has been on discovering and nurturing what makes him unique. Their support, encouragement, understanding, and acceptance of both his exceptional talent and his disability have been instrumental in Gareth becoming a self-confident, outgoing young man who is excited about the possibilities of life.

Attention Deficit Hyperactivity Disorder

Attention Deficit Hyperactivity Disorder (ADD/ADHD) is one of the most hotly debated and confusing issues surrounding gifted education. Can a child who is gifted also have ADD/ADHD? Of course. If somewhere between 2–7% of American children are affected by the disorder, there's no reason to assume that the gifted population is exempt. Can a child who is gifted seem to have ADD/ADHD even if she doesn't? Yes, especially if those making the judgment don't know the diagnostic criteria and assume that any child who is inattentive, distractible, energetic, impulsive, and intense must have the condition.

ADD/ADHD is now considered to be a biological rather than a behavioral issue, which is often welcome news to parents who have been led to believe that their parenting style is what has caused their child's poor school performance, tantrums, lack of control, and rudeness. ADD/ADHD is specifically related to the "executive" functions of the brain, especially the ability to control impulses and responses. There also are deleterious effects on the student's short-term memory.

The condition arises from abnormal regulation of certain chemical messengers within the brain, and to a large degree, it's genetic. Approximately 70% of cases appear to run in families.[10] Identification requires a comprehensive evaluation of behavior across a variety of settings and an interdisciplinary approach involving not only the teacher and parents, but also the pediatrician and/or any combination of other professionals, such as medical specialists, counselors, and psychologists. If giftedness is demonstrated, the multidisciplinary team should also include an expert in gifted education. ADD/ADHD is a specific diagnosis, not a catch-all for behavior that parents and teachers deem inappropriate.

ADD/ADHD is marked by inattention, distractibility, impulsivity, and hyperactivity and can be broken down into three types: (1) behavior that includes inattention, but not hyperactivity or impulsivity, (2) behavior that includes hyperactivity and impulsivity but not inattention, and (3) a mixed type that includes symptoms from both groups.[11]

To be diagnosed with ADD/ADHD, a child must exhibit at least six of the nine symptoms in Group One or Group Two below, and those symptoms must have persisted for at least six months *to a degree that is maladaptive and inconsistent with the child's developmental level.*[12]

A child with Group One (Inattention) symptoms may:

- Not pay attention to details and make careless errors.

- Have difficulty maintaining sustained attention when working or playing.

- Appear not to listen when spoken to.

- Not follow through or finish schoolwork, homework, chores, or projects.

- Have difficulty organizing what needs to be done.

- Avoid tasks that require sustained mental effort, neglecting homework or other school assignments.

- Lose belongings, such as notebooks, supplies, equipment, or books required for various tasks and activities.

- Be easily distracted by things going on around him.

- Be forgetful in everyday activities, neglecting to feed animals, pick up toys, or turn off faucets or stove burners.

A child affected by Group Two (Hyperactivity) symptoms may:

- Fidget, wiggle, and squirm when seated.

- Find it almost impossible to sit in her seat in the classroom for a long period of time.

- Run around or climb on things when that behavior is not desirable.

- Find it difficult to engage in quiet play.

- Seem to be driven by an internal motor that's stuck in the "on" position.

- Talk constantly.

Impulsivity symptoms include:

- Blurting out answers to questions that haven't been finished.
- Having difficulty waiting one's turn.
- Interrupting and intruding upon the activities of others.

In addition, some of these symptoms must have been present *before the age of seven* and must occur in *at least two settings* (e.g., home, school, club activities). There must be clear evidence that the behaviors *have a significant negative impact on the child's ability to function socially or academically.* It also must be established that the behaviors are *not* caused by other conditions such as anxiety, depression, or mental disorders of various kinds.[13]

It is important for parents of highly active or forgetful children to keep these diagnostic criteria in mind because others observing the child may suggest that he "has a touch of ADD/ADHD" and "might benefit from a trial of medication." Although ADD/ADHD is a recognized disorder, the United States accounts for 90% of worldwide prescriptions for the stimulants used to treat it. This may mean that we are recognizing and treating the disorder more frequently than those in other countries, or it means that we are overmedicating normal children who march to the beat of a different drummer.

There are stories of children who have made nearly miraculous progress on Ritalin® and other stimulant medication, and Ritalin itself is one of the most widely studied and understood medicines available. It is generally considered safe, although in 2006, concerns were raised about its effect on cardiovascular health, and more stringent labeling information was requested. For all of the beneficial effects of such medical treatment, however, there are also tales of children for whom medication has been ineffective. Too fast a leap to diagnosis, and pharmaceutical intervention may be detrimental. Relying solely on checklists of symptoms or listening to family and friends who are not experts in ADD/ADHD is usually a mistake.

For example, parents often hear that the child's ability to focus on anything for long periods of time is proof positive that she can't have ADD/ADHD. This is a false and misleading supposition. ADD/ADHD children, including those who are gifted, can often concentrate well, especially on activities that require little effort and are highly stimulating, changeable, and immediately rewarding.[14] Certain movies, television shows, and video games fall into these categories and can usually hold the attention of any child, even one with ADD/ADHD.

Also, any gifted student, even one with ADD/ADHD, can sometimes focus intensely on an interesting activity that the child himself selects.[15] In gifted students without ADD/ADHD, this state of heightened attention is often referred to as "flow."[16] In gifted people with ADD/ADHD, the condition may be referred to as "perseveration" or "hyperfocus." Whatever the term used, the child concentrates and pays attention, perhaps for a long period of time.

Identification: Why does it matter?

Although there is great concern about misidentification of ADD/ADHD, it's very important that gifted children who have the disorder be identified so that they can have access to the special services and accommodations that the condition requires. Experts tell us that gifted children with ADD/ADHD are often on the horns of a dilemma. Because their exceptional ability sometimes allows them to compensate for milder manifestations of the condition, parents and teachers may not notice the symptoms until the child shows severe impairment. By that time, the student may have spent years being inappropriately served in the classroom. On the other hand, the inattention and hyperactivity that characterize ADD/ADHD often hamper the students' abilities to excel on the tests that make them eligible for gifted programming. Once again, they are denied the optimal educational environment.[17]

If you're the parent of a gifted child, the list of ADD/ADHD symptoms may make your heart sink a little. Undoubtedly you've seen at least a few of these traits in your own offspring: forgetfulness, fidgeting, blurting out answers, constant talking, daydreaming, distractibility. So how do you tell the difference between a medical condition and the normal behavior of a gifted child? And how do you know if your child has both? The chart below may help you make some distinctions.

Gifted without ADD/ADHD	Gifted with ADD/ADHD
Shows asynchronous development—that is, the cognitive or thinking part of the personality races ahead of the social and emotional components, often causing misunderstandings with age peers. The child may be seem grown up at one moment and childish the next. Asynchrony may be greater if child is highly gifted.	Shows asynchronous development to a greater degree than the typical gifted child. Much greater variation in the child's ability to "act his age." Problems with peers may be more pronounced because of child's lack of ability to control behavior.

Gifted without ADD/ADHD	Gifted with ADD/ADHD
Symptoms tend to be setting-specific. Child may act out at school yet be attentive and in control elsewhere, like choir practice, scout meetings, or on a family trip. This behavior may indicate curriculum mismatch or other school-related issues.	Symptoms occur in most settings: school, home, scouts, restaurants, etc. Child often does well in novel situations because newness offers stimulation and engagement. After novelty wears off, it's back to business as usual.
May be inattentive and make errors because schoolwork is not challenging or tied to child's real life.	May be inattentive and make careless errors because of short-term memory deficits that make it hard for child to remember instructions or sequences. May have "output" problems—that is, it may be hard for her to express what she knows.[18]
Child is easily distracted because classwork requires little effort and leads to boredom; "hyperactive" behavior and excessive fidgeting may be a way that the child activates his brain in the absence of other meaningful stimulation.	Child is easily distracted because of inability to maintain focus, especially in an environment that taxes his attention, such as a busy schoolroom. Fidgets because of inability to control body; often up and out of seat, wandering around the classroom.
Speaks out of turn because she already knows the answers to questions and is eager to move on to further learning.	Speaks out in class because of inability to regulate her behavior and appreciate the consequences of her actions.
May not complete homework because he finds it repetitive and meaningless. Refusal to do work is a deliberate choice.	May not complete homework because he doesn't understand the assignment, can't organize his time, or misplaces the materials necessary to complete the work.
May show improved behavior when given appropriate classroom challenges and grouped with intellectual peers.	May show improved behavior in a quiet, structured, predictable environment.
May concentrate intensely on a task to master it. May have trouble moving between activities because of great interest in one topic. When interrupted, child can return to the task relatively easily.	May concentrate intensely on task because of inability to shift focus. May have trouble moving between activities because of difficulty in refocusing attention on a new subject. When interrupted, child may have great difficulty returning to the task.
Tends to make consistent effort in classes that interest her and with teachers who provide appropriate challenge. Makes good grades, at least in interest areas.	Effort is inconsistent in every class, and grades are usually substandard because of inability to concentrate on class discussions and homework. Acting out can cause problems with teachers and other students.

The combination of giftedness and ADD/ADHD is one of the most common dual exceptionalities and also one of the most problematic. Treating the medical condition while allowing the child to develop her areas of strength can be like walking a tightrope. Sometimes the strategies that mitigate the ADD/ADHD are detrimental to the flowering of the child's talent. For example, if a gifted child is comfortable with complexity (and most are), simplifying and shortening work to address her attention issues may be extremely frustrating for her.[19]

Finding the most appropriate educational setting for gifted children with ADD/ADHD may prove to be a bewildering exercise for both parents and teachers. For gifted students with mild symptoms, a school with stimulating, small classes may reduce symptoms to manageable levels, and the child's native intelligence may allow him to compensate for deficits and excel in areas of interest.[20]

However, students with moderately to severely impairing symptoms will need various types of support. Although they might benefit intellectually from advanced work, they will probably also need considerable instruction in note-taking, outlining, organization, time management, writing, and other strategies that will allow them to function in a challenging, higher-level environment.

Different children respond to different types of help, and there can be a long period of trial and error to determine which strategies—from occasional periods of physical exercise to listening to music while studying—are most useful for each child. Without question, the best strategies focus on developing the child's strengths while making allowances for the disability. Because ADD/ADHD is not restricted to the school setting, parents and teachers must work together in the interest of the child's total well-being. Communication is essential. ADD/ADHD is a long-term issue, and partnership is required to ensure long-term progress.

Another viewpoint

Although a diagnosis of ADD/ADHD may be upsetting to parents, it's not the worst thing that can happen. Indeed, if one looks at the flip side of ADD/ADHD issues, it's evident that the outlook doesn't have to be bleak. A dreamy, inattentive child can also be imaginative, creative, visionary, and inventive. A hyperactive child may at the same time be energetic, passionate, hardworking, and enthusiastic. Distractible? Try open-minded, adaptable, and unafraid to try novel ideas. Children with ADD/ADHD often excel in many professions and are sometimes the breakthrough thinkers who revolutionize a field. Their own struggles may make them especially empathetic and loving.

In the midst of the turmoil that may accompany ADD/ADHD, parents and teachers need to keep an optimistic attitude and let the child know that they believe in her abilities.

Success factors

All gifted children, and especially those with additional exceptionalities such as ADD/ADHD or processing problems, require help to keep them motivated and striving to achieve the potential that resides in them. The significant adults in a child's life must:

- *Provide consistent, loving, accepting support.* The importance of at least one person that the child can count on at all times and in all circumstances cannot be overstated. As we read the biographies of people who have overcome great obstacles to learning and achievement, there is invariably a mentor, a parent, a teacher, a friend, or a relative who looked beyond the disability—whether physical, emotional, social, or economic—and said, "You can." The more of these people a child can find, the better, but at least one is essential.

- *Respond to the child, not the disability.* Gifted children are more than a collection of brain cells, and gifted children with learning challenges are more than clusters of symptoms. Adults must take the time to know the child—his quirky sense of humor, her love of music—and appreciate these unique attributes. If most of the time spent together is related to repairing a deficiency, it's easy for adults to lose sight of the whole child, and it's easy for the child to think of himself as simply a problem or a burden.

- *Take the long view.* Many learning disabilities are for life. They are chronic conditions that, like diabetes, can be managed. The earlier such management begins and the more consistent the process, the better the child's chances for long-term success. Adults must not become so mired in the child's day-to-day struggles that they lose perspective.

- *Attend to the social and emotional issues, as well as the scholastic challenges.* Gifted children often castigate themselves for what they perceive as their imperfections and shortcomings. When they must also contend with a learning disability, their self-criticism can become relentless. They may become depressed and anxious, and these emotional needs require sensitive handling. Both the student and her parents may require professional assistance to break the cycle of blame and shame in which these children are sometimes enmeshed.

- *Help the child use his intellectual strengths to understand and modify the effects of his disability.* Intellectually gifted children have the capability to think about thinking, which gives them a big advantage when it comes to considering their learning blocks. They can see the logic behind certain learning strategies and often can use their innate intensity to persevere and persist in the tasks necessary to alter their behavior or build learning skills. When adults take the time to explain various courses of action and make the child part of the solution, they often gain a motivated, competent partner.

- *Be willing to try new ideas.* Parents and teachers must be ready to experiment with different approaches and strategies to help the child learn most effectively, and they must be flexible enough to look beyond standard methods. For example, the common wisdom is that children should do their homework in a study corner—a quiet place free from distraction. However, the child with ADD/ADHD may benefit from listening to music while she works. She may be able to function well in an area that looks like a rat's nest. Perhaps she'll respond better to short, timed tasks interspersed with activity than to a long study session. If she works on a computer, she might pay more attention to the documents she's producing if they are surrounded by stimulating, eye-catching "wallpaper" rather than by blank white space. Running counter to prevailing ideas can be difficult to explain, but parents and teachers should not be afraid to use what works rather than what's generally accepted.

- *Celebrate success.* Many times, the steps that move a learning disabled gifted child along the path to self-sufficiency are small: the child sits still through an entire classroom presentation or follows a simple set of instructions without an error. A private word of congratulations and encouragement from a teacher or the child's parents lets him know that his successes are noticed and valued.

- *Seek help themselves.* Bringing up a gifted child is exhausting in and of itself. These children are bundles of curiosity, energy, and questioning. They can wear out even the most patient adult. If the child also has a learning disability, the stamina required to deal with the child may be almost superhuman. Parents may find help and relief in a parent association, a support group, or from a counselor.

In short, adults should acknowledge the learning disability and its effect on performance. For example, parents and teachers must understand that a gifted child with ADD/ADHD may trail two to four years behind her gifted counterparts who do not have the disability when it comes to handling certain self-regulatory tasks, such as knowing where she put the supplies that she needs for a classroom project.[21] However, the gifted student must not be allowed to hide behind her other "label"; she must be challenged to the maximum that her disability will permit. Both sides of her unusual nature require attention and accommodation.

The enigma of identification

Giftedness may coexist with a variety of other conditions, and there is considerable overlap among learning disabilities themselves and with giftedness. It is sometimes very difficult to tease out what behaviors are related to giftedness and which might indicate a medical problem. If a child's behavior could suggest giftedness as well as a brain-based disorder, both should be investigated.

For example, a child can be gifted and both dyslexic and ADD/ADHD. Or just gifted. Or only dyslexic. Assessment by a clinician who understands giftedness is essential. A professional searching only for "pathology" can miss the giftedness half of the equation and recommend inappropriate treatment. The following chart shows some of the confusing convergences.

Typical Characteristics	ADD/ADHD	Dyslexia	Other Learning Disabilities	Giftedness
Difficulty paying attention	Yes	Yes, but often highly attentive to oral instruction to compensate for reading difficulties.	Yes, because of inability to understand or find meaning in what's being said or illustrated.	Sometimes, if topic is too elementary or not of interest to the child.
Poor impulse control and inappropriate classroom behavior	Often, in response to inability to regulate behavior.	Sometimes, in response to frustration and anxiety about classroom performance.	Sometimes, in response to frustration or anger about lack of understanding.	Occasionally, in response to boredom; student may be a "blurter" whose answers are usually correct.
Difficulty with recent memory	Yes	Yes	Sometimes	No; memory is usually keen and recall quick and accurate.
Difficulty following instructions, especially multi-part directions	Yes, especially oral instruction because of short-term memory deficits.	Yes, because of lag between hearing and action.	Yes, depending on type of problem and type of instruction.	Understands instructions; may choose to do work own way.
Poor handwriting	Yes, because of lack of attention to the task.	Yes, because of inability to manipulate letters. May grasp pencil awkwardly.	Yes, because of difficulty with letter formations.	Sometimes, because child's hand cannot keep up with his mind.
Poor self-image	Yes, because inability to control behavior makes child "different" and subject to ostracism of other students.	Yes; student can feel stupid because she can't do what others seem to do effortlessly.	Yes; student can feel incompetent because of lack of understanding of concepts.	Sometimes; most gifted children have a healthy self-image, but if the child holds herself to impossibly high standards and cannot meet personal goals, her self-image may suffer.

Typical Characteristics	ADD/ADHD	Dyslexia	Other Learning Disabilities	Giftedness
Poor relationships with peers	Often, because of inability to regulate behavior.	Often, because of poor self-image and teasing from other students.	Often, because of lack of understanding about what others are saying.	Sometimes, because of immaturity of age peers or the feeling that giftedness makes the student "special." May be more friendly with intellectual peers and adults, but may not be a very social being in any setting because he is so engaged in the life of the mind. However, many gifted children have no difficulty with peers at all.

Establishing the physical reasons that gifted children may lose their motivational thrust can be an arduous, time-consuming task because it is often difficult for parents and teachers to figure out the boundary between normal and abnormal behavior. It's this difficulty that often leads parents, teachers, or physicians to believe that a "wired" child has ADD/ADHD or another medical issue.

What is most important is the degree to which the unusual behavior affects the child's ability to function in the world. To adults, a gifted child may seem more excitable or more introverted than others, and parents may worry about their child's differences. However, if the child is doing well in school, has even one or two friends, and derives enjoyment from out-of-school activities, there's little reason for alarm. On the other hand, if the child is miserable in school, isolated, and lonely, adults must intervene. If a physical cause for a motivational issue is discovered, it is the job of the adults to accommodate the child's needs and to expand her learning as far as possible, for it is gifted children, including those with disabilities, who become the gifted adults who change the world.

In summary

- Motivational issues may have their origin in physical problems, such as vision and hearing difficulties, visual and auditory processing problems, and brain-based issues, such as dyslexia and ADD/ADHD, that affect how the student learns.

- School screenings may not uncover these issues, and professional intervention may be necessary.

- Although gifted children may also have ADD/ADHD, sometimes the behavior that is typical of profound giftedness resembles the symptoms of ADD/ADHD. A professional who understands both issues can help parents and teachers sort it all out.

- Gifted students with learning disabilities are called twice-exceptional and require accommodation for both their giftedness and their disability.

- Although meeting the needs of a twice-exceptional child may be difficult, an optimistic, long-range perspective is helpful for both adults and children.

Chapter 4
Emotional Reasons for Loss of Motivation

If there's one word that almost everyone uses to describe gifted children, it's *intense.* An average-ability child probably notices a spectacular sunset, but a sensitive gifted child may see, feel, and revel in the colors. The tints and hues themselves may trigger a cascade of connections to pieces of art the child has seen, previous experiences of other sunsets, vivid emotional memories connected with those experiences, and a burning desire to recreate what she has seen in new and different ways. The artistic child may want to paint the sunset as seen from the sun's point of view, the child gifted in language arts may be moved to write a poem, and the scientifically gifted student may want to understand the light refraction that resulted in the brilliant colors.

For many gifted children, it's as if the intellectual, sensory, and emotional receptors are always open and active. There's so much that these children want to explore and learn that they can barely sit down—unless, of course, they are studying one of their passions in depth. Then it's next to impossible for parents and teachers to pry them away from what they're doing.

Many gifted children are constant talkers, working out concepts by discussing them for long periods of time and monopolizing adults' time and attention. Often bumptious and demanding, they may be impatient with classmates who are slower to grasp concepts, as well as with teachers whose efforts are directed primarily at average-ability students. Passionately interested in things that other children don't even understand, these students are stereotypical gifted children.

Others, however, are quiet, compliant students who fit into any classroom situation. Their intensity may not be visible; it's internal. One parent says, "I watch her stare at her computer for as much as 15 minutes, silent and lost in thought. I can almost see the wheels turning in her head. Her level of concentration is so deep that I think I could set off two dozen alarm clocks and she wouldn't hear one of them. Then she rouses herself, and what she's been thinking about just flows out of her hands, through the keyboard and onto the screen. It's fully formed work. Though she's a relaxed and engaging child, I would certainly say that in those minutes, she's the most intense person I've ever known."

It's important for parents to realize that their child's extreme intensity and sensitivity do not *necessarily* predispose him to emotional or social deficits. A variety of research studies conducted by an array of experts over long periods of time have shown that while individual gifted children may have specific issues and challenges, gifted children as a group are not particularly at risk for psychological problems. In fact, many studies have shown that children with exceptional ability are at least as well-adjusted as their average-ability peers. When researchers study specific factors, such as depression, suicide, or levels of anxiety, they find few differences between gifted students and those who are less intellectually able.

Whether a gifted child is plagued by emotional problems often has to do with how a constellation of factors comes together: the type and degree of giftedness, the degree of educational fit, the child's home environment, and the child's personal characteristics.[1] Sometimes these factors combine to create anxiety or other psychological issues. Many of these issues boil down to one primary problem: fear.

The consequences of fear

Fear of failure

Although we might believe that high intelligence should make a gifted child less fearful of learning tasks than a student of average ability would be, the reverse is often the case. Gifted students, particularly those who are highly gifted, often are afraid of many things about school, and one of their biggest fears is that they will fail.

They sometimes have good reason to be afraid, for failure is usually measured by an arbitrary standard like a quiz or test score. If the students answer all of the questions on a test within the confines allowed by the answer key, they succeed. Most students can "read and regurgitate" well enough to answer appropriately and pass the test, some with higher scores than others. However, a gifted student may fail the test because her answers fall outside the guidelines allowed by the key. She may over-answer, answer only a portion of the question, question the question, or choose to write multiple answers, justifying them all with facts and conjecture. The test can scarcely be graded, and the student's score may be reduced, perhaps to the point of failure, no matter how thoroughly she knows the subject matter.

In some cases, gifted children may think and move too fast to take the time to read test instructions. For example, a directive to "round to the nearest hundredth" may be buried at the end of the instructions. The child may not notice this detail, if he reads the instructions at all. He works diligently, doing the work correctly, but not rounding. Depending on the teacher's degree of insistence on students' following instructions to the letter, the child may obtain only partial or no credit at all for work on the test, even if all of the answers are accurate. In some cases, his grade may be a zero, even though he has perfect understanding of the concepts and skills.

The gifted perfectionist

An inordinate fear of failure may be fed by *perfectionism*, which is perhaps one of the most common—and misunderstood—components of the gifted child's makeup. Although striving for high goals and excellence is a laudable endeavor, perfectionists cannot make the distinction between excellence and perfection. For a perfectionistic gifted child, a grade of 99 on a history test is a failure. The only acceptable grade is 100—or even more, if there happens to be an extra-credit question that could add additional points.

Perfectionism may arise early in a child's school career. Because the classroom curriculum is so easy for her, the only way she can exercise her brain and create learning excitement is by completing every test and assignment perfectly.

Perfectionism also may be fueled by the child's asynchronous development. A second grader with the mental ability of a fifth grader knows what fifth-grade essays should contain; he can see what a fifth-grade art project looks like. He will use the fifth-grade models to establish his second-grade goals and strive after a standard that other students may not reach for three years or more. He is able to discern excellence and has the desire to attain it. He may feel unfulfilled if he does not reach the level of performance of which he believes he's capable, even if that level is unrealistic for his social, emotional, and physical development.

Some gifted perfectionists may wish to do well in class but be so immobilized by their need for perfect performance that they become fearful that they've misheard assignments, asking for clarification again and again. They may not complete classwork or homework because they become nearly obsessed with making each aspect—from letter forms to margins to research—complete and perfect.

These children may do so poorly that they have to repeat a grade, often with no change in their performance. Unless a parent or teacher recognizes the child's gifts, such "paralyzed perfectionists"[2] may never succeed in school. Conversely, when challenged appropriately, given choices and an opportunity to explore, and supported in achieving excellence rather than perfection, such children can make nearly unbelievable progress in a very short time.

Other gifted children may be highly competitive, comparing themselves to students who appear to grasp concepts and skills more easily. If the gifted student keeps pace with her peers, she can feel good about herself and her performance. If she perceives herself to be falling behind, her self-image may go into freefall. Her feelings and behavior are often dependent on the environment in which she finds herself. She may be flying high one moment and down in the dumps the next because she hasn't developed a consistent self-concept that allows for mistakes and human frailty.

Natalie is such a child. When she entered a gifted language arts program, she lagged behind four other gifted students in writing and interpreting some types of poetry. She became afraid because she couldn't keep up with the others. Her mother reported that Natalie cried uncontrollably almost every night because she believed that she wasn't as able as the other students in her class.

Natalie's teacher spent a great deal of time assuring Natalie that she was mastering the essentials (remembering that those essentials were far beyond what was going on in the standard language arts classroom) and that understanding what she was doing was far more important than the speed at which she accomplished her work. She gave Natalie choices about when she would tackle the more complicated curriculum expansions. It took several months of reassurance, but by the middle of the second semester, Natalie's confidence improved, and she began to ask for more complex assignments. She finally realized that pace had little to do with quality and that her work actually measured up well against that of the students who moved faster.

Perfectionists may be plagued by thoughts and feelings of unworthiness if their performance does not always meet the highest possible standard. Today's test-heavy environment may contribute to these children's discomfort, as the classroom emphasis shifts from long-term learning goals to short-range test performance. Perfectionistic students can view every test as yet another opportunity to fail.

Parents and teachers sometimes inadvertently fan the flames of perfectionism with statements such as, "If you're so smart, why did you get a B in social studies?" "You have the best brain in the class. You should have the highest grades," or, "You understand the topic thoroughly. I'd like you to join this group of students and help them finish their project."

Although it's appropriate for parents and teachers to encourage students, praise that identifies them as "the best" or "the most brilliant" or sets them up as assistant instructors can result in the child's believing that he must always perform exceptionally to gain adult acceptance. These internalized expectations often lead to severe anxiety about having to measure up to what he perceives as an impossible standard. There are several ways that the student may respond to adults' demands for consistently excellent performance.

When a child views her parents and teachers as overly demanding, she may rebel openly, defying their insistence on high achievement. She may deliberately fail tests and be confrontational and argumentative with those who have such lofty expectations of her. She may be dragged off to a counselor because school personnel think she has Oppositional Defiant Disorder that requires treatment.

In fact, if the adults look closely, they'll see that the student is not universally defiant. Her obstreperous behavior usually involves issues related to school achievement. Rather than fail in her attempt to meet others' standards, she uses her prodigious energy to reject their expectations altogether. It's a tragic misdirection and waste of energy and creativity, but it's understandable.

A child may also fight back from unrealistic expectations through passive aggression. A passive-aggressive child is not overtly defiant. He remains pleasant, agreeing to everything the parent or teacher asks, but then "forgets" a test, "overlooks" a question, or "misunderstands" an assignment, and his grade suffers. His parents and teachers are disappointed and sometimes annoyed at his performance, and in his heart of hearts, the child is very likely unhappy as well, but he sees failure, or at least poor performance, as a way to relieve the unremitting pressure for perfection.

One dangerous method that gifted students may use in an attempt to take control of their own lives and at the same time seek perfection is an eating disorder. Although not typical in young children, bulimia and anorexia nervosa become more common in adolescence. Usually thought of as a disease of females, anorexia is affecting more males. Approximately 10% of patients are boys, and the number is rising.[3]

Some studies have shown a correlation between high intellectual functioning and eating disorders, although others indicate that giftedness is not an issue in developing such a disorder. However, there appear to be some traits that both groups may share: intense sensitivity, an acute awareness of others' expectations of high performance, perfectionism, and a sense of loss of control. Certainly these common traits do not indicate that a child will become anorexic. It means only that in adolescents who are both gifted and anorexic, these characteristics often exist.

If parents and teachers demand excessively high levels of performance within a severely restricted curriculum in which the child has little choice, she may become restless, anxious, and even irritated. If schoolmates also tease her about being "different," an eating disorder may fill a variety of needs: the child becomes thinner (and therefore more acceptable to peers, for whom body image is crucial); she seizes control over a portion of her life, no matter what parents or teachers may be telling her is best; and she works continuously toward the goal of a perfect body—thin and athletic. She eats little, often exercises excessively, and is out of touch with what is really happening to her health. Once an eating disorder has taken hold, professional help is essential. There are many centers around the country, both private and hospital-based, where children work to overcome such disorders.

Perfectionistic children often learn quickly that one of the easiest ways to escape failure is to avoid attempting anything too difficult. Although they may continue to excel in an area of expertise, they may refuse to risk embarrassing themselves in areas outside of their comfort zone. If they excel in science and it is their passion, they may shirk assignments in other areas, such as writing a poem or memorizing multiplication tables. Or if they have exceptional talent in playing the piano, for instance, they may seek out only music that is within their ability so that they always sound good, never challenging themselves with more difficult pieces on which they may make mistakes. This avoidance is often accompanied by procrastination.

Fear and procrastination

Gifted perfectionistic children can be superb procrastinators. Faced with a big project, they sometimes put off beginning the work because the assignment seems too overwhelming to complete perfectly. As the due date approaches, they continue to procrastinate, because now the deadline is too short for them to do what they consider to be an acceptable job. The date for completion arrives, and they're left with nothing to turn in.

Conversely, other perfectionist students plunge in with enthusiasm and high spirits but then turn the project in late, if at all, because no matter how hard they work, they see their final product as flawed. They need to fix just one more thing, and then another, and probably another. "It isn't quite done yet," is the mantra for these students. What they mean is that it isn't done to perfection, and they can't let the project go until it is.

Fear of success

As much as they fear failure, gifted children may also be leery of success. If they do the work that they are capable of on an assignment and the product is exceptional, they may worry that even more will be expected of them the next time, and it might be expected every day in every subject. As Ashley, a gifted eighth grader observed, "I'm much better in math than anyone knows because I kind of keep it under wraps. I mean, I qualified for the gifted math program and everything, but no one knows what I can really do. Even the gifted program isn't very challenging for me.

"I don't want to move ahead of the program, though, because everyone assumes that if you're good in math, you're probably good in science, too. They're supposed to go together or something. Well, I'm not good at science. I don't like science, and my grades aren't all that great. If I suddenly started showing people the kind of math I can do, I know my science teacher would want me to improve my grades in her class. I'd rather just go on doing my math than spend a lot of time trying to be a scientist."

Ashley's reasoning is impeccable, and she's right. Teachers and parents often expect students who are gifted in one subject to be brilliant in all subjects. "Take us off the hook," one student implored. "Teachers need to know that we're not good at everything."

Jared, a highly gifted college student, is another example of a student who's afraid of too much success. Although he has tested in the profoundly gifted range, he turns in average work in his classes. "It's not that

I can't do better," he says. "It's that I don't always want to work so hard. My major is an extremely taxing subject. If I were to outperform at every turn, my advisor would expect that from me all of the time. I'm very motivated to learn more and succeed in my area of expertise, but if all I ever do is spend time in the physics lab, then I'm missing a valuable part of the whole college experience. I want time to do other things, too—fun things."

Children who do consistently achieve at high levels sometimes find themselves in a paradox. The more success they experience, the more anxious they may become about making sure that the next challenge is met with success as well. When the anxiety becomes too much to handle, they may be unable to muster the motivation required to go on. They may suddenly quit trying. Parents and teachers complain that these students are lethargic and careless. In reality, however, their sluggishness is a result of fatigue. They are burned out from keeping up with their own internal demands and from the expectations that their parents and teachers may hold because of their exceptional ability. Even if they are still highly motivated in their areas of interest, they may be too emotionally exhausted to participate.

Depression

The majority of gifted children, like the majority of all children, are not depressed. In fact, many gifted children are very happy people because they are engaged in pursuits—from collecting butterflies to writing short stories to figuring out how to mitigate the effects of greenhouse gases—that fill their lives with meaning, challenge, and excitement.

However, gifted children's extreme sensitivity may be a good news/bad news proposition. Although it can make them intuitive and empathetic to the needs of others, it also can predispose them to depression, especially if they are highly self-critical and perfectionistic.

While an average-ability student may feel abashed at making silly errors on a test, a sensitive gifted student may be unable to forgive himself for such carelessness. He may reproach himself harshly for mistakes, and his negative self-talk can trigger feelings of insignificance and inadequacy. Turning his anger and frustration against himself, he becomes depressed.

Sometimes depression can arise because of over-commitment. Gifted students often take a heavy course load, and because they have so many interests and an abundance of energy, they may also involve themselves in a wide spectrum of out-of-class activities that are meaningful to them. Over-commitment can lead to fatigue, confusion, and absent-mindedness. The child becomes too tired to compete well in an athletic contest, forgets an important after-school meeting, or performs poorly on a test. If the child is also a perfectionist or is being pressured by parents, teachers, coaches, or peers, she may view these very human mistakes as unforgivable and slip toward depression. Parents and teachers need to be on guard and help children learn to say no to activities that may wear them out and not give them the satisfaction they desire.

Children who are involuntarily isolated may also suffer from depression. Some gifted children like and need long periods of reflection and time to themselves. Others thoroughly enjoy spending most of their time with adults or much older intellectual peers. However, some gifted children find themselves alone because of their asynchrony. They want to play with neighborhood children and have friends at school, but the other children may not play with them because they don't understand the gifted child's interests. The child may face rejection ranging from indifference to teasing to outright cruelty, and if his self-image is not sufficiently strong to withstand this kind of buffeting, depression can be the result.

Gifted children may be more prone than others to suffer from a particular type of depression—a sort of mid-life crisis that may hit them as early as middle school and is referred to as "existential depression."[4]

An existential depression is not triggered by a specific event such as the death of a family member or a divorce. It arises out of the child's search for meaning. Because gifted children are so aware and so empathetic, they often feel the pain of others—victims of war, natural disasters, famine, poverty, and illness—and they are moved to help. However, they may be disheartened by the magnitude of the world's suffering and their limited ability to address global, or even community, issues. They also see and understand the greed, hypocrisy, and political agendas that stand in the way of solutions—factors over which they have little influence.

Therefore, some especially sensitive gifted children begin to question the meaning of their own existence. If they can't do anything about pressing needs, why are they here at all? Because their peers are usually unconcerned about world affairs, gifted children may conclude that they are alone and must struggle with the issues that concern them by themselves. They may feel estranged from the rest of the world. Their pervading sense of powerlessness can result in moderate to severe depression.

It stands to reason that the stress of dealing with depression saps motivation. The child attempts to go on, but it's just too hard. Grades may drop, and she may lose interest in things she once enjoyed. She may become irritable and restless. Her eating habits may change; she may stop eating or suddenly gain a great deal of weight. Sleep issues are common, ranging from sleeping too much to middle-of-the-night wakefulness to early morning waking to periods of insomnia. She may reject family and friends and stop doing chores or homework.

Extreme depression may be accompanied by behavior that is injurious, such as cutting or threatening suicide. Any mention of suicide, even if the parent suspects it is simply an attempt at manipulation, must be taken seriously. Do not delay in seeking help, even to the point of taking a child to the emergency room if necessary. Brilliant suicidal children can use their intelligence to mask their symptoms from others. They playact effectively, assuring their families, teachers, and friends that there's no reason to worry. They know the right things to say to each audience, so their deaths are often shocking and unexpected.

Depression can be short-term, long-term, or forever. Although medication and psychotherapy may be necessary, what is even more important is the parents' unwavering support. When a child feels unworthy of love, he may test parents by trying to alienate them. If he succeeds, he proves to himself that his initial assessment was correct: he is unlovable and undeserving of affection. Therefore, no matter how hard the child resists, parents must be persistent in their attempts to show their love and concern. They can help by encouraging the child to talk about his feelings; listening, sometimes for protracted periods of time; and demonstrating consistent caring, whatever the child's mood may be.

Obviously, gifted children's emotional states have an impact on their ability to motivate themselves to learn in school and to achieve the academic results of which they're capable. In most cases, gifted children are highly motivated to learn, but if psychological issues erect barriers to learning in school, parents, teachers, and other professionals must work together to build the child's coping mechanisms, resilience, and emotional health.

In summary

- Gifted children are almost always intellectually and emotionally intense, even if they are quiet and compliant.

- Gifted children's sensitivity does not necessarily result in emotional problems.

- The most common emotional issue in gifted children is perfectionism, which can be fed by adults' unrealistic expectations when they discover that the child has unique talents.

- Gifted children are more likely than other students to enter an existential depression, during which they question the meaning of life and their place in the universe. This period can be marked by both great pain and great growth.

- Parents and teachers must be prepared to intervene if any emotional issue has a marked effect on the child's ability to function in school or at home.

Chapter 5
Social Reasons for Loss of Motivation

Because of their innate intellectual ability and voracious curiosity, gifted children can often learn and thrive even in less than optimal conditions. Like dandelions growing through a broken sidewalk, these students bloom, absorbing knowledge wherever they find it. Children who are able to surmount disability, a complicated family structure, poverty, or other potentially limiting situations are said to have *resilience*—the ability to bounce back again and again in the face of adversity. Research indicates that between one-half and two-thirds of children growing up under trying conditions overcome the odds against them. Their resilience mediates the risks to their learning and growth.[1]

Resilient children tend to have several common characteristics. They are likely to be:[2]

- Very intelligent, with strong reasoning and problem-solving abilities.

- Autonomous—that is, capable of handling tasks by themselves and maintaining a strong self-concept.

- Highly motivated and persistent in their desire to achieve; able to plan and solve problems.

- Optimistic and positive, with a strong belief in the future.

- Interested in spirituality or religion.

- Ethical.

- Somewhat more androgynous than other children—that is, girls may be more assertive and boys more demonstrative and sociable than is typical.

Gifted children manifest many of these qualities as well. They generally combine high intelligence with a strong motivation to learn. They usually want to achieve, and they are frequently more androgynous in their choice of activities than other children. Therefore, in whatever setting they find themselves, gifted children whose resilience has been fostered by concerned parents and teachers have the ability and potential to accomplish great things.

Poverty

For every resilient child, there are others whose motivation to learn in school is obliterated by life circumstances. One of the chief causes a child may not be identified as gifted or receive the educational opportunities that go with exceptional intellect is poverty. Gifted children living in poverty may never be able to take advantage of the enrichment opportunities that spark the curiosity and creativity of more affluent gifted students. Although they are very bright, their minds and bodies often have not been adequately nourished. Parents may frequently be absent because they must work; there are scant possibilities for meaningful communication with Mom and Dad. There may be few books in the home and even fewer opportunities for trips to the museum, the science center, or the symphony. However devoutly the parents may wish to provide these occasions for their child, reality dictates that heat, light, and food take precedence. Even low- or no-cost opportunities such as libraries may be far away and not accessible by public transportation.

Many highly dedicated teachers are found in poverty-blighted areas, but the school buildings themselves may be dilapidated, the textbooks outdated, and technology nonexistent. Children who must attend such schools begin their academic careers at a disadvantage, and the disadvantage may persist for years.

Children who are poor are usually highly mobile; they often move from town to town, school to school, and shelter to shelter. They may live on the streets. This mobility affects their ability to attend school regularly, put down roots, make friends, or develop the skills to study and learn. In addition, if these children learn to equate success only with the attainment of money, there are many other ways to make money—crime, drug dealing, and prostitution among them—that don't require an education.[3]

Parental involvement in the child's education does much to foster learning and resilience. Although some parents who live in poverty make concentrated efforts to connect with the child's schools and teachers, many others cannot or choose not to. The child doesn't experience the affirmation of adults working together to create the best environment. As she fends for herself, she may come to believe that no one cares about her life and dreams. No matter how gifted she may be, the conditions in which she finds herself conspire to rob her of her resilience, self-confidence, autonomy, hope, and motivation.

Experts agree that the most crucial factor in the formation of resilience is the presence of at least one strong, concerned, and understanding adult in the child's life. While poverty and hardship may have a significant impact on any child, a consistent, caring adult with whom the child is safe can counterbalance many negatives. This person, who may be a parent, teacher, social worker, grandparent or family member, coach, boys' or girls' club leader, neighbor, or specially chosen mentor, gives the child a sense of belonging and importance, which in turn enhances his self-worth and allows him to develop a positive outlook and a belief in his ability to succeed. The adult looks beyond the child's current circumstances and sees his potential.

This adult may also help the child develop *self-efficacy*—that is, the ability to direct his own activities and choose his own path. The mentor shows the child that he has the power to make decisions that will allow him to move beyond the confines of his current conditions. Many successful adults who have transcended poverty, hardship, disordered families, and other difficult situations have nothing but praise for the one person who helped them see a way out.

Dr. Benjamin Carson, Director of Pediatric Neurosurgery at Johns Hopkins University, points to the one such person in his life: his mother. Dr. Carson's mother had only a third-grade education and married at age 13. Left alone to raise two children while barely more than a child herself, she was devastated by her sons' grades and study habits. Although she could not read (a fact unknown to her children), she required her sons to turn off the television, read two books a week, and submit written book reports to her. She would then pretend to read the reports and check them off.

"I hated it for the first several weeks," says Dr. Carson, "but then all of a sudden, I started to enjoy it, because we had no money, but between the covers of those books, I could go anyplace, I could be anybody, I could do anything.... Once I recognized that I had the ability to pretty much map out my own future based on the choices that I made, and the degree of energy that I put into it, life was wonderful at that point."[4]

Pulitzer Prize-winner Frank McCourt, author of *Angela's Ashes*, had an alcoholic father, and the family lived in a squalor that most people would find hard to imagine. However, a teacher called McCourt "a literary genius," and though other children teased him about this designation, it was a comment McCourt never forgot.[5] The passion for writing was already in him; his teacher's comment helped direct it.

An illegitimate child who lived in poverty, was raped by a family member, and was continually molested by others, teenage Oprah Winfrey gave birth to an out-of-wedlock child who died shortly after birth. Today, Winfrey is one of the country's most respected and influential voices. She credits her resilience to her grandmother, who taught her to read; a teacher, who inspired her to believe that she could be and do anything; and her father, who put her back on the straight and narrow path after she slid into promiscuity as a teenager.[6]

Clearly, these gifted adults were also gifted children who, at critical times, were influenced by strong, loving mentors. Their lives are a testimony to the power of at least one person to fire and maintain the child's motivation, perseverance, and resilience.

Complicated families

Stepfamilies

Rich or poor, all children find it easier to give attention to their intellectual pursuits when they live in a stable environment. Unfortunately, in many of today's homes, stability is far from the norm. Multiple divorces; the creation—and sometimes the dismantling—of families of origin and subsequent blended families, which may include step- or half-siblings; and temporary partners who become part of the family structure may confuse and disorient the child.

This is not to say that stepfamilies cannot contribute to a child's stability. If a child is supported as she works through the crises that sometimes accompany the formation of a new family (moving, accommodating the presence of a new parent and siblings, changes in family routine and discipline techniques), she can develop positive relationships with the stepparent, and if parents and stepparents cooperate in decisions related to the child, little damage may be done to her functioning.

However, during a divorce and remarriage process, it's likely that there will be at least temporary emotional upheaval—anxiety, anger, confusion, fear, or depression—that may affect the child's ability to concentrate and achieve in school, or even to care about doing so. Since motivation ebbs and flows and is to some degree dependent upon outside conditions, it may dip as children struggle with the difficult task of finding themselves in a new family structure. Some social setbacks should be expected as well.

Single-parent families

According to the United States Census Bureau in 2002, nearly 20 million American children grow up in homes in which parents have never married or are now divorced or living apart.[7] And this statistic does not include children who are in the unfortunate circumstance of have one parent who is deceased. These children often are subject to economic hardship, as statistics show that single parents are often young themselves, are less educated, and are likely to hold low-paying jobs. Children of single parents may find their standard of living lowered dramatically, especially if they live with their mothers. If non-custodial parents refuse to pay child support, the child may be economically deprived.

Parenting is often difficult for single adults. Because of economic constraints and the need to work, sometimes at several low-paying jobs, single parents may have less time to spend with their children. They may be less emotionally supportive, simply because they are frequently absent from home. Their children have less supervision and are often subject to inconsistent discipline from an exhausted mother or father.

However, the effects of single parenting because of divorce or estrangement can be mitigated if the parents put aside their differences and work together for the good of the child. It's important that children not lose contact with the non-custodial parent unless there is sufficient reason, such as abuse or neglect, to sever the relationship.

In addition, the parents should try to come to an agreement on discipline and rules to maintain a steady, predictable environment for the child. They should attempt to model respect, kindness, and cooperation. The child will then learn that even in difficult situations, civility can be maintained and problems solved. These traits build resilience and serve children well as they navigate relationships with peers and other adults.

Because of their intellect, gifted children may cope well even in complicated family structures. Their academic passions may provide a welcome relief from the stresses that often accompany a complex or contentious family life. School, the library, or a laboratory may be a haven for them; their motivation to learn remains high. However, the opposite may be equally true. Because of their exquisitely honed sensitivity, gifted children may have extreme reactions to instability in the family structure or to an intact family in which parents are constantly at odds.

We know that stress and threat inhibit motivation in the classroom, so it's understandable that the threat of losing one's family and the stress of living in a "war zone" or under new circumstances and even with new people can defuse motivation in a variety of settings, including school. Interest in achievement may falter as the child deals with life issues that he perceives to be of greater importance: Will the family have to move? Will he have to attend a new school? Where will he find friends? Will he ever see the non-custodial parent again? Do his parents love him if they no longer love each other? Will the family have enough money for necessities, let alone niceties? An adult would be hard-pressed to find motivation in these circumstances, and it is no less difficult for a child.

Too-busy families

Affluence, while it may make it easier for a child to receive enrichment opportunities, does not create a hedge against lack of motivation. Today, many intact families are headed by parents who work long hours—not just to put food on the table, but to enjoy a high standard of living. Although there surely is nothing wrong with pursuing the American dream, these parents' heightened concern with material goods can result in too much emphasis on work and not enough interaction with the children.

It's not surprising that children who are relegated to spending short bursts of "quality time" with their parents may feel less than valued and validated. A lack of self-worth may result in a sense of hopelessness and a diminution in the desire to excel.

In too many families, primary contact with parents occurs in the car as the parents and children dash from one sport, lesson, class, or appointment to another in the hope of making the students "well-adjusted." Drowning in activities, worn to a frazzle, and with little time for introspection, these stressed-out youngsters can lose their way and their motivation to learn in school and elsewhere.

Although some gifted children, particularly those who are talented at leadership and friend-making, may be interested in many of the same things that intrigue average-ability students, many others are so fascinated by a particular subject—math, biology, government, journalism, drama, or music, for instance—that they will be drawn in that direction for the rest of their lives. While they may have many interests, their passions will predominate. These children may never be what society considers well-rounded. It's far better for parents to enrich the child's experience in the area of her interest than it is to try to mold her into something she isn't. In the end, the child is who she is, and parents should encourage and find beauty in her uniqueness rather than attempt to make her more "normal."

If a child has a particular passion that can be cultivated with lessons, classes, or a workshop, then parents who can afford to provide these opportunities might talk with the child about the possibility of enrollment in these activities. That's good stewardship of both money and the child's talents. But overwhelming a child with activities that are of little interest to him can result in boredom, resentment, and disengagement. It's far more important that parents spend time with the child than it is to drag him to one more lesson in an area that doesn't interest him.

However, some gifted children are just the opposite. Because they may be talented in many different areas, they may find that they want to participate in a wide spectrum of activities, filling up their schedules with classes and programs and participation in clubs and groups. Their schedules are so full of what they want to do that they have little time and energy left to fully enjoy any of it. In these cases, parents need to help the child learn to discriminate between what is truly of interest and what needs to be left by the wayside—at least for the moment.

Whether a child's schedule is unrelentingly full due to a parent's push toward multiple activities or the child's own inability to discern which activities would be better left for another time, many families simply cannot find the time to have much meaningful interaction. Although gifted students can and probably will locate others to nurture their talents, it's most appropriate for a parent to be "the one person" that resilient, successful people mention as being significant in their lives. However, being that person is difficult if the parent does not carve out sufficient time to know and appreciate the child in the present moment.

Gifted children often need far more time than other youngsters—time to talk things over, try out ideas, explore their passions, and even to go down blind alleys as they investigate brainstorms and difficult concepts. The most precious gift that a parent can give such a child is to listen, and listening takes time and attention.

Often a gifted child is so eager to think out loud with another person that the listening becomes very tiring. There's no question that a gifted child can tax a parent's reserves. However, gifted youngsters are also fascinating and rewarding. Taking the time to listen can be a pure delight because gifted children are often witty, insightful, and just plain fun.

Friendships

Children's friendships grow in stages. Very young children engage in parallel play—that is, they play next to each other rather than *with* one another. As they grow slightly older, they look for play partners—those who will share toys and offer help. It's the type of friendship that might be characterized as "What's mine is mine and what's yours is mine, too." The friendship is relatively one-sided on both sides, as each child looks to the other to meet her own needs.

Around the age of 10, children begin to share interests, thoughts, and feelings. They develop a more mature friendship, in which assistance and affection flow in both directions. Finally, children begin to build friendships that involve the sharing of confidences, trust, and accept-ance—what one author calls "the sure shelter."[8]

Because of their great sensitivity and asynchronous development, highly gifted children may be ready for deeper levels of friendship ear-lier than their age peers. At quite a young age, they may want to share thoughts and feelings with a friend, while the friend just wants to borrow the gifted student's water colors.

Cut off from what they consider meaningful relationships, gifted students can become isolated and lonely. This isolation is particularly poignant in the early grades, when gifted children can be as much as three years ahead of their peers in their concepts of friendship. Some highly gifted students may be even further out of step regarding their expectations of their friends. School placement with chronological rather than intellectual peers can make this sense of isolation even more devastating.

When a highly gifted student does find a friend, he tends to over-invest in the relationship. If the friendship then fails, the child can be nearly inconsolable. Teachers and parents must be alert to this poten-tial hazard and be available to listen and support the child when necessary.

A Quick Look: Joella

Joella was a highly gifted third grader whose social immaturity caused even other gifted students to consider her odd. Exceptionally talented in music and math, Joella was unkempt and seemingly oblivious to her environment.

Joella's conversation with other students was limited to discussing very arcane aspects of music, and most of the other students found this unnerving. She would interrupt conversations about basketball or an art class assignment to discuss an obscure composer that the other children didn't know or care about, so she was usually excluded from other students' informal chats.

The teacher spent some private time with Joella, explaining to her that conversation involved listening and showing interest in what other people liked, as well as talking about what she liked. They role played some conversations about events at school, and Joella worked hard to pay attention to what the teacher was saying.

Over a period of several months, Joella became more adept in relating to her classmates, and they began to accept her as a member of the class. "She's still not as attentive to others as she should be at her age," says her teacher, "but she's improved. Her parents and I are working together to develop a coordinated plan to increase her social skills. She was a very solitary child, which in itself is not that unusual in cases of extreme giftedness. But I think she was also lonely and confused about why the other kids didn't gravitate to her. She will probably never have a huge group of friends, but I was heartened the other day when one of the boys in the class, who is usually quite introverted but also a very laid back, accepting kind of child, asked her to be his partner in a project. It was the first time she'd experienced being chosen for something. I could see a change in her right away. She just beamed. She's taking small steps, but it's small steps that can lead to success."

Teachers who don't understand the nature of gifted children's need for friendship may think that the child who cannot find friends is anti-social and immature. In fact, the child may be more emotionally grown-up than age peers and struggling to find like-minded classmates.

The teacher might be surprised to see how well the child functions within an older, more socially mature age group.

On the other hand, greater intellectual ability is no guarantee of mature behavior, and in some cases, gifted children are socially inept, unable to understand the idea of give-and-take in conversation and activities. They may interrupt, insist on their own way, boss other students around, or try to control every game and activity by instituting a set of complex rules. They may also act silly and try to gain attention by showing off. None of these traits wins many friends.

Gender differences also affect gifted children's friendships. Whether gifted or not, girls are generally faster at climbing the friendship hierarchy than boys, arriving at the sharing and intimacy stage much earlier. Highly gifted boys may also begin the search for intimacy much earlier than their classmates and thus be estranged from other boys their age.[9] Therefore, in the early grades, gifted boys may prefer the company of girls, which can set them up for teasing by both sexes.

For highly gifted children to find friends, it's important that they be in the company of true peers who have similar intellectual powers and interests. It's not enough to assume that older children will be good potential friends for a young gifted child because older children still may not be as intellectually mature as the gifted student. In some cases, an adult may be the only peer the child can find. And some highly gifted children are perfectly happy with that arrangement.

Parents who worry about their children's social lives should be consoled by the knowledge that as other children in the class mature, they will eventually reach the same expectations of friendship that the gifted child has held for years. Children who often were alone in elementary school may have an ample number of friends by the time they reach high school.

Parents are often inordinately concerned about the ramifications of giftedness. They are afraid that their children will be "nerdy," "weird," "geeky," and subject to the merciless bullying of cruel schoolmates. In general, however, this is not the case; the majority of gifted children do well socially. Highly or profoundly gifted children, who are a small subset of the gifted population, may have more complex social and emotional issues and may require special attention and gentle handling. Teachers can sometimes serve as the catalyst in putting together combinations of students who will benefit from and support one another, and if the children are supported by loving, involved parents willing to make the effort to model and explain the give-and-take of friendship, even a highly asynchronous child will find a place to bloom.

In summary

- A caring, concerned adult can foster resilience and hope in a gifted student.

- Poverty is a significant problem in identifying and motivating gifted students. These children often lack the most rudimentary learning tools and have difficulty demonstrating their talent.

- Today's single-parent and blended families offer both challenge and opportunity to gifted students.

- Over-committed children can become unmotivated because too many activities can keep them from following their true interests.

- Because of differing understandings about what a relationship entails, friendship can be a problem for highly talented children.

Chapter 6

School Reasons for Loss of Motivation

It seems almost heretical to suggest that schools and educational policies, which should promote learning in all its forms, can instead demotivate and discourage gifted students. However, the evidence mounts that many schools are not adequately serving their gifted learners. These inadequacies usually can be traced to:

- A rigid, unbending curriculum, with little or no differentiation for gifted learners.

- A definition of giftedness that is so narrow it excludes many types of learners, especially minority children.

- Staff members who do not understand the special intellectual, social, and emotional needs of gifted students.

The old school

In the 19th Century, American children were generally taught in a one-room schoolhouse. The teacher, often with little education beyond high school, effectively managed the instruction of children from age five to age 16. Although no one used the term, each child was on an Individual Education Plan. Children worked on their lessons until they mastered them, often with the help and mentoring of older students. Some students zoomed through their lessons, understanding concepts and skills quickly. Others moved more slowly, but it was the children, rather than the teacher, who set the pace of learning.[1] There was a curriculum to be mastered, but there was no rigidly enforced timeline by which a student was to accomplish each task.

In the tight confines of the one-room school, teachers often conversed with individual students, guiding and supporting their efforts. Hands-on learning was common, and feedback from the teacher was immediate. The teacher was paid by the parents and often boarded with students' families, creating a natural alliance among the adults who were concerned with the child's education.

These schoolhouses, which also served as community centers, churches, and meeting halls, prepared students to be productive citizens and produced leaders who changed the course of our country's history. The graduating examinations that children were expected to pass were reflective of the learning tasks that were relevant for the time: reading, writing, and mathematics.

The world has changed. Most students live in cities, not on farms. Our society is far more diverse, and that diversity is reflected in the nation's classrooms. School buildings no longer look like the community's homes; they now resemble factories, frequently housing thousands of students and intimidating parents who come to discuss their children's futures. Instead of being daily occurrences, parent–teacher interactions may be restricted to twice-a-year conferences.

So is 21st-Century education really better than it was in the 19th Century? Yes. We know more about how children learn, and we provide more learning opportunities for a wider spectrum of students, including English Language Learners and students with physical and learning disabilities. Curricula are far more comprehensive, encompassing world literature and history, calculus and other higher math classes, foreign languages, and rigorous science courses. In many classrooms, technology has revolutionized instruction.

Although nostalgia colors and romanticizes the past, no one suggests a literal return to one-room schooling. "Back to basics" learning will not work in a rapidly changing world. Relevant education today must prepare students for life in the global village rather than a small community of like-minded neighbors.

Nonetheless, what we have forgotten in the era of government-mandated standards, accountability, proficiency testing, and benchmarking is that students are individuals with unique learning needs. As always, there is a curriculum to be mastered, but American schools too often expect all children to accomplish each task at the same pace and at the same time. Unfortunately, because of the emphasis on preparing students for high-stakes testing, the focus of instruction may be very circumscribed.

Teachers may present material in many different ways, but differences in style of instruction cannot disguise the fact that students are simply recycling the same ideas until each student has at least a rudimentary grasp of concepts that will be tested. The gifted child is asked to learn at the pace required by average-ability students or, in extreme cases, by the least able members of the class. This narrow approach to learning denies gifted children the educational fit they need to reach their potential, and it dampens their motivation to learn in school.

"It's so discouraging," says a middle school teacher. "*No Child Left Behind* is having some unintended consequences. The proficiency tests stress the one right answer, and when districts and teachers are rewarded—or severely sanctioned—not for how children learn, but how well they perform on a test, the teacher is going to teach students how to get those right answers, often to the detriment of inquiry and exploration, which are the very areas gifted kids need if they are to develop intellectually.

"All the emphasis on right answers is also having an effect on how students study and learn across the curriculum. They often go to the Internet to find one specific answer to one specific question and have no interest in additional research or connecting what they've discovered to a larger context. They've found the correct answer. Why go farther? It's chilling.

"Kids need to learn how to learn, and some schools aren't teaching that anymore. And it's gifted children who suffer the most from this kind of constricted thinking. In their talent areas, they're not so concerned with the right answer. They want to think. They want to examine *all* of the answers. They want to study widely and understand deeply. So in many cases, they just don't fit in."

This teacher has identified the number one school-related problem facing gifted children: lack of fit. Except in schools in which their physical safety is threatened, no other issue even comes close.

Educational fit means that classroom instruction challenges students in their "zone of proximal development"—that is, just far enough above their comfort level to ensure that they are neither bored nor inordinately frustrated. Finding the best match between the child and the learning challenge is essential if the student is to be motivated to learn and achieve in school. Although she may excel and earn excellent grades if work is easy for her, a gifted child will not learn such important skills as persistence and intellectual risk-taking—not to mention study skills—in the absence of adequate academic challenge. In fact, the student actually may be learning next to nothing.

It stands to reason that intellectually gifted students are ready for—and will thrive on—more complex challenges than their average-ability classmates. To be fully engaged in learning, these children require more choices in how they learn, greater depth of instruction, and a faster pace. Many gifted learners come to the classroom having mastered 50% or more of what they will be studying during the school year. A highly gifted student may be able to demonstrate mastery of the entire year's curriculum on the first day of school, at least in the area in which he is gifted, such as mathematics or language arts.

Asking such children to spend an entire school year learning what they already know puts them on a treadmill to nowhere, and equally important, it *requires* them to underachieve. Yet when they *do* under-achieve, teachers, parents, and administrators seem shocked that such bright children aren't fulfilling their potential. That the students are becalmed shouldn't be a surprise. Striving to learn in institutions that restrict what, when, and how they learn, these talented students are simply living down to the expectations set for them. There could be no more effective way to dampen a gifted child's enthusiasm for learning in school.

Stymied, thwarted, and trapped in a curricular straitjacket, some children may withdraw and become passive, inert, and nearly impossible to reach. Deep within their own shells, they do just enough to get by. Classes are something to get through; the world of meaning and signifi-cance is outside the schoolhouse door.

Other students act out, become argumentative and defiant, or seek attention by becoming class clowns. In more serious cases, a child may become so disruptive, fidgety, anxious, and distracted that the school system recommends medical intervention.

Differentiating instruction

What most gifted children need is not medication, but a differenti-ated curriculum. Differentiation of instruction is not a new concept. In the 1920s, the Winnetka Plan, devised by educators in Illinois, included a variety of self-paced instructional materials, as well as diagnostic tests and self-tests that helped both students and teachers assess each student's readiness to learn. The job of the teacher was to develop specific learn-ing objectives and create an instructional plan that allowed the students to reach the objectives at their own pace.[2]

Today, a differentiated classroom offers instructional choices based on each child's readiness to learn, areas of interest, and/or learning style.[3] These options allow students to learn the essential concepts and skills at the level that is most meaningful for them, while also providing different ways for them to demonstrate what they know. Differentiated instruction is good for all children because a differentiated curriculum ensures that *each* child, from those who are struggling to those who are advanced, is provided with learning challenges that stretch his abilities but do not overwhelm them.

Some teachers believe that they are challenging gifted students appropriately if they simply give them more work or "reward" them with enrichment activities *after* they have completed the specific assignments required for all students. Other teachers require their gifted students to answer additional or harder questions on tests without providing instruction that differs from what other students receive. None of these options is effective. Asking a gifted student to do more of what she has already mastered is torture for the child. In effect, it punishes her for being gifted. And demanding that she demonstrate a higher level of test performance without preparing her to do so is unfair.

A differentiated curriculum allows all students to learn, understand, and expand key concepts at the level of which they are capable and helps to keep intrinsic motivation active. Differentiation can occur in a variety of ways. For example, if a teacher decides to differentiate a unit on students' specific interest areas, the students can study a particular subject from many perspectives.

Suppose the topic is the English Industrial Revolution. A student whose passion is mathematics might design a study of productivity measures before 1750 and after 1830. A student gifted in language arts might prefer to write a short story about how a family was changed by moving off an isolated farm and into a crowded factory town. A student with an interest in science could choose to research changes in the incidence of various diseases during the period. A child with an aptitude for mechanics might elect to study how an inventor designed one of the machines that hastened the mechanization of work.

The required standards remain the backbone of study, but students take different paths to reach those standards. In some classes, teachers share the standards with the students, who then write a proposal that demonstrates how their work will meet the standard. And when students share their various projects with the class, all of them benefit.

When the curriculum is differentiated, every student, from the most to the least able, is engaged in inquiry that is personally meaningful. Although they have no choice in deciding *which* concepts they will learn—state and national standards are non-negotiable—the teacher may offer myriad choices in determining *how* they will learn them. Obviously, while differentiated learning benefits every student, it is most helpful to gifted students, who are finally able to study in the depth they require for maximum intellectual development.

The curriculum can be adjusted in nearly limitless ways, and options for gifted students are usually more abstract, complex, and multifaceted than those provided for their classmates. Gifted learners are typically more ready to handle independent studies and topics that require multi-dimensional thinking across a variety of disciplines.

Differentiated instruction allows teachers to make the curriculum fit the child, rather than shoehorning the child into a prescribed course of study. It makes allowances for differences in readiness to learn and in the amount of knowledge students already possess. Learning challenges differ with the students' ability levels. Learning tasks may range from simple teacher-directed units to autonomous projects during which the students check in with the teacher only at specified intervals or when they have specific questions. Projects may require only grade-level resources—textbooks or library materials—or above-grade-level technology and research techniques. Learning tasks may be paced differently, with fewer repetitions for those who master the information easily. Some tasks may require quick-hit research, while others are multi-step, long-term learning opportunities.[4]

Gifted children are capable of understanding why schools have mandated certain outcomes for all students. They generally will cooperate in mastering the curriculum if they are given some degree of choice in the way they do so. When they have ownership of and accountability for a learning task, they work much harder to achieve their goals. In addition, when students are given choices, the emotional impact can be stunning. The positive impact of feeling respected and valued builds self-esteem, releases creativity, and greatly increases motivation.

In a differentiated classroom, a teacher must take care to ensure that each student's work is interesting and appealing.[5] No student should perceive his work as dull and humdrum while others are involved in tasks that he believes to be more exciting and fun. Although teachers cannot be responsible for students' attitudes toward classroom activities, they can provide learning opportunities that engage students of varying ability levels in work they consider important and relevant.

Before a unit of study can be differentiated, the teacher should administer a pretest that assesses what students already know and what gaps need to be filled with whole-class instruction. Based on the results of the pretest, the teacher then designs learning tasks to be assigned to individual students or groups. For example, suppose a language arts standard requires students to "read a wide range of literature from many periods in many genres to build an understanding of the many dimensions (e.g., philosophical, ethical, aesthetic) of human experience." This standard may be enacted in a variety of ways:

- Average-ability students may be asked to read a specific American poem and write an essay that explains how the poem's content reflects the historical period in which it was written.

- More advanced students might be required to read two poems they choose from an appropriate list of titles from a specific historical period and construct a chart that demonstrates where the poems diverge on an ethical or social issue. Then, writing as one of the poets, they might prepare an essay that explains why that poet takes a different view from his or her contemporary.

- Students who are capable of even higher-level thinking could read three poems from the prescribed list from three different periods of history that deal with the same theme—love, honor, evil, death, or aspects of daily life, for instance. Working in small groups, they would interpret the poems and create a timeline that shows which ideas have remained constant across time and which concepts have undergone change. They would then analyze the historical events that might have had sufficient impact to change the concepts and their artistic expression. Each student would extend the process further by writing an original poem that presents what she sees as today's prevailing attitude about the theme she selected.

Many gifted students work well in groups, exploring and discussing concepts with others. Others are highly motivated when they work alone. A differentiated curriculum allows for both group work and individual assignments, and every assignment advances the standards and provides opportunities for students to be appropriately challenged.

In a differentiated classroom, teachers are not simply reciters of facts ("the sage on the stage"); they are facilitators who work with individual students on various aspects of their learning ("the guide on the side"). They ask questions; listen to the students' answers; provide immediate, relevant, and understandable feedback; and measure progress toward stated goals. All of these processes are good for every student, but gifted students may glean the greatest benefit. Their motivation to learn is fanned by an interested, involved teacher who attends not only to their intellectual growth, but also becomes aware of their social and emotional needs. It's the most exciting way for a child to learn and the most rewarding way to teach.

A Quick Look: Teaching to the Passion

Matthew was a sixth grader who was gifted in mathematics and also a kinesthetic learner—that is, he learned best when he could use his body and manipulate materials. He also happened to have a passion for tennis. He was both a player and a student of the game, with a vast storehouse of knowledge about all aspects of its rules and history. Because Matthew's gifted math program was small, his teacher became well-acquainted with all of the students, and he knew how to ignite their interests to keep their mathematics motivation high.

When Matthew began to struggle with some geometric concepts, the teacher was prepared. He had Matthew draw a tennis court and use checkers to represent the players in both singles and doubles matches. By moving the checkers, Matthew could create the angles, planes, and measures that were confusing him. As he visualized the game and placed the checkers in various configurations, the concepts became clear, and he later had little trouble translating them to paper and pencil. In standardized testing, he placed far above grade level and helped raise his school's rating in mathematics.

An interesting side benefit was that Matthew became a better tennis player once he understood the geometry of the game. His ball sense improved because he knew the angle that the ball would take after it was struck by his opponent and he could be in position to return the shot more quickly.

Matthew is now a freshman in high school, still taking advanced mathematics and enjoying his participation on the tennis team.

The politics of giftedness

There is no question that minority children—Black, Hispanic, and non-native speakers of English—are under-represented in programs for gifted and talented students. There is also no question that the techniques that work for gifted children, primarily curriculum differentiation—should be available to every child. Many students miss the cutoff for gifted programming by only a point or two, and their parents are rightly concerned that their child's experience in a mixed-ability classroom might not be sufficiently challenging or interesting.

Some of the inequities in identifying gifted children come from over-reliance on achievement tests, which tend to favor economically advantaged children and those who test well. It is far more likely that gifted children of all races and backgrounds will be included in gifted programs if identification is multi-factored and also includes ability testing, behavioral rating scales, and a mechanism by which parents, teachers, or counselors can nominate students for screening. Portfolios are an excellent way of demonstrating students' work over time, especially those who are artistically gifted.

We must move from relying solely on cutoff scores to weighing evidence from multiple sources, and we must consider the environmental factors that affect severely disadvantaged children.[6] Some districts consider opening the door to students who fall outside of the criteria for inclusion in gifted programs by bringing such cases to an Intervention Assistance Team, which makes the final decision on whether the program is appropriate for the child. This sort of intervention requires careful documentation and clear guidelines.

Equity in education is essential, and new understandings about the nature of giftedness are forcing changes in how children are identified and served. When the field of gifted education first developed, many assumptions were made about gifted children: they were genetically superior, gifted in all subject areas, and were identified primarily by intelligence and ability testing that was performed when they were relatively young. Educators Dona J. Matthews, Ph.D., and Joanne F. Foster, Ed.D., call this viewpoint the "mystery" model of giftedness, because the children were identified by a global test that had little direct relationship to specific classroom activities. It was assumed that once designated "gifted"—based on a somewhat mysterious IQ test score—these children would always be gifted, whether or not they mastered the school's curriculum. This mystery model created confusion in the minds of gifted students, those who taught them, and the community at large. It was difficult for teachers and parents to justify why these children deserved special programming because the definitions of giftedness using the mystery model were so imprecise.[7]

Today we understand that giftedness arises from a complex mixture of genetics and environment and that intellectually gifted children, though they may outpace other students in every class, are generally not equally able in all areas of learning. We also know that, like their physical and emotional growth, children's intellectual development is uneven, proceeding in fits and starts. Gifted children often make great cognitive strides in their area of expertise and then level off for a time—as if they're consolidating their learning gains and resting—before taking off again. Assessing giftedness is therefore part of an ongoing process of talent development, not a one-time-only occasion that marks a child as gifted or not gifted.

As educators seek to include all children whose exceptional talents require intervention, they now look beyond multidisciplinary pull-out classes to new and creative ways to provide learning options for them. Rather than placing the child in a so-called gifted program, which may seem just fluff and fun and unrelated to the curriculum that other students follow, newer options include subject-specific acceleration in the student's areas of talent, whole-grade acceleration, working with a mentor, participating in a cross-grade classroom, or a combination of these strategies designed to meet the needs of a specific child.

These options reflect a "mastery" perspective regarding gifted students. The mastery viewpoint stresses that the student has shown exceptional mastery of a subject and requires special programming to meet his learning needs.[8] It eliminates implied value judgments concerning a child's overall "superiority" and is more equitable for every student.

Adopting a mastery perspective allows for curricular options that are of great benefit not only for the child, but also for the teacher. Various types of grouping for advanced study mean that the classroom teacher may not need to differentiate every lesson for every child every day. Students with exceptional ability in a particular area may be taught by another teacher, perhaps a gifted specialist or a classroom teacher in a higher grade. This team works together to ensure coordination of the student's regular classroom regimen and the differentiated portion of her school experience.

An additional benefit of the mastery perspective

However gifted children are identified, grouped, taught, and assessed, there are some persons who, in the name of equality, want to do away with gifted programming altogether. They believe that many times, those who are identified as gifted or talented are simply children who have had opportunities.[9]

This argument doesn't hold water. Although it is widely accepted that a rich, nurturing environment can actually raise a child's IQ a few points, consider this: many advantaged children have every opportunity for enrichment, from young people's concerts to art lessons to trips to natural history museums. They're often world travelers, accompanying their parents to exotic locales. They're proficient with computers and every other kind of electronic device. In spite of all that enrichment, these children may still be average-ability students. They're intelligent, they're good kids, and they'll probably succeed in whatever they undertake, but they don't have the combination of traits that characterizes gifted students.

On the other hand, there are many children from disadvantaged backgrounds who are intellectually or artistically gifted. They also may exhibit strong leadership traits. Of course they would benefit from the enrichment that more affluent youngsters receive, but even in its absence, they show an immense capacity for growth. With good teaching and strong mentoring, they blossom, achieving great success in science, the arts, politics, and business.

The mastery orientation makes gifted education seem far less elitist because each child is viewed individually, regardless of race, color, socioeconomic standing, language preference, or sex and is provided with enrichment related specifically to that child's domain of giftedness.

Whatever their talent areas, gifted children, like other exceptional children, are special needs students, and we cannot deprive gifted students of the education they deserve simply because every other student in the school isn't able to navigate the same intellectual challenges. Without question, we must raise the bar for everyone—and everyone includes the gifted students in our schools. If they are grouped indiscriminately with students of lesser ability and not provided with the curriculum adaptations they need to enjoy their learning experiences, their motivation to learn in school diminishes, and if it is not revived, they may give up and never share their unique gifts with the world.

The point of talent identification is not to give parents bragging rights or to make children feel superior. It is to help students understand and develop their strengths and to assist them in making choices that provide them with satisfaction and growth.

The child and the teacher

Teachers who have not had training in the special needs of gifted children—and that's a majority of the country's teachers—may need support in working with these students. Because so few teachers have had exposure to sufficient information about gifted children, it's not unusual to hear them make statements like:

- "He can't be gifted. He does very well in math, but his spelling is atrocious."

- "I can't see putting her into a gifted class, in spite of what her test scores say. I can name four other children who make far better grades than she does."

- "I really don't like most so-called gifted children. I think labeling children 'gifted' just gives them an excuse when they don't want to do the work the other students have to do."

- "She never turns in her homework on time. I don't see how that equates to giftedness."

All of these statements indicate a teacher who is out of touch with the characteristics of gifted children, who confuses ability with achievement, and who doesn't understand that giftedness doesn't always result in good grades. But these teachers' confusion is sometimes understandable because gifted students who aren't achieving might look quite ordinary when compared with highly motivated average-ability students who work hard, finish their assignments, and meet the standards.

Those who teach gifted children must understand that a student with an IQ of 130 is as different from the norm as a student with an IQ of 70. Teachers would not hesitate to modify their instructional methods to accommodate a lower-ability child who is not capable of learning the way average-ability students do. The same consideration must be afforded to exceptionally bright students who are hampered by an unchallenging curriculum.

Good teachers of gifted students welcome the child who is intense, sensitive, driven, competitive, perfectionistic, empathetic, fair-minded, and often very funny. They are exhilarated by the child who questions, challenges, and sometimes actively disagrees. They provide an atmosphere of optimism, acceptance, and safety, never belittling the gifted student's uniqueness. They create a shared sense of responsibility—a "we" feeling that allows the students to participate in setting the classroom philosophy and guidelines.

Those who teach the gifted must be a mixture of humor and steel. The sense of humor helps get them and the students through tough times, and the steel gives them an unbending commitment to advocacy for their students.

Parents can serve as great resources to teachers as they talk with them about their gifted children's behavior and interests at home. Many parents of gifted children do their own homework: they attend meetings of organizations such as the National Association for Gifted Children or SENG (Supporting Emotional Needs of Gifted), where they learn the latest strategies for dealing with the intellectual and emotional needs of their children. They read the websites of these organizations (www.nagc.org and www.sengifted.org) and others, such as Hoagie's Gifted Page (www.hoagiesgifted.com), The Davidson Institute for Talent Development (www.ditd.org), and the Gifted Development Center (www.gifteddevelopment.com), which contain articles and features related to all aspects of gifted education. Committed parents also contribute to online chat rooms and subscribe to listservs that follow legislation affecting gifted students. They know about talent searches, summer institutes, and competitions for talented youngsters.

Simply by virtue of their daily interaction with their children, parents often discover particular strategies that work best with the child. They understand the student's particular quirks—for instance, she's so afraid of making a mistake that she wants explicit directions and a scoring rubric before she begins a project; he's passionate about baseball as well as mathematics. All of these observations assist the classroom teacher in making informed judgments and decisions when working with the child in school.

Parents who wish to be helpful should remember to approach the teacher in a respectful, non-adversarial manner. Insinuating that a teacher is incompetent or does not understand one's child is not the way to engender cooperation and a good outcome. Most teachers will be happy to hear parents' perspectives and work with them for the student's benefit, but they're much more willing to participate in a discussion if parents create a team atmosphere. Parents can share books and resource lists, serve as classroom volunteers, or suggest experts to speak at parent meetings.

When parents and teachers are united in their effort to make the child's learning meaningful, everyone wins, but especially the child. In fact, in the absence of such teamwork, the student's intellectual and social progress can be halted. Parents, teachers, counselors, and administrators must work in concert to provide the instructional options and supportive strategies that keep the student on track and moving ahead.

In summary

- Many American schools do not adequately serve gifted children because of inadequacies in identification, curriculum, and instruction.

- Differentiated instruction can be based on the child's interest, readiness to learn, and learning style.

- Some parents and teachers believe that gifted education is inherently elitist. Adopting a mastery perspective helps integrate gifted programming into the general curriculum, removing the stigma of elitism.

- Parents and teachers should share their perspectives and resources for the good of the child.

Section III

Enhancing Motivation

Chapter 7
The Four C's in Action

Have you ever been so wrapped up in an activity that you lost track of time? You were completely engaged, happy, and peaceful, even though the activity might have been quite demanding. You felt challenged, but not overpowered, and were committed to the task. During those hours, you were in a psychological state called *flow.*

The pioneer of flow theory, Mihaly Csikszentmihalyi, says that the flow experience occurs "when a person is completely involved in what he or she is doing, when concentration is very high…when the person knows moment by moment what the next steps should be…. There is the feeling that…challenges and skills are pretty much in balance. When these characteristics are present, a person wants to do [more of] whatever made him or her feel like this…and that seems to explain why people are willing to do things for no good reason—there is no money, no recognition—just because this experience is so rewarding."[1]

In short, flow is the satisfaction that bubbles up when people are called upon to use their skills at the highest level of which they're capable. Being "in flow" is the most effective and efficient way to learn. The student is, to a high degree, intrinsically motivated.

Students will build their intrinsic motivation to learn in school if they have opportunities to enter into the flow state during the school day. Their enthusiasm for learning will increase; they will stay with tasks longer and learn better.

Sailing the C's

Several conditions must be present for flow to occur. Obviously, the first prerequisite is adequate and appropriate *Challenge.* If there is insufficient challenge, the learner isn't engaged; learning tasks become routine and boring. Motivation drops, and unless challenging work is substituted for repetition and rote memorization, the student's motivation may disappear altogether. On the other hand, if the challenge is too great, the student may become frustrated, frightened, or demoralized and just give up.

Control is also important in creating a state of flow. If there's too much external control, the student may concentrate on doing the job "to spec," never venturing outside the lines to set his learning in context or to apply it to his real life. However, giving the student too much control without sufficient guidance can cause him to become perplexed about how to approach a task because there seem to be so many possibilities.

Control also implies considerable choice in how learning tasks are carried out. Students must have choice in the way they do their work and demonstrate their competence. Their choices are not limitless, of course, but within the guidelines laid out by parents and teachers, students may be given wide latitude, and they will respond with increased motivation and effort because they will gain a sense of responsibility for their own learning.

The third prerequisite for creating flow is *Commitment*. The students must believe that the learning tasks are important enough for them to invest their time and effort. Students are far more likely to be committed to learning in school if they see lessons as relevant to their own experiences and interests. Tying lessons to real-life situations is self-rewarding to students and motivates them to continue learning. Simply teaching facts and data to prepare them for the next test doesn't inspire much commitment and, in fact, may cause students to dig in their heels and refuse to complete assignments to which they feel no connection.

Gifted students' intensity and sensitivity require a fourth C: *Compassion*. More than some other students, gifted children need understanding and support as they work through the myriad issues related to their asynchronous development. The first three C's are critical to the intellectual growth of gifted students; compassion is necessary to enhance their social and emotional evolution.

Compassionate home and school environments combine high scholastic expectations with an understanding of children's psychological needs. Students are expected to perform at the level of their ability, and they are never ridiculed, put down, made fun of, or pointed out as bad examples. Why would anyone, child or adult, want to put forth effort for someone who makes her feel small or inadequate?

All four C's have a critical impact on students' social and emotional development and response to school. Challenge, including the importance of learning that mistakes and failures are necessary for great achievements, enhances a student's self-image as a problem solver and an able person. Control is central to developing the student's belief in his ability to influence circumstances in his own life. Commitment feeds a sense of responsibility and discipline that is ego-enhancing and rewarding. Compassion helps gifted students learn to honor and respect their uniqueness and come to terms with their human imperfections.

Schools, teachers, and flow

In their book *Talented Teenagers: The Roots of Success and Failure*, Mihaly Csikszentmihalyi and his colleagues reported on their four-year study of gifted teens. They found that students' sense of flow was highest in extracurricular activities, such as band or orchestra, drama, athletics, the newspaper or yearbook staff, or interest-based clubs in which they participated by choice.[2]

In the academic realm, students reported flow most often when working on team projects. The activities that presented the lowest flow potential were lecture and audiovisual presentations—the very stuff of which most schooling is made. These activities offer little challenge, inspire little commitment, and are compulsory, so it's hardly surprising that they produce no sense of engagement or flow.

Csikszentmihalyi and his colleagues also discovered that enjoyment was a critical factor in keeping students interested in developing their talents. Enjoyment is not the same as "making learning fun." In an age of shortened attention spans, many teachers feel they must become combinations of Robin Williams and George Lucas to capture and maintain students' interest.[3]

That's not the case. The highest enjoyment—the state of flow—is not created by a teacher's being amusing (although there's nothing wrong with laughing while learning). The best thing a teacher can do to motivate students is to continue learning in her own area of expertise and to share her excitement about her subject to her students—in short, to provide flow experiences for herself and extend them to her students.

Next, she should involve students in their own learning by devising challenging, relevant lessons based on students' interests. She can offer opportunities for hands-on work and projects that engage students' minds. If she also articulates clear expectations and goals; offers timely, helpful feedback; and is aware of students' changing needs as the year progresses, she increases the chances for students to be in flow and to want to continue learning.

Parents, too, can help students enhance flow and intrinsic motivation by providing a blend of challenge and support. Csikszentmihalyi's research showed that gifted students who reported frequent flow states had parents who held high expectations for them and believed that their children could achieve great things. They encouraged them to grow and change. At the same time, they built a stable environment by encouraging cooperation within the family.[4] These parents sought the middle ground between not paying enough attention to the talent area, thus depriving the child of adequate challenge, and paying too much attention to the student's strength, thereby depriving the child of an identity beyond his area of giftedness.[5]

Just as it helps to build a strong internal locus of control, freedom within limits promotes achievement, maintains motivation, and makes it easier for children to experience flow. Parents of motivated students provide opportunities for their children to learn, often by restricting television and video games. They respect their children's privacy and give them spaces in the home where they can read, study, experiment, create, and try out ideas. Like good teachers, parents provide immediate feedback and correction, especially when it comes to discipline, without making the child feel stupid or self-conscious.

"The chief impediments to learning," Csikszentmihalyi says, "are not cognitive in nature. It is not that students cannot learn; it is that they do not wish to."[6] And they don't wish to because, in general, too many schools still depend on lecture, rote memorization, unyielding age-based classroom assignment, and an orientation that leans toward imparting information as if it were factory piecework. To make learning effective, we must abandon the model of children as vessels to be filled with facts. This model makes intrinsic motivation nearly impossible for children to achieve.

To motivate students, we must create opportunities for them to feel responsible for what they learn, to become fully involved in learning, and to derive satisfaction and joy in the process of learning. We must bring the Four C's to the center of the learning experience—and watch students flourish.

In summary

- A flow state is characterized by an optimal match of challenge and ability. It produces a feeling of psychological well-being and enjoyment.

- Learning is enhanced when the learner is in a state of flow.

- Students report that flow experiences are more common in extracurricular activities than in the classroom.

- Enjoyment is critical to the learning process, yet for many gifted children, classes offer little enjoyment because students have no control or choice in how they learn.

Chapter 8
Creating Challenge

To the gifted child, challenge is essential. A gifted student who faces few learning challenges has little opportunity to enter into a flow state, to feel the enjoyment of intrinsic motivation, or to develop the study skills and patience required for mastery of her area(s) of talent—with the result that she may suffer emotionally and even physically. Without adequate challenge, she may become depressed, anxious, explosive, or nearly mute.

For some gifted children, however, challenge may be a double-edged sword. They may actively desire more opportunities to use their cognitive skills, but at the same time be fearful of their ability to master learning tasks that stretch their abilities. This can be the result of the child's never having been confronted with real challenge in the school setting before. He may avoid the difficult tasks or the opportunities that force him outside of the boundaries in which success is assured. Adults must therefore do all they can to fit the task to the child and encourage the child to reach beyond his customary comfort zone.

The following points help children find the challenges that will free their hearts and minds.

Let them be with others like them

Gifted children are challenged when there are other gifted learners in the class. Being grouped with other talented youngsters alleviates the stress of always being the smartest child in the room and allows the teacher of these students to broaden, deepen, extend, and pace instruction much more efficiently than if each teacher must differentiate for only one or two students in the class.[1]

Socially, grouping helps students find intellectual peers and friends. Forming friendships can make the difference between a child who resists school and one who enjoys attending class. The school districts that group gifted students may do so in myriad ways, including full-time gifted programs; clustering in a mixed-ability classroom, which means placing all of the talented learners at each grade level with a specific teacher who has been trained to work with advanced students and to differentiate the curriculum; single-subject or multidisciplinary pull-out programs; in-class ability grouping, such as a higher-level mathematics or reading group; and mixed-ability cooperative learning groups.

All of these groupings except mixed-ability cooperative learning groups have been shown to increase achievement and provide academic gains for gifted students. Mixed-ability cooperative learning groups are often helpful for average- or low-ability students, but they may be detrimental to gifted children.[2] In too many cases, these groups become experiences in which the gifted student teaches others and learns little herself.

While groups may promote classroom socialization skills, they may be of no value in stimulating achievement in gifted students if the curriculum provided for the group is not deeper, richer, and broader—and often faster. Gifted children learn faster than other students. They may already have mastered much of the curriculum that other students haven't yet studied, and the pace of learning must be appropriate if they are to remain challenged and motivated to learn in school.

One of the most effective and easiest to implement methods of grouping for gifted students is clustering. Clustering for bright children may be of two basic types: (1) a "talent cluster" for those who far exceed the academic norms for their grade in a particular discipline, such as math or science, and (2) a "gifted cluster," for those who are strong in abstract thinking and problem solving. In a talent cluster, the students are identified by scores on *achievement* tests, and the accommodations made for them may be restricted only to acceleration in their specific subjects. This type of cluster can be a daily class in the particular discipline.

The gifted cluster would include students who have demonstrated intellectual giftedness on *ability* tests and other measures. They might be achievers with high grades, but the group could also include underachieving gifted students who teachers, parents, and counselors feel would benefit from exposure to a deeper, broader curriculum. This group would carry out more independent and problem-based study. The differentiation of their curriculum would probably include some acceleration, but it would primarily allow for more in-depth examination of the subjects that the entire class is studying.

These two types of clusters are quite different from one another, and participants must be chosen carefully. Some gifted students might not be able to maintain the speedy pace of the single-subject accelerated students who generally whiz through the curriculum. The talented students may balk at the slower pace required for studying a problem or issue from multiple perspectives.[3]

Although clustering can be very helpful in unleashing gifted students' cognitive power, those who are struggling with perfectionism might be intimidated by the brain power of others in their group. They may see themselves as inadequate or not measuring up to the rest of the class. Teachers must be aware of this possibility. It's important that they model and emphasize the value of individual differences and ensure that all of the students in the cluster treat one another with courtesy and respect.

Acceleration

Acceleration continues to be a hot button in education circles because the term often is applied only to whole-grade acceleration—that is, grade skipping. However, according to the authors of the most comprehensive study of acceleration, there are at least 18 go-ahead options that can be combined in nearly limitless ways.[4] There is no reason today for a child to be held back by a ball-and-chain curriculum that impedes his ability to find enough challenge.

Acceleration options include, but are not limited to:

- Early admission to kindergarten, first grade, middle school, high school, or college.

- Whole-grade acceleration.

- Subject-matter (or partial) acceleration, in which the child is given opportunities either to explore her area of talent in a higher-level class, such as taking fifth-grade math in the second grade, or to receive the higher-level curriculum in her regular classroom at the time her classmates are studying the same subject. Her other subjects may continue to be at grade level.

- Combined classes, which can include mixed-grade or mixed-age classes.

- Curriculum compacting, which involves streamlining the regular curriculum to allow time for enrichment or independent study. The student usually qualifies for this option by demonstrating mastery on a pretest.

- Concurrent/dual enrollment, in which a student is enrolled in classes in more than one building—for instance, an elementary school and a middle school. This option is often used at the end of high school, when students may be dually enrolled in twelfth grade and in university classes.

- Post-Secondary Enrollment Options (PSEO), which allow students to take college courses for high school and/or college credit. These courses are not designed to replace high school courses, but to offer students an opportunity to enhance their learning in a particular field. Most colleges have relatively stringent requirements for acceptance into their PSEO programs.

- Advanced Placement (AP) or International Baccalaureate (IB) classes, in which students are allowed to receive college credit for classes taken in high school. Students may amass a great deal of credit, which compacts their college experience and saves them and/or their parents considerable time and money.

These classes allow students to accelerate their learning, but not necessarily their departure from high school. Many gifted students enjoy other facets of high school—sports, cheerleading, student government, yearbook, or student newspaper work. Some want to participate in national competitions open only to high school students or are finishing a long-term research project. For these students, AP classes are an academic bridge between their high school interests and the rigors of university life.

The subject of acceleration has been examined perhaps more than any other issue in gifted education, and the results of multiple studies indicate that the benefits clearly outweigh the disadvantages. Educators tend to be more accepting of limited acceleration than of whole-grade skips, but unfortunately, some feel that all acceleration rushes children and is too hard on them psychologically. They believe that social justice and equity in education are best maintained by giving all students the *same* opportunity, and that age is a better criterion for class placement than readiness to learn.

The facts argue otherwise, so long as acceleration options are wisely chosen and the children are not forced into an acceleration program they don't want. Study after study shows that when the program is matched to their abilities and levels of maturity, the vast majority of students thrive in the atmosphere of challenge provided by acceleration. They do not suffer psychological damage or contend with friendship issues any more than they would if they were not accelerated. In fact, because they are far less frustrated in school, they are usually much happier. They view themselves more positively, which makes them more likely to participate in various school activities.

This is not to say that acceleration is always seamless or easy. A first grader who is accelerated to third-grade math may have a period of severe anxiety because he is no longer always the top student. However, as he learns to navigate the subject matter and enjoys the company of intellectual rather than age peers, much of the fear dissipates. His motivation zooms, and he begins to develop the disciplined habits of study necessary to excel in the advanced work of his accelerated curriculum—habits he would not have learned had his work continued to be too easy and repetitive.

Where educators and parents have the greatest doubts about acceleration is the whole-grade option, and in some cases, they are rightly concerned. First of all, if a child is gifted enough to require whole-grade acceleration, it's possible that a skip of only one grade may not be enough to provide adequate challenge. While the new classroom may be slightly better, the child may require a much more radical jump to be truly engaged in learning. Although many children can make a two-grade skip or even more and still excel and be comfortable, some emotionally immature youngsters may not do as well.

Additionally, some children simply don't want acceleration, and those who fight vigorously against it should not be forced to accept it. A patchwork of other solutions may be necessary to give the child the intellectual challenge she needs while allowing her to remain with her class.

The *Iowa Acceleration Scale*[5] is a comprehensive instrument that helps determine which students might benefit from whole-grade acceleration. In its 10 sections, this instrument illuminates all of the factors required to make such an accommodation successful: the child's age, maturity, interpersonal skills, interests, experiences, and attitude; the school's ability and willingness to offer the necessary curriculum and teachers; family information; and an assessment of the student's desire to be accelerated. The scale is a neutral guide that keeps parents and educators from overlooking potential problems and allows them to weigh their decision more rationally and less emotionally.

Of course, there have been some failures in acceleration, and adults point to those missteps as a reason to keep children in age-based classrooms. However, using age as a criterion for what children are allowed to learn makes no more sense than using their height. We don't assign children to first or second grade based on how tall they are, and we shouldn't herd them into a situation in which they won't learn based solely on their age.

Acceleration is a multifaceted process requiring appropriate pupil selection, coordination and cooperation between sending and receiving teachers, and good communication among all those involved—teachers, parents, gifted resource teachers, and administrators. There may even be transportation issues if the child is traveling between different buildings.

Although most children don't require acceleration, those who would benefit from it should have the option available to them. Overwhelming evidence points to the fact that acceleration is one of the most cost-efficient, useful ways to keep children motivated, learning, and growing at a pace that meets their needs.

Encourage them to excel, but not to be perfect

Students achieve when adults have high expectations for them and believe that they can master learning challenges. However, there is a line between expecting children to do well and expecting them achieve perfection.

Gifted children may already be whipsawed between the desire to be perfect and the realization that perfection is impossible. These children often see things in black and white, and if they are not perfect, they may believe that they are worthless. Perfectionism may lead them to a great deal of negative self-talk: "I'm worthless," "I'm stupid," "If I can't do it perfectly, there's no reason to do it at all," and "Mistakes are for other people." They may feel a great deal of shame, anger, or self-loathing.

Perfectionism arises when *doing* becomes more important than *being*—when the child comes to the belief that he is acceptable to others only when he is performing perfectly.[6] The cure is to create a climate of acceptance in which mistakes are embraced as opportunities for learning. Although adults may think that they are creating such an atmosphere, their actions may have quite the opposite effect.

"My dad always checks my report card," says Meg, a talented ninth grader. "The first thing he always notices is what isn't perfect. Last grading period I got all A's except for one B. He never said, 'Great job.' He said, 'How come you got a B?' I got the feeling that he never saw the rest of the report card. It was like the B had a big spotlight on it, and that's what he focused on. I did really well, but that's the way he always is. I don't think he means to be hard on me, but he could have at least mentioned all the A's. I think that's the standard he expects, and he only notices if I deviate from that.

"Other kids' parents praise them for grades that are much less out-standing than mine. It would be nice sometime if he would comment on what I do right or on how hard I work.

"I'm a gymnast, too, and he comes to my meets. I'm glad he's inter-ested, but if I fall or miss an element, that's what we talk about all the way home. He never brings up the improvements I made on my dismount or the new tumbling pass I tried. I always feel like I'm letting him down."

Meg's dad isn't an evil man, but he's noticing the wrong things. By constantly stressing what's wrong with her performance, he's not encouraging his daughter to risk anything new. She has internalized that perfection is what's expected. In time, she may become timid about trying more difficult things because she doesn't want to look stupid to herself or others.

Encourage them to take risks and enjoy rewards

Perfectionistic students are often the ones who shy away from learn-ing challenges that might benefit them because they are afraid of not doing the work to perfection. They may avoid Advanced Placement courses because they worry that the rigor of such classes might result in their not making a top grade and perhaps ruining their GPA or their chance to be valedictorian.

One successful writer says, "My family heritage is German, so I decided to take intensive German in college. One of the things we were supposed to do was meet the other students and the professor for lunch several times a week and converse only in German. I never went. I was so afraid of making a mistake and being ridiculed that I missed the oppor-tunity to be comfortable with conversational German. I can read it, but I don't speak it very well.

"With the benefit of hindsight, I realize that the only person who would have ridiculed me at those lunches was me, because everyone else was in the same boat, but I couldn't get past my fear. I had always been a successful student, and it was more important for me to protect my image than to learn a valuable skill. Of course, today I know how silly that was."

Parents and teachers can take advantage of gifted students' superior abilities to think about themselves and their learning as they help them evaluate relative risks and rewards. When the students focus on the worst that can happen, adults can help them figure out the other side of the equation: What's the best thing they could accomplish by taking an aca-demic or social risk?

For example, gifted children, like everyone else, can get themselves tangled up in the "What if?" conundrum. "What if I fail the test?" "What if my friends think I'm stuck up when I make the grade skip?" "What if I can't handle the work in the new class?" Adults can serve as sounding boards, urging the child to play out the "What if?" to its conclusion. What will *really* happen if he fails the test? Parents and teachers can point out that perfect work is not required to pass the test and that a passing grade represents success. They can also talk about the minimal impact of one failure on a total school career.

Parents and teachers can also probe for solutions. Is there a specific learning gap that needs to be addressed before the test? Is there something specific in the construction of the test that will have a negative impact on the child's ability to do well? Could the student speak with the teacher about the learning gap and the difficulty that he fears it will pose on the test? Can the test be delayed until the gap is addressed? Would the teacher allow the child's learning to be assessed in another way?

Discussions like these allow the child to use his intellect to consider all aspects of a choice, and once he understands how his exceptional cognitive power can be used to overcome challenges and achieve success, he is often more willing to try a riskier course of action and to accept the consequences—even failure—that may accompany greater daring.

To keep children from falling into the perfectionism snare, parents and teachers need to focus on the process rather than the product, on learning rather than results, on effort rather than potential, and on failure as a bridge to success. "When this experiment didn't go as you planned, what did you find out, and what do you think should be your next step?" is a much more encouraging statement than, "Well, that bombed, didn't it?"

Gifted children are often very successful without much effort, and they need to understand early in life that this will not always be the case. As learning becomes more complex, they will not experience such immediate understanding and achievement. As adults, we need to help them see that failure, far from being something to fear, has much to teach—namely, persistence, a strong work ethic, and the ability to see what needs to be kept and what should be discarded on the way to one's goals.

For example, WD-40®, one of the most recognizable brands in the world, stands for *Water Displacement, 40th Attempt.* The chemist who created the product was trying to develop a rust prevention solvent and degreaser, which required water displacement. His first 39 attempts failed. Had he stopped there, the product never would have seen the light of day, but he was persistent and undoubtedly incorporated the lessons he'd learned from his failures. The next formula worked—and it became the cornerstone of a very prosperous company.[7]

Sometimes a child has a hero she admires: a business leader, an entertainer, a scientist, or a sports figure. Encourage the child to read biographies of this hero, looking specifically for instances of learning and persistence in overcoming failures. How did this model handle setbacks and times when performance was less than perfect?

If the hero is local, the teacher might be able to ask him or her to speak about success and failure to a class or at an assembly. The student might also write to the admired person, asking a question about how he or she learned to take risks and deal with both success and failure. Many well-known people respond to children's questions.

A "near peer"—that is, a student who is slightly older than the gifted child—can be a powerful role model in helping children learn not to fear appropriate risks.[8] "I remember my first baseball game," says one tenth grader. "I got a hit, but instead of going to first base, I ran over the pitcher's mound straight to second. Everybody was laughing, and I felt like a dork. But the next time I got a double, I didn't make that mistake again. I did it right. Go ahead and try. You'll probably make a lot of mistakes, but that's okay. Just don't make the same one twice. That's how you get good." Statements like this from an admired, slightly older peer can be worth their weight in diamonds.

Children also must learn that doing one's best isn't always necessary. Sometimes it's fun just to play around with new things, like trying a new recipe or making a mess with some unfamiliar art supplies. The goal is to have a good time experimenting, not to create a culinary or artistic masterpiece. Slam the oven door and watch the soufflé fall. Laugh and eat it anyway. It won't be perfect, but it will still be delicious. Brainstorm the most outrageous solutions you can imagine to problems—and then see if any of them have the germ of a great idea. If they don't, pick the one that's the silliest and award a prize for it.

In short, parents and teachers can help defuse some of the detrimental effects of perfectionism by modeling the joys of imperfection, the satisfaction of reaching a long-term goal, and the excitement of exploring without worrying about how well you do.

A Quick Look: What Famous People Say about Success and Failure

Anyone who has never made a mistake has never tried anything new.
~*Albert Einstein*

Failure is success if we learn from it.
~*Malcolm Forbes*

The greatest glory in living lies not in never falling,
but in rising every time we fall.
~*Nelson Mandela*

There is no such thing as failure. Only giving up too soon.
~*Jonas Salk*

A physicist's best tool is his wastebasket.
~*Albert Einstein*

We are not retreating. We are advancing in another direction.
~*General Douglas MacArthur*

Success is not final; failure is not fatal.
It is the courage to continue that counts.
~*Winston Churchill*

Build their resilience

To some degree, resilience appears to be inborn. Some children recover quickly from untoward events; some crumble. Those who have trouble rebounding tend to be highly sensitive children who may be burdened with perfectionism. When they fail, it's hard for them to get up again.

This constellation of qualities describes many gifted students. However, possessing great intelligence can also make it possible for students to reflect on positive ways to meet challenges and surmount difficulties. Therefore, the sensitivity that often accompanies giftedness does not necessarily predict fragile resilience.

One of the most effective strategies for building resilience is biblio-therapy—using books, usually novels, to help gifted children understand their differences, their reactions to others' expectations, their need for solitude, and other issues. By making an emotional connection with characters in books, children can learn how to accept themselves and their unique qualities, create and sustain friendships, and rise up when life's circumstances knock them down.

Developmental bibliotherapy involves students meeting with a teacher, counselor, or librarian to help "resolve normal developmental issues of adjustment and growth…through changes in attitude and/or behavior resulting from reading and discussion."[9] By identifying with characters who are resilient and then connecting the characters' experiences to their own, children can try out various coping strategies, often with great success.

Judith Wynn Halsted's *Some of My Best Friends Are Books: Guiding Gifted Readers from Preschool to High School* offers an exceptional anno-tated bibliography of children's and young adult literature organized by categories such as aloneness, arrogance, drive to understand, identity, moral concerns, perfectionism, and relationships with others. Halsted further subdivides the literature by grade level, which makes choosing an appropriate book a relatively simple matter. In addition, she offers practical advice for parents and teachers who wish to organize book dis-cussion groups.

But books, no matter how wonderful, cannot take the place of human beings, and as previously mentioned, a child needs at least one person who is "crazy about him"[10] and fosters his belief in himself. That person—a parent or non-parental adult—does more to build resilience than any other single factor.

Resilience is also created by meeting and mastering anxiety and fear. Gifted children may be sensitive, but they are not hothouse plants to be shielded from any situation that might "singe their leaves" a little. Gifted students should be subjected to developmentally appropriate anxiety-pro-ducing situations. The experiences of spending a week at a sleep-away camp; participating in a school program such as a mathematics bee, in which they might be eliminated in an early round; or stepping out on the stage in a dramatic or musical presentation that holds the potential for forgetting lines or missing a note can all create a certain amount of anxiety. Once a student has passed through the challenge, however, she feels stronger and more capable. She might not have won the competition or sung a perfect solo, but she experienced fear and walked through it.

In a study of high-achieving and underachieving students in an urban high school, researchers found that resilience was "the ability to experience stress and adversity, while simultaneously experiencing protective factors that may have helped them to develop positive personal characteristics necessary for high achievement in school."[11] The achieving students believed in themselves, had great determination and motivation to succeed, used their time well, participated in extracurricular activities and sports which exposed them to positive peers, and had "the one person" in their corner at all times.

Those who underachieved lacked many of these factors. They had few positive peer relationships, their siblings often had dropped out of school or had substance abuse problems, they had not been involved in any program for talented youngsters in their elementary schools, and they did not experience the positive regard of at least one adult. They had far too much discretionary time and no involvement in extracurricular activities or sports.

To build resilience in gifted and talented students, then, adults should first provide them with a solid base of unconditional positive regard and then urge them to participate in experiences that allow them to overcome fear and stress. It's helpful that gifted children be identified relatively early so that their intellectual, social, and emotional needs can be attended to before they reach high school.

Provide them with mentors

Nothing excites or motivates a gifted student more than working with someone who has a passion for the same thing he does. Mentors provide a model of what the student can aspire to become. They help him sort through options and develop focus and direction. These benefits are particularly useful for the child who is gifted in more than one area and is confused about how to make choices about his life, vocation, and coursework.

Mentors are also a wonderful support for parents who, though they love their child extravagantly, may be unable to understand or guide her in her talent area, particularly if it involves a field in which the parent is not an expert. A father or mother who is not a science whiz simply is not prepared to handle questions about particle physics. Calling in a mentor may lift a frustrating burden off the parent-child relationship.

However, it's important to remember that even if a child's interests are different from a parent's, the parent can often be a powerful mentor in modeling and teaching life skills such as friend-making, community service, kindness, inclusivity, empathy, industriousness, and optimism.

If a student lacks appropriate family role models, a mentor can become "the one person" who helps create resilience, promotes the student's self-confidence, and fires his intellectual curiosity and growth.

For mentoring arrangements to be most effective, both the student and the mentor must want and be committed to the relationship because it may last far beyond the time either one expects. Mentor-student relationships can grow to become colleague relationships. For instance, one talented high school student who worked on cancer research during his high school years will return to the lab where he began when he finishes his college and medical school studies—and he will undoubtedly work with his mentor for years to come.

Finding appropriate mentors may take some work. Parents can begin with their own friends and then extend the search to business colleagues, local educational institutions, associations, and organizations. If a child is enrolled in a specialized program such as a magnet school, the school probably has information on mentorship programs.

Once potential mentors have been identified, parents and teachers should interview them to see if they are truly interested and capable of investing the time and attention required to work with a challenging and unusually talented student. For the mentor, flexibility and adaptability are essential characteristics. When a mentor relationship fails, it's often because the adult is rigid and tries to "mold" rather than guide and inspire the student. Optimism is also a positive trait for a mentor to possess. Optimism breeds a can-do attitude in the child, helping her to overcome inevitable missteps and failures.

The student also must understand his responsibilities and not miss appointments or otherwise disrespect the mentor's contributions of time and expertise. A mentorship is not a right; it's a privileged relationship, and the student must hold up his end of the bargain.

Parents and teachers should not simply establish the mentorship and walk away. They should monitor the relationship to see if the child is comfortable, learning, and developing confidence. They must note and intervene if the mentor is too demanding just because the student is highly intelligent. Continual conversation among the parents, teacher, and mentor takes the pulse of the relationship and allows for corrections—or, if necessary, discontinuation of the relationship.

Not all mentorships are formal arrangements. Some students have a genius for finding adults to help them explore certain interests at various points of their school careers. They may ask to "shadow" a neighbor for a week during summer vacation to get a look at the life of a doctor, physicist, editor, or professor. Or they might just want to spend an evening discussing a subject with someone who's an expert. Gifted youngsters can be resourceful in locating and asking for what they need, and adults are often willing to assist them in their quest for knowledge and understanding.

Sometimes an informal alliance may develop between a young student and a custodian, office worker, or playground aide—in short, someone who is not necessarily an expert in the child's area of talent or interest. Nevertheless, all people have valuable life lessons to teach, and a child may remember the wisdom of that special person for the rest of her life.

The importance of active, concerned adults is critical to the development of motivation to learn in school. Parents and teachers are the perfect supports for one another as they motivate and advise the gifted child.

In summary

- Gifted students must learn to take appropriate academic risks and to embrace mistakes and failures.

- Grouping gifted students feeds their motivation, helps them find friends, and allows for more efficient differentiation of instruction.

- Accelerations options can be combined to provide gifted children with academic challenge and increased motivation to learn in school.

- Parents and teachers can support students' motivation by rewarding experimentation and progress, not perfection.

- Teachers and parents must help the child develop resilience by providing stability and encouragement.

Chapter 9
Creating Control

To be motivated to learn in school and be able to experience flow, gifted students must have some sense of control over their lives, both in the classroom and beyond the school. Yet finding opportunities to control their destinies can be difficult. Because of their asynchronous development, gifted students often have the mental ability to think as logically and clearly as most adults. However, those advanced abilities are combined with the experience and maturity levels of a child. Therefore, the gifted child frequently is unable to accomplish the feats he can understand intellectually—because he is still a child, society often will not let him try the things of which he is capable.

Meaningful differentiation of classroom instruction allows these children a sense of control. Once a learning task is established, students may be given the freedom to choose among a variety of attractive alternatives to accomplish the goal: working in a learning center, completing an independent project, using a computer program, or engaging in a group research experience. As long as they can demonstrate mastery of the required concepts, there's no reason to restrict their method of learning. Learning is far more effective if children are permitted to learn in the ways that are most comfortable for them.

Students also feel a greater degree of control over the learning environment when teachers actively solicit their input and assistance. Teachers can ask students to:

- Keep track of their own work as assignments are completed.

- Serve as a class student council to let the teacher know which individual and group learning experiences work best and which are not so useful.

- Give a full-class presentation of an independent study they've completed for a science fair or a competition.

- Help make the rules for classroom conduct and operation.

- Be responsible for some daily classroom routines, such as lunch counts, clean-up procedures, and the organization of the classroom.

- Assist with audiovisual equipment.

- Create and set up displays for bulletin boards.

Taking ownership of some of the operational details in their classrooms gives students a sense of importance, belonging, and satisfaction, all of which work together to keep motivation high.

The goal of all teachers of the gifted should be to develop students' autonomy in school and in life—to help them become self-directed, lifelong learners, such as those described in the Autonomous Learner Model developed by George Betts, Ph.D. An autonomous learner is a student "who solves problems or develops new ideas through a combination of divergent and convergent thinking and functions with minimal external guidance in the selected areas of endeavor."[1] In his very comprehensive model, Betts defines gifted students' goals as:

- Developing more positive self-concepts.

- Comprehending their own giftedness in relationship to self and society.

- Developing the skills appropriate to interact with peers, siblings, parents, and other adults.

- Increasing their knowledge in a variety of subject areas.

- Developing their thinking, decision-making, and problem-solving skills.

- Participating in activities selected to facilitate their cognitive, social, and emotional development.

- Demonstrating responsibility for their own learning in and out of the school setting.

- Becoming responsible, creative, independent learners.

These traits should be evident outside the classroom, too, and for autonomy to grow, gifted children need some degree of control in their non-academic pursuits. Certainly control is not absolute, and parents must tread a fine line between being too authoritarian and ceding too much authority to their children. Like other children, gifted students need limits. No child should ride rough shod over the rights of other family members or friends. But within those limits, gifted children thrive when they are given choices in charting the direction of their lives. For instance, a child who wants to study music may be given a choice of instrument; a student who wants dance lessons may choose between ballet and jazz.

A sound mind in a sound body

A facet of control that is often overlooked is control of the body. A student cannot contribute much to family life or accomplish what she wishes if she eats poorly, doesn't get enough sleep, and rarely exercises.

In the early years, parents can decide what a child eats. By limiting sweets and modeling good nutritional practices themselves, parents can start the child down the path to healthful eating. Very early, they can offer a child a choice between two nutritious alternatives: an apple or a banana, a bowl of oatmeal or a scrambled egg. If all options are beneficial, then the choice can be the child's, and he is on the way to a stronger, healthier life. Allowing him to make choices also engenders the understanding that his decisions matter in the conduct of his life.

Exercise is crucial to optimal physical development. Childhood obesity has become a national epidemic and a major public health issue. Children with Type 2 diabetes, heart conditions, high cholesterol, and high blood pressure are not unusual these days, and most of these conditions can be traced to overeating and a lack of exercise. Hours of television and computer and video games conspire to rob children of outdoor activity and turn them into spectators rather than actors in their daily lives.

To keep children physically active, parents must take the responsibility to set limits on sedentary activities and join their children in outdoor activities. Organized sports are often a good physical outlet, but not all children like them, participation can be expensive, and when the season is over, the child may revert to lolling on the couch with a video controller in her hand. Investigate activities that the whole family can enjoy year-round, and take the time to be a role model. Walking, biking, swimming, cross-country skiing, and hiking are all aerobic activities that build strength and stamina and that children can enjoy for a lifetime. Tennis and golf are sports that families often play together for years.

A Quick Look: Training the Body, Training the Mind

James was a talented second grader whose energy level was so high that his teacher thought he must surely have ADHD. His mind was also very restless. It was hard for him to maintain concentration, and his in-class assignments and homework were often incomplete. James was small for his age, somewhat uncoordinated, and a target of mean-spirited teasing.

After observing James in gym class, the physical education teacher suggested to James's mother that the child might benefit from martial arts training to improve his balance, coordination, and self-discipline. James thought it was a great idea, and his parents enrolled him in a carefully selected school where he studied tai kwan do.

James took his new activity seriously, going to class and studying his forms for hours each week. Earning new belts gave him specific goals. His concentration improved as he practiced, participated in class competitions, and progressed in his quest for improvement. He carried his new self-discipline into the classroom as well and was able to manage his fidgetiness more effectively.

James understood from his tai kwan do teacher that he was never to seek a fight and that this form of martial arts was only for defense. However, within a year, when word got around school that James could break a board by kicking it, he was physically assaulted by a child two years older and much bigger than he. James later discussed the encounter with his mother, saying, "I didn't hurt him, Mom, but I was able to use what I know to keep him off balance. He finally fell down on his own, and I just walked away. I don't think I'll have any more problems with him, but if I do, I think I can handle them myself."

The bully did try once again, and this time he brought a friend, with the intent that one of them would hold James while the other pummeled him. It didn't work any better the second time. James knew many escape techniques and used them. The bullies were unable to land a hand on him. This time when James walked away, he did so proudly. He felt in control of his body and his ability to confront and manage difficult situations.

That confidence was evident in the way he carried himself, and even though he was still one of the smallest students in his class, he was never the target of bullying again.

James earned a black belt at the age of 10 and as a teen now instructs younger students. Socially, he has a group of friends he enjoys, and his academic work is exceptional. Although his language arts projects are on par with others in his class, he will finish all of the math classes offered by his high school during his sophomore year and will be concurrently enrolled in university math classes while he continues his high school activities.

Getting enough sleep is essential for good health and can be problematic for gifted children. Many parents report that as infants, their gifted children never took naps or gave them up long before their contemporaries. They often don't get nearly the amount of sleep recommended by their pediatricians. Since parents cannot force a child to sleep, it's useless to get into power struggles about the issue, unless the child's night owl habits have an impact on the rest of the family. Parents simply must learn to make provisions for the child to have some periods during the day when she can relax, read, listen to music, and recharge.

Some gifted children sleep better if they have a period of time before bed when they can decompress with a parent, talking over the events of the day and their reactions to them. They may have bottled up their emotions all day long, and they need to release their feelings, both positive and negative, before they can sleep. These decompression periods are sometimes lengthy, and the parent may fall asleep before the child does, but they help the child process feelings and discharge emotions. Sometimes a short massage, combined with conversation, can relieve the physical tension that keeps the child awake.

Bedtime can be negotiated within limits. Some parents offer a "window" of bedtimes, and the child makes the choice within the times allowed—for example, between 8:30 P.M. and 10 P.M. If he can't sleep, he may be permitted to read, but he must remain in bed to rest. If the child wakes up easily in the morning, remains alert in school, participates in activities, and seems generally happy, a later bedtime should not be considered detrimental.

Not all gifted children need less sleep than average-ability children. In fact, some need more. Sometimes these children are so intense during the day that they simply wear themselves out and need more time to recharge their batteries. However, even if their children typically require less sleep than normal, if parents notice insomnia (the child cannot get to sleep or stay asleep, and the lack of sleep affects functioning) or sleepiness that occurs nearly every day and makes it difficult for the child to carry out daily activities, it's wise to check with the child's doctor to see if there's a need to investigate a sleep disorder.

Skills for living

By definition, gifted children are bright academically, but because they are children first, they need the same instruction in life skills that other children do. They may require considerable help in learning to manage their time and handle stress.

The time trap

Time management is often a thorny issue for gifted children. In the beginning of their school careers, they usually zoom through class assignments and schoolwork and come to believe that academic success is easily attained. As they grow older and work becomes more difficult, they often don't allot the amount of time they need to complete assignments adequately. Their work can become slipshod, and their grades may fall. Motivation drops, and the child may start down the path of underachievement.

Some children run into time management difficulties because they are so wrapped up in their passion for one discipline—math or poetry, for example—that they simply don't complete tasks that are related to areas in which they are less interested.

On the other hand, some gifted students have so many interests that they take on too much. They want to enroll in every advanced class, participate in student government, play in the orchestra, take up a sport, volunteer in the community, sign up for a mentorship, and join a variety of interest groups. It's exhausting to think about, let alone do. In addition, a child like this may put an unfair burden on parents and other children in the family. Choices must be made, and adults can share strategies for making good decisions.

Parents and teachers create the guidelines for the child's use of time, but they must be prepared to be flexible within the limits they set. To create a workable time management plan:

- *Involve the child in planning.* Work together to create a schedule. Don't expect the child to figure it out on her own. And don't expect her to accept your schedule for her without discussion.

- *Decide which aspects of the plan are non-negotiable.* For example, schoolwork must be a number one priority, so homework and class assignments must be scheduled before any other activities. For some families, music lessons or religious instruction are also not up for discussion. Other families require home chores, from setting the table to folding laundry to feeding the cat or walking the dog. Some chores must be completed every day; some are once-a-week occurrences. But the child is responsible for them, and the tasks must be scheduled and completed.

In addition, many parents refuse to allow the child to schedule anything that disrupts the family dinner time because they know that studies show that having dinner as a family every night reduces the odds that children will smoke, drink, or use illegal drugs. Also, in today's busy world, dinnertime may be the only hour the family has together, and some families guard it jealously.

Some parents set a limit on the number of activities in which the child may participate, but they do allow him to choose what those activities may be. If the parents allow two activities, the child may select soccer and scouts or music and dance lessons, but nothing more. The forced choice often helps children decide which activities they really value.

Whatever your family non-negotiables may be, make sure the child understands that those items must be part of any time management discussion, and be sure to explain your reasons for insisting that they be included. Most gifted children are quick to challenge the rationale, "Because I said so," but they often respond well to a parent's cogent reasoning.

In the classroom, non-negotiable aspects of the schedule may include when the child works with a group of students or uses the computer. There may be other specific periods of whole-class instruction or assessments such as spelling tests or math quizzes that the student must accommodate. However, once the essentials are scheduled, the child may choose the order in which he does other work: math first, then reading, or another combination that best meets the child's needs.

At the end of each day, the child should assess how well and effectively he used his time: What goals did he accomplish, and what behavior allowed him to complete the goals? Did he chatter less to his friends during work periods? Did he develop a system for managing supplies so he didn't waste time looking for scissors, markers, and paper? Did he handle routine tasks more efficiently so he could spend more time on his favorite subjects? These self-assessments may be part of the parent-teacher reporting process. Helping a child formulate a plan and then giving him accountability for carrying it out breeds responsibility, autonomy, and motivation.

- *Be sure the plan includes downtime.* Every calendar, even a child's, must have some white space—unstructured time—built in. Children must have time to play, relax, read, talk with friends, sleep, and just *be.*

  And just as adults sometimes ease off a bit in the workplace, children occasionally need to do so at school. After particularly intense periods of work and concentration, a break is essential to regain energy, relieve tension in the body, and restore physical and mental equilibrium. In many classrooms, break time includes a choice of activities: working in a learning center, going to the media center, having an additional opportunity to work on a favorite subject, or even a brief period of exercise.

- *Examine every activity in which the child participates.* Once homework and relaxation are on the docket, discretionary activities can be discussed. Make a roster of everything the child is currently involved in, from scouts to chess club to outside instruction. You can place the activities in a list or on calendar pages. Sometimes when a gifted child sees a visual representation of how she spends her time, she immediately grasps the reality of her time pressures and starts the process of simplifying her schedule by herself.

- *Teach the child to rank priorities.* At home, ask the child to designate which things he wants to keep in his schedule. Use different colored markers to choose Priority 1 items (things the child says he can't live without), Priority 2 activities (things he enjoys but could give up), and Priority 3 items (things he won't miss at all).

Many children will end up with too many Priority 1's. If this happens, make a list of only those priorities, and rank them again until the child is able to refine the list to a manageable size.

Priority ranking is equally important in the classroom, and teachers can help active students priority rank school assignments to fit within the child's overall schedule and family activities. Within the classroom itself, a color-coded system can helps students keep priorities in order. A child might choose red for high-priority or near-deadline tasks; yellow for things that must be done, but not immediately, or for individual steps that must be taken to accomplish a high-priority assignment; and green for activities that the student might want to do but are not necessary to reach her goals.

Nonetheless, choice-making is often difficult for talented children because they have such an abundance of ability. Selecting among alternatives may be wrenching and stressful for a child who is capable in many fields. He may wonder if he's closing a door too soon or making a decision he'll regret later. Adults should help him think through the potential consequences of his decisions, but also remind him of the relief he'll feel when he is no longer overstressed and overtired. They should also offer a substantial dose of empathy as the child wrestles with these hard decisions.

Once choices are made, parents and teachers can help the child devise a schedule that keeps her on track. They can also teach her practical time management skills, such as breaking down large assignments into manageable chunks that she can fit easily into her available time.

Figuring out how to assign priorities is one of the most important lessons a student can learn. It helps him focus, makes him aware of when his life is becoming too crowded with activities, and allows him to downshift before he becomes over-committed and tense. Managing their own schedules feeds students' self-confidence and independence while it prepares them for real life.

The stress trap

Because of their heightened sensitivity, intensity, and tendency toward perfectionism, gifted children often experience more stress than other students. They may be tense, anxious, and fearful, and if they don't develop the skills to cope with stress, they may feel both helpless and hopeless. These feelings may significantly drive down their motivation and ability to learn in school. If the quality of their work declines, their perfectionism can become even more torturous. They may feel as if they're in a whirlpool, unable to control their lives or their emotions.

Although greater than average sensitivity characterizes most gifted children, there is a subset of these children who are even more sensitive to environmental stimuli. For example, many young children go through a phase in which they find the tags in their clothes uncomfortable and demand that their parents remove them. A highly sensitive child might also be upset by wrinkles in her socks that "hurt" her feet, or fabrics, even denim jeans, that "scratch" her skin. Dressing such a child can be an exercise in frustration as choice after choice is rejected.

Other children report being distracted by the hum of fluorescent lights or overwhelmed by the noise of a television set, even if the sound is muted. A ticking clock in the room can irritate them and cause them to lose focus. Some children cannot bear even cartoon violence, and they will do all they can to create quiet and peace in their environment. Their sensitivities to such stimuli may seem unreasonable—or even incomprehensible—to many adults.

According to experts such as Elaine Aron, Ph.D., author of *The Highly Sensitive Child*, sensitive children notice more about every aspect of the environment in which they find themselves. Because they take in so many more impressions than the average person, they need time to work through all of the stimuli before they act.[2] These are the children who hang around the edges at a birthday party, observing the others before plunging into the games and activities. If the party is particularly noisy and confusing, they may never participate at all. There simply isn't enough time for them to process everything that's coming at them. They protect themselves by remaining on the sidelines.

When they withdraw or back away from stimulating situations, highly sensitive children may appear to be tentative and shy, even if they're really quite sociable. If they're forced into an over-stimulating environment, they may become very upset. Others often consider their reactions "babyish" and overly dramatic. Clearly these children need special help in the classroom and from their parents. At school, a "quiet corner" that faces away from classroom activity may help them relax and regroup. Some children do better if this corner includes a set of earphones; as they work, they listen to quiet music to block out the normal noise of a classroom.

Both parents and teachers must realize that extreme sensitivity is not a disability. It's a trait, often hereditary. The child will probably grow into a highly sensitive adult who will always require a greater degree of quiet and orderliness than the general population. Highly sensitive people are found in every walk of life and enjoy as much success in every field as those who can tolerate more chaos in their environment.

Aside from the stresses of outside stimuli bombarding children with intense sensitivities, much student stress comes from a mismatch between challenge and ability. That is, the child may be unchallenged by the curriculum or, at the other end of the spectrum, may have taken on too heavy a course load and find himself unable to keep up with classroom demands. This inability can be a severe blow to the ego of a student for whom learning has always been a breeze. He can begin to feel tentative, insecure, and highly stressed.

Parents and teachers can build students' ability to control stress by:[3]

- *Encouraging regular exercise.* Exercise is a powerful stress-reliever, relieving muscle tension and flooding the body with natural chemicals that create feelings of well-being.

- *Teaching relaxation and stress-relieving techniques,* such as progressive muscle relaxation. Progressive muscle relaxation is a powerful tool for stress relief during the day and can also be very useful at bedtime if a child has difficulty sleeping. The technique involves tensing and relaxing each set of muscles in the body in turn, starting with the eyebrows and ending with the feet. The parent may serve as a coach the first few times the child tries muscle relaxation, but after the child learns the skill, she can manage it on her own.

Another useful way to deal with anxiety is with the HALT technique, which teaches the child to isolate causes of stress. When he feels anxious and tense, he can ask himself if he's **H**ungry, **A**ngry, **L**onely, or **T**ired and then take control by alleviating the stressors. He can have a snack, walk off annoyance, talk things out with a friend, or find a quiet place to relax for a moment.

With instruction, gifted children can learn the bodily symptoms of stress—racing heart, sweaty palms, lightheadedness, memory issues, headaches and stomachaches—and employ a whole battery of strategies to relax and unwind. These strategies include:

- Purposeful procrastination, which means delaying (not forever) an activity that may cause the child to become overloaded.

- Breaking a task into small segments, such as learning only the right hand line of a piece of piano music today, the left hand line tomorrow, and not attempting to put them together until the third day.

- Providing a self-reward when a stressful task is completed.

- Using meditation, deep breathing, or prayer to re-establish a sense of balance and relax the nervous system.

- Doing a small act of kindness for someone else, like holding a door open for an elderly person, smiling at a store clerk, playing a simple game with a younger sibling.

- Remembering that they are more than what they do (or don't do).

- Using humor—reading an amusing author, watching a situation comedy or blooper tape—to keep from dwelling on the stressful situation.

Anxiety clouds judgment and reduces the ability to think clearly, but if a child has a repertoire of coping mechanisms he can use immediately to pull the plug on stress, he will feel more secure about his abilities to manage himself in all sorts of circumstances. He strengthens his internal sense of control and becomes more self-sufficient.

- *Replacing negative self-talk with positive alternatives.* Young people, even those with exceptional reasoning ability, often believe that the way things are now is the way they will always be—and if they are sad or anxious now, they will be sad or anxious forever. Adults can help them see another perspective by reframing the context.

For example, suppose a gifted student's best friend must move away. Gifted children take friendship seriously, and because they are ready for deeper levels of friendship earlier than most other young people, they usually have a relatively small circle of friends they can trust and confide in. The loss of one of these friends often is devastating, and the child may suffer intensely. Adults can recast the situation by acknowledging the child's feelings and then helping her get beyond them. The discussion might go like this:

Parent: "I can see you're broken-hearted because Lauren is moving." (Showing empathy.)

Child: "I'll *never* get over this. I'll *never* have another friend like her." (Catastrophizing, making things worse than they are.)

Parent: "You're right. Lauren is special. You've been friends for a long time, and it's hard to think of her not being here." (Validating feelings.)

Child: "I don't know what to do. I'm going to be lonely *forever.*"

Parent: "I know you'll be lonely for a while. It will be different, but that doesn't mean that your friendship will disappear. (Reframing.) You won't see each other every day, but long-distance friendships are easier these days. When my best friend moved away, we had to rely on letters and an occasional phone call, but with e-mail and cell phones and all the other ways to communicate, Lauren won't seem so far away.

"And let's make plans for you two to get together when she gets settled. Maybe you can save up your babysitting money to visit her this summer or she can come here for a weekend. (Creating hope and positive energy.)

"I suppose it's possible you might grow apart, but that might have happened even if she lived here. If you want to maintain your relationship, you can. It just takes a little creativity."

This kind of thoughtful, positive communication can go a long way toward helping a child take a longer view and feel more in control and resilient in the face of negative circumstances.

- *Teaching the child to ask for help.* Sometimes stress is simply a matter of too much to do at a particular moment, and it often can be relieved simply by asking for help. Can his coworker switch shifts so the student can finish an important paper? Will the teacher consider a one-day deadline extension? Can the student reschedule a music lesson to make time to complete his science fair project? Once the logjam is broken, the stress abates.

Perfectionistic gifted students may believe that asking for help or special consideration is an admission of weakness. Adults should reframe that point of view: asking for assistance is nothing more than an admission of humanity. They should also model the behavior, taking care to provide relief for themselves when they become over-committed. Children learn from what they see, not necessarily what adults tell them.

The joys of solving problems

Gifted children often exhibit extraordinary empathy and possess a moral code that impels them to try to eliminate injustice, poverty, hunger, war, and disease. As adults, we too often discourage them from attempting to make a difference. We say, "Yes, that is a big problem, but there probably isn't too much one person can do." And sometimes we're right. An eight-year-old cannot rid the world of hunger by herself.

But an eight-year-old can accompany her parents to a soup kitchen to serve meals to the homeless. An eight-year-old can bag groceries at a food pantry. An eight-year-old can initiate a food drive at her school. And all of these appropriate activities will feed the child's need to participate as they feed the hungry.

Children, often very young gifted children, have raised thousands of dollars to drill water wells in Africa and fund cancer research in the United States. Others have organized book drives and enticed people to give money to build libraries in developing nations. They have created their own foundations to build community centers in the Third World. They have launched food, clothing, and teddy bear drives for the victims of natural disasters. They have spoken boldly at community meetings to interest others in their causes. They have given back and paid forward.

What all these young philanthropists have in common is the unqualified backing of their parents, teachers, and mentors. They were encouraged by significant adults to take the steps to realize their dream of helping others realize theirs.

Nothing gives children a greater sense of control over their own life than solving a problem great or small, to say nothing of the enormous self-satisfaction their projects bring to them. Before we defeat our gifted children by telling them that the world's problems are too difficult for them to manage, we should instead say, "I'm so glad and so proud that you care. What do you think would be the best thing to do, and how can I help you do it?"

When we offer support to such endeavors, we tell gifted children that their ideas have worth and value. We let them know that they matter to the world. Helping them carry out their philanthropic work may take time and effort, but the rewards of joining a dedicated child in his pursuit of justice and equity are immeasurable. What better thing could we do?

In summary

- The goal of gifted education is to develop self-aware, autonomous, lifelong learners.

- To protect themselves from burnout, gifted children must follow good health habits and be conscious of their physical and emotional limitations.

- Gifted students often need instruction in the skills of everyday living, such as time management, and they can learn and use stress-reducing techniques to help them calm themselves down.

- Gifted children should be encouraged in their attempts to affect social change.

Chapter 10
Creating Commitment

Gifted students become committed to learning in school when they feel a sense of belonging and importance and are engaged in activities that hold meaning for them. They want to know that they are valuable, both in themselves and as members of their classes. They also want to learn and grow to the limits of their ability, and to do so, they require autonomy—the freedom to explore, analyze, synthesize, infer, and work independently or in small groups with other able students. They respond enthusiastically to performing at peak intellectual levels on projects that intrigue them.

One of the joys of teaching gifted students is that they master the basics very quickly and are ready for the kind of substantive assignments that are also exciting for teachers. The following suggestions are practical ways to foster gifted students' commitment to learning in school.

Tie investigations to real life and let students plunge in

Connecting academic pursuits to students' real-world interests guarantees relevance and student involvement from the outset. For example, suppose a history class is studying the First Amendment of the U.S. Constitution, particularly the right of free speech. Students can begin to wrestle with issues related to the amendment even before they learn the factual details about who wrote the document and when. The teacher will make sure that this information is covered, but commitment to understanding the importance of the amendment begins when students see the subject as relevant for them.

Perhaps the topic could be tied to the issue of bullying. The First Amendment says that Congress shall make *no* law abridging the freedom of speech, so what is the relationship between free speech and verbal abuse? Is one student free to intimidate and threaten another, even if the threat is never carried out? Does the Constitution allow people to spread rumors and gossip that may not be true? Where does teasing end and bullying begin? These are the types of questions that will keep gifted students moving forward because bullying and its effects are a hot issue for many school communities, as well as for many gifted students who have been the victims of unpleasant encounters with others.

The questions can be investigated in many different ways. A student may choose to write an individual paper on a specific aspect of the topic or work with a small group to devise a new anti-bullying code for the school. Other students may want to engage in a debate. One might decide to design a survey to assess the level of bullying in the school or the coping methods students use to deal with bullies. A larger group of students might set up a mock congress and draft legislation—from creation of a bill to its enactment as a law.

In this type of learning, the possibilities for flow experiences are virtually endless, not only because the projects themselves inspire commitment, but also because the challenges are carefully matched to students' abilities, and the students have considerable control over both the process they employ and the product they create.

A Quick Look:
Making Commitment Personal

"Many of my gifted students enter the school science fair, and I'm the one who's supposed to sign off on their project proposals," says a gifted coordinator at a Midwestern elementary school. "Of course, they have to do the standard things: develop a question to be answered, create a hypothesis, provide a context or background for the project, gather materials, set up an experiment, manipulate variables, use the scientific method, record data, and arrive at conclusions. Then they have to complete an extensive report in a style that the judges will want to read.

"However, I also ask for one more thing. All of my students must write a personal statement about why they've chosen their particular project. Why does this topic matter to them? Is there a reason this subject ignites their curiosity and compels them to investigate it in depth?

"This year, one of my fifth graders wanted to study the effects of antibiotics on germs. I asked her to detail the reasons why this was important to her. Her answer was that she wanted to be a surgeon someday, and she knew that post-surgical infections are common and that some antibiotics are becoming less effective against 'super germs.' She didn't want her future patients to have successful surgery and then suffer from a terrible infection.

"Although I can't quantitatively measure the effect of her personal statement on her project, I know that the statement mattered to her. She took a long time considering the question and sharing her reasons for wanting to tackle this topic. I believe that the investment of time she made in finding her personal meaning made her more committed to the project than she otherwise might have been. Her entry was stunning in its originality, depth, and complexity.

"I find that all of my gifted students enjoy this part of the preparation. They think long and hard about their engagement with particular issues, and I believe that sometimes they're a bit surprised to discover unexpected reasons why certain things matter to them. Those reasons might start them down a whole new path of inquiry, and that's exciting for them and for me."

Assess and grade fairly

Nothing kills commitment to learning in school faster than grades that do not reflect a student's learning, and in many American schools, extraneous measures make up a large part of students' grades. Teachers must make concerted efforts to avoid common unfair grading practices and observe the following recommendations.

Avoid giving non-academic factors too much weight

For a grade to be meaningful, it must be linked to a clearly defined learning goal or an essential skill that the student has mastered. Too often good grades mean only that a child behaves well in the classroom, participates in discussions, turns in assignments on time, and makes life easier for the teacher.[1]

Therefore, two students can receive an A for different reasons. One student may be gifted, touchy, and argumentative but demonstrate exceptional performance that cannot be denied the top grade. The other may be an average-ability student whose achievement is less outstanding but whose pleasant classroom demeanor and dependability are taken into account in calculating her grade. She too may receive an A.

This type of grading is unfair to both students. Each will probably be demotivated by her grades—the first because she sees inferior work rewarded with the same grade as superior work, and the second because she's been taught that what matters is not learning but charm. Both will be less committed to working hard the next time.

The converse may be true as well. A student may be able to demonstrate proficiency on the task that's being graded, but his writing may be messy and his thought process disorganized. These issues should not be part of his grade. If he can show that he's mastered the learning task, his penmanship is not germane (unless, of course, the task is related to letter formation). The grade should be based on the result, not on extraneous details. If it isn't, how likely is he to want to continue giving his best effort?

Because a student's preparation, class participation, and attitude toward learning—in short, her work habits—will contribute to her success in the real world, the teacher's observation about the quality of these attributes should be included in the report that goes home. However, this "effort" indicator should not be part of the grade that the student receives for mastery of the standards and goals. Instead, this part of the report is often a basis for useful discussion among students, teachers, and parents, especially in the case of extra-bright students who are achieving without effort.

Resist averaging grades

If all grades are given equal weight and averaged, the final grade is not accurate. Suppose, for example, that a student is trying to master multiplication. During the course of the grading period, the teacher administers two tests to measure progress. On the first test, which occurs early in the period, the child is unsure of the strategies required to multiply quickly and accurately. On a 100-point scale, he receives a 65. On the next test, the student has figured it out. He understands the principles, and he's worked hard to memorize the tables so that he can solve problems at a rapid pace. On this test, he receives a 92. When his grade card comes out, however, his work is rewarded with a C because that's the average of his two test grades. If the goal of learning was to demonstrate facility with multiplication, then the student has accomplished it. The grade is misleading.

Experts say that teachers should evaluate students' achievements later in the learning cycle. If students achieve the goal later in the marking period, they should not be penalized for not doing it earlier. The goal of learning, after all, is mastery.[2]

Base grades on individual rather than group performance

Students should be graded on whether they achieved the goals for the grading period, not on how well they did in relationship to other students in the class. In fact, if all students meet the challenge and reach the goal, then all students should receive the grade that reflects that achievement.

On group projects, assign individual grades to students rather than a single grade for the entire group. Students who are motivated to achieve a high grade sometimes carry the weight of the children in the group who care less about grades, with the result being that the high achieving student may end up doing a substantially greater amount of work than others in the group. Assigning individual grades to those in the group relieves some of the pressure of these students to perform highly on all parts of the project, not just the part to be done by that student.

Set clear learning goals

Gifted children are quick to grasp what they must do to receive excellent grades and the reasons they are supposed to meet specific goals. To a greater degree than other students, they understand the realities of curriculum design, standards, *No Child Left Behind*, and other issues related to their learning.

Explaining the learning goals in detail—and allowing the students some meaningful choices in how they may meet and demonstrate mastery of the goals—goes a long way toward ensuring their cooperation and effort. Students should know what they are to learn, the dimensions of learning that will be measured, and the quality of the work expected.

A rubric is a carefully constructed device that allows both the student and teacher to see how well a child is progressing toward meeting a standard, and it works well to help clarify learning goals. A rubric for the language arts grade on a multidisciplinary project, for example, may be set up as follows.

In this project, the tasks are to design an imaginary animal that is likely to be endangered in the future. The students must create a set of illustrations of the animal; a detailed description, including its physical appearance, habitat, and behavior; and an explanation of why it is endangered. They must also write an adventure story told from the perspective of the animal. The students must do considerable research, and the research must be consistent with the animal they choose to design. If their animal is a reptile, it must exhibit reptilian characteristics, and the first-person story must be based on the factual research about the animal.

The written description of the animal and the adventure story about it both support the language arts standards related to the students' knowledge of language structure and conventions, such as spelling and punctuation, as well as their ability to gather, evaluate, and synthesize data and communicate what they know to an audience.

Ideally, the students work with the teacher to establish the rubric. They use it as a continuing self-assessment device to see how well they meet the quality standards of the project, and the teacher uses it as a guide for feedback and encouragement of the child during the learning phase, as well as for the final grade. An example of the rubric for this project is shown.

Endangered Animal Project: Language Arts Standards

Factors Assessed			
Accuracy of Description	Explanation of Threat	Spelling	Punctuation
Criteria for Excellence: Exceptional Work			
Animal fully described, including size, weight, hair, fur, or skin; swimmer, walker, or flyer, etc. All characteristics of imaginary animal consistent with type of real animal model, e.g., live birth vs. laying eggs. Habitat fully described and consistent with imaginary animal's characteristics.	Threat fully explained and consistent with imaginary animal's characteristics and habitat.	All spelling accurate.	All punctuation marks properly applied.
Criteria for Excellence: Good Work			
Animal well-described, with only minor omissions, such as weight or length, which are easily corrected. Habitat description accurate and consistent with animal.	Threat generally well-explained with only minor errors or inconsistencies.	Fewer than three misspelled words.	Fewer than five punctuation errors.
Criteria for Excellence: Needs Attention			
Description too superficial. More research required.	Threat isn't related to the stated facts about the animal.	Multiple misspellings.	Multiple errors in punctuation.

When a project is completed, students may also be given the opportunity to assess their own work: What did they learn? What did they do best? What could they have done better? What grade do they think they deserve? If they believe that they deserve a better grade than the teacher does, a discussion of the discrepancies will probably help resolve the issue.

When students believe that the grades they receive are fair and measure their efforts and achievements accurately, they are usually motivated to perform well. Occasionally, some gifted students may opt to do less than excellent—but still acceptable—work on a given project, and for the short term, such an effort may be sufficient. However, parents and teachers will want to probe for other reasons if a gifted child is consistently performing at less than her best. Is it a perfectionism or peer issue? A time management problem? A learning gap? Fatigue? Outstanding performance is usually the norm for these students in their talent areas, and they frequently perform at very high levels across the curriculum. If their day-to-day effort begins to slip, it's important to uncover the reasons for their stall.

Help children understand how grades relate to life goals

Adults often tell children that if they do their best, the grade doesn't matter. In fact, grades do matter. Good grades can make it possible for a student to play on a team, enter a competition, or be admitted to the college he wants to attend.

Although parents and teachers should encourage students to follow their bliss and explore their passions, they must also be realistic about the fact that giftedness does not give children a pass when it comes to the expectations the world may hold for them. Although the children may be sensitive and intense, they will not be able to use those traits to excuse themselves from work and family responsibilities when they reach adulthood. When they are grown, they will be held to the same standards as others, and they must learn the skills that will equip them to navigate life and excel in the real world.

Grades can sometimes be explained to students using the analogy of a salary. Parents and teachers work, and if they meet certain standards, they receive a paycheck. They aren't paid for effort; they are paid for results. Grades may be seen as academic currency. If the student achieves the standard, her payment is a good grade.

Because they are skilled at making connections, gifted students are usually quick to catch on to the fact that grades can take them where they want to go. They understand that making good grades is not an end in itself but simply a waypoint on the path to a higher purpose. This understanding can keep gifted students from becoming "grade slaves" and help them maintain their intrinsic motivation.

Modeling commitment

To build commitment *in* gifted students, adults must demonstrate commitment *to* them. This commitment is of two types: personal and academic.

For teachers, personal commitment involves creating positive relationships with students by becoming acquainted with their interests and family backgrounds, as well as trying to keep abreast of major life events, such as a death in the family or a significant personal achievement, that might affect the student's social and emotional well-being.

Gaining personal knowledge of each student isn't an easy task, and it takes time, which is scarce in today's schoolrooms. Nonetheless, something as simple as standing by the door when students enter or leave the classroom and speaking to them by name is an indication of a teacher's interest. Perhaps even that tiny gesture will embolden a timid student to speak up and become an active classroom participant.

For parents, personal commitment is exemplified by relishing the child's personhood in the here and now. Too often, parents become overly concerned with popularity and how well the child fits in. They fret unduly about how the student differs from other kids, and they often try to coerce the child into activities they value but the child finds undesirable, frightening, boring, or silly.

In most communities, there's some activity that immediately elevates a child to being a member of the "in" group. These activities are often sports, cheerleading, or the performing arts. Some parents feel that their children should participate in sports from a young age so they can be scouted and selected for teams from elementary school through high school. Parents who focus on the performing arts may force the child into public performances or look for an agent to make the student the next teen idol. Parents may push their children too hard, expecting that these activities will make the children popular and admired.

Some children, however, don't want to be part of these groups, which often feature very unhealthy competition, and these students should be validated and supported for their differences. Community expectations must not be permitted to set the agenda for the child and the family.

Stefan, a talented eight-year-old, told his mother, "I don't want to play pee-wee football this year. I liked flag football, but I don't want to be in the league this year."

Surprised, his mother asked why. Virtually every boy in the third grade participated in the junior football league.

"I have an allergy," he said.

"That's news to me," his mother answered. "What are you allergic to?"

"Pain," he replied.

When his mother stopped laughing, they discussed his reasons further, and he was excused from further participation in football. "What was really funny," Stefan's mother says, "is that a few years later, he was the photographer for the high school yearbook and was covering a football game. He got bowled over by some really big kid who was running the ball out of bounds. The camera was jarred loose and soared over his head, the film flew out, and Stefan was knocked clear onto the cinder track that circled the field. Without missing a beat, he jumped up, reassembled his camera, and went back to work.

"Apparently, he was the hit of the game films that week. The coach ran that play over and over, saying, 'That's the toughest kid on the field. No pads, no helmet, no whining. He has an assignment, and he gets the job done. You guys could take a lesson from him.' We laughed about that around the dinner table for weeks.

"Sometimes, as parents, we're not sure we're doing the right thing, but listening to Stefan and letting him opt out of football was one of the best parenting decisions I ever made. In middle and high school, it did cut him out of some social groups, but he found his own friends and participated in activities he liked. Even at a young age, he knew what was important to him and what wasn't, and as his mother, I felt it was important to honor that."

The importance of parents' and teachers' commitment to the personal lives of their gifted children cannot be understated. Also of great importance is academic commitment. For teachers, academic commitment to students means creating an environment in which they can learn most effectively, continually assessing their readiness for new challenges, articulating clear and specific learning goals, providing guidance on how to reach those goals, discovering how the students learn best, and letting them demonstrate mastery in a variety of ways.

Parents can model commitment to academics by showing respect for the child's teachers, even if they disagree with them. Differences should be ironed out in private so that the child doesn't become embroiled in a parent-teacher difference of opinion. Parents should also stress the importance of their child's completing her assignments and doing the best work she can. However, they must be mindful not to make their love or approval conditional on the child's achievement.

When those who are responsible for a child's education combine equal measures of challenge, control, and commitment, they make it much more likely that the student will come to value learning in school for its own sake and motivate himself to set continually greater goals.

In summary

- Gifted children can learn curriculum basics within the context of high-level projects.

- Commitment is increased when a teacher grades students fairly on the basis of what they know, not on their behavior or their work relative to others in the class.

- Gifted students become more motivated when they understand classroom goals and are given the tools to measure their own progress.

- Gifted students must understand the relationship between goals and grades.

- If adults expect commitment from students, they must model commitment to them.

Chapter 11
Creating Compassion

Challenge, control, and commitment are critical to the growth and development of gifted students' academic motivation, but these unusual children are more than the sum of their cognitive attainments. They are children first, and they require understanding and support as they work through the social and emotional issues that may arise because of their giftedness and asynchronous development.

Therefore, the fourth C—compassion—is essential. If children who need it do not receive the bolstering they require from significant adults, their social and emotional difficulties can make it very hard for them to exercise their abilities, focus on academic achievement, and fully realize their talents.

However, critical though it is, compassion is not more important than the other three C's. Nurturance and rigor must coexist in relative equilibrium. Gifted children's minds must be honed by demanding, relevant learning experiences, while their social and emotional development must be tended to with sensitivity, tact, and kindness.

Compassionate homes and classrooms that balance understanding, high expectations, and constructive discipline are critical elements in the lives of gifted students because the world at large isn't particularly compassionate to them. Most people aren't deliberately uncaring, but a majority of the population is unaware of what giftedness entails. They equate being gifted with earning top grades and don't know that an achieving child may not be gifted and a gifted child may not achieve.

Many people, including teachers, may not understand that being intellectually advanced does not guarantee superior social and emotional behavior. They may be mystified by a child who can carry on an adult conversation at one moment and have a tantrum the next. They are often impatient with the child's incessant questions. They may consider her mouthy and rude if she interrupts, challenges explanations, and fidgets. On the other hand, they may believe that a quiet, introverted gifted student is antisocial and maybe even a potentially dangerous loner.

And it's not just adults who don't understand. Age peers are often perplexed by gifted students. They have difficulty relating to a classmate with an advanced vocabulary and interests that may be far removed from their own—and what they don't understand, they may avoid. Gifted students often comment on their feelings of being different from other children and speak eloquently about how those differences can create feelings of isolation and friendlessness.

Since friendship is such a critical need for children, one of the most compassionate things we can do for young people is to provide direction as they attempt to manage peer issues. To assist gifted students in this endeavor, we need to help them understand themselves and others. Their great intelligence allows them to reflect on their own traits and behaviors and how those characteristics might affect others' views of them. Once they have a grasp of the issues surrounding peer relationships, they often are able to make changes that invite friendship and closeness to others. They may also come to a greater awareness and acceptance of their own interests and needs, which allows them to feel more comfortable with their place in the world.

Parents can explain to their children that intellectual giftedness is similar to talent in art or music and that these talents are inborn. They should emphasize that having this kind of ability may make them different from other children, but it does not make them superior to others. Nor does it make them "weird," any more than being a great violinist or even a talented quarterback makes a classmate weird.

Adults should make it clear that having a prodigious talent is not an excuse for rudeness or a nasty temper. If the child is out of line, he should expect to be disciplined and corrected. He will eventually have to make his way in the world, and people will not welcome him if he is surly, supercilious, and haughty.

In general, such egocentric, insensitive attitudes grow up as a defense mechanism to protect the child from rejection, criticism, or failure. The child may be extremely perfectionistic and fearful that others may discover her imperfections. If adults treat her compassionately and model compassion in encounters with others in her presence, they may witness the emergence of tender feelings hidden behind the veneer of indifference.

Where are my friends?

Giftedness does not prevent a child from having friends or taking part in school activities. In fact, most moderately gifted children are involved in sports, clubs, student government, or other endeavors that may have little do to with their areas of expertise.

These children usually contend only with the friendship issues that are common to all children. An occasional misunderstanding or spat is normal. Because of gifted children's ability to show kindness and empathy, they frequently have a wide circle of friends. Classmates may admire and emulate them. Many gifted children emerge as class leaders and are popular with other students, teachers, and members of the community.

However, more highly gifted students, especially the profoundly gifted, can have difficulty cultivating and maintaining friendships. Problems often arise because of the great discrepancy between the students' mental and chronological ages. They are intellectually too advanced to enjoy the enthusiasms of their age peers and emotionally too immature to fit in well with older students, except sometimes in class.

Parents and teachers should be sensitive to a child's being involuntarily shut out of peer interactions. Although some children are quite content with their own company, there's a vast difference between being alone and being lonely. Adults should monitor the amount of time that the child is alone, how he feels about that, and whether there seems to be a great imbalance between periods of isolation and episodes of social interaction.

For a lonely child, an interest group or club can sometimes be the answer to a prayer. Parents or teachers should not push the child into just any group; they should search for one that will truly engage her. An interest group such as a multi-age chess club, a Junior Great Books discussion series, a fencing club, or a drama class in which the child can meet and form friendships with other like-minded children can relieve loneliness. It can also assuage some of the odd-person-out feelings that may later lead the child to underachieve academically because of a focus on trying to find friends.

A summer institute or camp for gifted children allows attendees to discover and interact with others like them, which makes them feel less peculiar. Today's wealth of communication options allows young people to maintain the valuable friendships that begin at camp. These relationships are sometimes immensely valuable when a child is feeling particularly vulnerable. A caring, compassionate friend who understands the challenges of giftedness and with whom the child can share his deepest thoughts—even at a distance—is often the perfect safety valve and, in extreme cases, literally a lifesaver.

Adults can help gifted children wrestling with friendship issues learn to function socially by:

- Explaining the different types of friendships that exist at different ages (such as those mentioned in Chapter 5—parallel play, give-and-take friendships, and "sure shelter" friendships) so the child can understand why age peers don't respond in the way that he might expect them to.

- Helping the child learn to appreciate others' attributes: kindness, good manners, friendliness, responsibility, or a special skill, such as woodworking, sketching, or cooking. Intellectually gifted children need to understand that all people are worthwhile, not just those who are exceptionally smart, and that all talents are to be prized.

- Encouraging the child's interest in a sport or activity that requires her to work with others. Sports are often fertile environments for teaching a child about teamwork and valuing others' contributions. Even an individual sport such as swimming, gymnastics, or tennis puts the child on a team. Although she will be expected to do her best for the team, the pressure to excel that she feels in the classroom may be lessened. She may feel more "normal" and come to enjoy the company of others who like what she likes, even if they aren't as smart as she is. As one gifted student explains, "Sports makes people equal. Even if you're not that good, the team will accept you with or without your intellect."

- Other kinds of activities, such as choir, band, orchestra, or the drama club, also put the child in contact with others who are working together toward a common goal in an arena beyond the classroom.

- Allowing the child to have older friends who share his interests. Just because a child is segregated by age in school is no reason to keep him in such an artificial environment beyond school hours. However, it's possible that chronologically older children, particularly those in middle and high school, may be involved in experimenting with activities such as smoking, drug-taking, or drinking that are inappropriate and dangerous. Monitor the child's activities closely and call a halt to any relationship that has the potential to damage him.

- Helping the child become more socially aware and agreeable by overt instruction in taking turns, speaking politely, and listening to others' points of view.

A Quick Look: The Joys of Optimism

Because of their capacity for empathy, many gifted children are compassionate and sensitive to the needs of others. However, they may have to learn how to treat themselves compassionately, because they can be very dour when it comes to assessing themselves and their relationships with others. It's not uncommon for parents and teachers to hear a gifted child declare that no one likes her and no one ever will. She's too weird, too different, too ugly, too smart, or all of the above.

Martin E. P. Seligman, Ph.D., believes that children can be encouraged to replace such negative beliefs with some that are more positive and optimistic. He suggests that students become aware of the self-defeating things they say about themselves and then imagine that those statements were made by an external person who is trying to make that student miserable.[1]

Seligman says that making negative self-statements causes the student to believe and act as if they were true. His solution is for students to dispute their pessimistic self-talk just as they would if they were hearing these opinions from an outside source. "We generally have the skill of disputing other people when they make false accusations, and we can learn to do so with ourselves as well," he says.[2] This strategy calls upon gifted children's cognitive ability, which they can employ to examine the validity of their self-defeating assumptions.

Studies prove that optimism is positively associated with intrinsic and extrinsic motivation and indirectly associated with satisfaction with school and commitment to schoolwork.[3] Expecting a favorable outcome affects how students may react to adversity. Optimistic students believe they have more control over their fate than those who think they are controlled by the whims of fortune.

Parents and teachers can indicate that they believe in the student's competence to succeed in meeting high expectations. They also can show students how to assess situations realistically yet optimistically and emphasize that a can-do spirit increases the chance of success in any endeavor. A cheerful approach and appropriate humor—never at the expense of the child—can help a gifted student lighten up, relax, and overcome many obstacles.

Issues with introverts

Gifted children are not necessarily introverts. Many are extroverted and happy in large groups of other children; they aren't put off by loud, confusing environments; and they're free and open about their emotions and feelings. However, just as in the general population, there are some gifted students who are introverted.

Adults must be careful in their use of the word *introvert*. Introverts are not misfits who live by themselves in the woods and can't get along with others. They are simply people who processes information and experiences internally.

Extroverts draw energy from being around other people. They like to try out and refine their ideas in the presence of others. Introverts draw energy from being alone and quiet. They like to think things through by themselves or in the presence of only one or two trusted confidants.

Introverts are not necessarily shy or socially backward, but because American society tends to be extroverted, those who are more contemplative or reserved are often viewed as bashful, uncertain, and somehow "less than" extroverts. Parents sometimes worry that an introverted child is unhappy because he isn't surrounded by a gaggle of other children. Teachers may push quiet children into social interactions that they neither need nor desire in an effort to make them "friendlier" and "better adjusted."

In fact, introverted children may already be friendly and well-liked. They just choose to deal with their friends in small doses, playing with one or two at a time in a corner of the playground rather than joining in a large-group game of dodgeball. If they have only a small number of reciprocal friendships but are content with the quality of these relationships, there's no reason for adults to be particularly concerned.

Introversion is not a bad thing. Introverts can be deeply sensitive and kind. They may be excellent observers, able to pick up nuances and subtleties in others' behavior. Their quiet nature and astute observations are often assets in the classroom and elsewhere. It's not necessary for teachers or parents to push them on to the stage if they are happier in the wings.

Compassionate adults will accept and value introverted children as they are and will provide the following for these children.

Time to process events and ideas

In the classroom, the introverted child will not be the first one with her hand in the air when the teacher asks a question. If the teacher wants to hear the child's opinion, he should call on other students first to allow the introverted student time to consider her answer. Or the teacher can meet with the child privately to gauge her understanding of a skill or concept. An otherwise introverted child often opens up if the teacher provides a safe, non-threatening arena for one-to-one discussion.

At home, parents might notice that the introverted gifted student needs considerable time to complete assignments. The pace is dictated by the student's need to ponder and process the dimensions of the assignment. When developing a time management plan for such children, it's wise to allow extra time for homework so the child doesn't feel rushed during the cogitation phase. Once the thinking is done, the child may complete the work rapidly, but shortcutting the "mulling over" time may make it difficult for him to finish the assignment.

Transitions between events may be difficult for introverts because of their need for processing time. Letting them know in advance that a transition will occur in a specified number of minutes helps them move between activities. The teacher may say, "There are 15 minutes left for this project," and repeat the countdown at 10 and five minutes so that the child has enough time to wind down, put away materials, and prepare herself to tackle the next subject.

At home, a parent may tell the child, "We're leaving for Grandma's in a half-hour, so please choose what clothes you're going to wear and make sure you leave time to brush your teeth. We have to get on the road on time." Once again, a reminder at 15 minutes will help the child disengage from what he's doing and allow him to shift his focus.

Larger transitions, such as from elementary to middle school or moving to a new house, may require a great deal of preparation. When the child is changing schools, familiarize her with her new surroundings as far in advance as possible. Show her where the school is. Find out how many students attend, how she'll be transported to and from the building, and what extracurricular activities and teams await her there. Take her to the new school several times, or if she has a choice of schools, which is possible in districts in which there is open enrollment, make sure she has the opportunity to visit several schools and time to talk over her reactions to each one. Give her a real voice in the selection.

Privacy

Gifted introverts can be over-stimulated by an exciting—or even mundane—day at school. They need a place of their own where they can get away and be by themselves to think, relax, and rebuild their energy stores before venturing out again.

If it's not possible for a child to have her own room, try to find a corner in the home where she can hide out for a little while to read, do an art project, meditate, or whatever other activity helps her refuel. Like highly sensitive children, introverted students can benefit from a "thinking space" in the classroom where they can go to work or restore a sense of inner calm in the flurry of classroom activity.

On school projects, introverts sometimes work best alone and usually do better working with a partner than in a large cooperative group. Although group work may be required, if it's preceded by time-limited partner investigation that offers a sense of privacy and allows the child to test ideas with one other person rather than with a crowd, he may be more comfortable when the whole group begins its work.[4]

Both at home and at school, correction, discipline, feedback, and even praise should be handled privately. Gifted introverts can feel intensely ashamed if their mistakes are pointed out publicly. Conversely, they can be miserably uncomfortable if they are singled out for praise. In fact, being singled out for any reason can feel like torture to them.

Assistance in managing others' perceptions

Because of gifted introverts' need for privacy and their reticence to share their deepest thoughts with a crowd, other children may view them as snobbish, stand-offish, and superior. These perceptions can translate into the child's being ignored or taunted by classmates.

Compassionate adults can help gifted children moderate others' perceptions. Sometimes all a gifted child requires is an explanation of why others may have received a wrong impression. Be specific so that the child can see precisely what behavior caused the misperception, and then strategize with her to develop alternatives. For example, a teacher might say, "Do you remember the other day when Tarik tried to ask for your help with a math problem? You walked right by him without even acknowledging that he was speaking to you. When you do something like that, it makes other people think you're stuck up—that you don't have time for them. What could you do differently the next time someone asks for help?"

Once the issue is pointed out, a gifted child probably will be able to generate several alternative behaviors. The teacher can help her select those that balance her needs for privacy against her being receptive and cooperative with others. A child doesn't have to turn into a garrulous glad-hander to be polite and friendly, and parents and teachers can give her the tools to maintain her private identity while exhibiting courteous public behavior. One-to-one role play can be a powerful way for children to try out different styles of relating to others and receive feedback in a private, non-threatening environment.

Dumbing down and fitting in

Most gifted students will admit that, at least occasionally, they deliberately hide their talents. They fail a test, don't turn in their homework, or work at less than their capacity so that they won't always outpace their classmates. Because they want to fit in and be part of a peer group, they deny their individuality and play down their ability.

Girls especially may make the disturbing choice to hide their intelligence to avoid social isolation. Boys may mask their brain power with humor. It seems a shame that children feel that they have to choose between being smart and being liked, but oftentimes they do.

Gifted African-American students who participate in advanced classes may be accused of being an "Oreo" or "acting white." American Indian children sometimes face the same taunts, being referred to as "apples" (red on the outside, white on the inside). Asian students often want to stay in a group because being viewed as exemplary is antithetical to their cultural values. To keep themselves in good standing with their peers, some of these children try to appear less intelligent than they are. They achieve at a level far below what they are capable of in school. Others adopt a dual identity: one for school, and one for the neighborhood. Such a bisection of their personalities can be disorienting and exhausting.

Peer influence appears to be affected by the stability of the family structure. Although all children will pull away from their families and begin to individuate as they mature, they will reject parental influence to a greater extent if the parent-child interactions are composed mainly of squabbling and conflict.

Parents and teachers must send a strong message that gifted children are acceptable as they are. Because they sometimes worry about their children's socialization, parents may send an unconscious signal that a student must be popular as well as talented. However, as Sylvia Rimm, Ph.D., insightfully points out, our society's unhealthy emphasis on popularity ends at high school graduation.[5] Once college begins, no one cares if the student was in the "right crowd" in high school. Thus, for many gifted students, college is the oasis they've longed for as they struggled through the desert of high school immaturity.

The pressure to be popular and to fall in with the crowd can be somewhat mitigated if parents begin early to engage their children in discussions about what real friendship looks like. By the time the child arrives at middle or high school, he should understand that real friends don't ask others to indulge in risky behaviors such as smoking, drinking, or premature sexual behavior. They aren't rude and cruel to one another. Real friends respect one another's rights, talents, and differences. They don't ask friends to sacrifice their own goals and ideals in the name of friendship.

When a young child is gifted, it's good for parents and teachers to encourage friendships with other students who are eager to learn. These children can lean on each other when the pressure to underachieve crops up in later years. The child's significant adults also must model an interest in learning for its own sake. If parents only talk a good game, children will consider them hypocritical and inauthentic.

In later years, when children are more independent, it's harder to monitor every friend and situation. Nonetheless, parents can continue to stress the importance of associating with other students who are looking toward the future, setting positive goals, and taking action to attain them. They can role play how their children might handle negative, but perhaps attractive, influences. They can encourage the child's participation in community activities that contribute to the public good, and they can join them in these worthwhile projects. They can provide healthy options and allow the child to select the one that is most interesting: working as a youth docent at a local museum, serving as a summer nanny for young children, or attending an art class for non-artists.

There are no guarantees that even the finest parenting will prevent a child from succumbing to negative peer pressure, but the more parents and teachers can strengthen the student's sense of worth and self-sufficiency, the more likely she is to resist inappropriate behavior.

Dealing with taunting and bullying

It's nothing short of tragic that smart children, particularly the profoundly gifted, are so often the target of both verbal and physical abuse. In a study funded by the Supporting Emotional Needs of Gifted (SENG) Foundation, researchers looked at the effects of bullying on gifted students. Sixty-seven percent of the 432 gifted eighth graders in the survey reported that they had been the target of bullying in the first eight years of school.[6]

Despite the fact that this number is in line with the general population, in which 60% to 90% reported that they had been bullied,[7] gifted children appear to be more adversely affected than others, especially by teasing about their appearance. Perhaps this is because of their sensitivity. "The words...tend to stay with them the rest of their lives," says Jean Sunde Peterson, Ph.D., who conducted the survey. "Many are intense, sensitive, and stressed by their own and other's high expectations, and their ability, interests, and behavior may make them vulnerable. Additionally, social justice issues are important to them, and they struggle to make sense of cruelty and aggression."[8]

Although most of the gifted students contended with bullying nonviolently, 11% of them reported responding with violence and had violent thoughts regarding their tormentors. The consideration of violence as a strategy for dealing with bullying should be taken seriously by parents, teachers, administrators, and the community, especially in the aftermath of highly publicized school shootings and other violence.

Because gifted children may be intensely sensitive, adults must show them how to differentiate between the teasing that children may engage in when, for example, a student starts wearing glasses or braces, and the more serious taunting that is directed toward inflicting emotional pain. Parents and teachers can point out that good-natured teasing may be a sign of affection and acceptance. Bullying never is.

Bullying involves repeated incidents of physical or psychological aggression. It can consist of words, gestures, isolation or exclusion, rumor-spreading, and name-calling. It is threatening and relentless. The victim suffers nearly every day. Bullying often involves a leader who incites others to carry on the torture while the leader remains above it.

Cyberbullying, a relatively new phenomenon, can comprise using the Internet to send threatening or intimidating messages or pictures to the victim or sharing personal information or embarrassing pictures of the victim with others. Sometimes online polls are taken as to which student is the ugliest, fattest, dumbest, or smelliest, and the results are sent to the victim, along with the polling information about how many people voted. This kind of bullying is in some ways the most destructive of all. Gifted children may spend considerable time on the Internet, and this interruption of their work and enjoyment amounts to nothing less than persecution. The cruelty is agonizing.

Students many be loath to tell adults that they're being bullied because they think that they should be able to handle the issue on their own. This may be especially true of gifted children. They might believe that their intellectual prowess should be enough to see them through the problem. They may also be afraid of seeming weak or babyish. Students with low self-esteem may believe that the taunts have elements of truth to them and thus be embarrassed at their own shortcomings.

Parents and teachers therefore must be alert to both physical and emotional symptoms that indicate a child is being bullied. Obviously, bruising or abrasions that are more serious than one would expect from playground activities should be investigated. Headaches and stomach-aches that resolve themselves when the child is allowed to stay at home can be a clue that something is wrong at school. If the child develops a sudden aversion to riding the bus, wants to change his routine (take a different route to school or be driven instead of riding his bike), or seems to be "losing" his lunch money or belongings frequently, parents need to keep their eyes and ears open. They may have to seek answers indirectly, asking such questions as:

- Have you seen anyone having trouble on the bus or walking to school?
- Have you heard any ugly rumors about kids you know and like?
- How do the kids act on the playground?
- Have you ever heard anyone threaten another student?

Teachers and administrators must enforce a no-excuses ban on physical and emotional abuse. Unfortunately, many of the country's most popular situation comedies feature disrespect, insults, and outright cruelty, so children may be unaware that such behavior is unacceptable.

In addition, some children are bullies because it's what they've seen all their lives. They may have grown up in a home in which screaming and hurting one another are everyday acts. They may not know any other way of dealing with others. For these children, bullying must be defined, the limits clearly explained, and a zero tolerance policy enforced without exception.

But a policy isn't enough. Students must know what to do when they're in the midst of a bullying situation. Many parents tell their children to fight back. The problem with this suggestion is that, while it sometimes calls the bully's bluff, it just as often brings about an escalation of violence. More students can be drawn into the conflict, and life-threatening injuries can be the result.

Better, more effective, suggestions abound. Adults may advise a child to:

- *Maintain your personal power.* If the bully can generate an aggressive response, he's gotten what he wants and he's in charge. Be indifferent to anything the bully says or does. When he realizes that you will not respond, he may back off. Calmly walking away from taunts and threats can sometime deactivate a bully.

- *Use your brain and speak up.* Sometimes a student can look a bully in the eye and say, "You can have any opinion of me you want. What you think doesn't matter to me. It doesn't affect my opinion of myself. You aren't bothering me, so you might as well forget it." Occasionally, a simple, "Stop talking to me that way," can be effective, but sometimes it isn't.

- *Stand confidently.* Bullies pick on students who look vulnerable, so maintain a relaxed, assured, and non-confrontational stance.

- *Intervene if another student is being bullied.* If it's safe to do so, stand up to the bully, which may encourage others to join you in ending the incident. If it's dangerous to try to stop the bullying, seek immediate assistance from an adult.

- *Allow parents and teachers to help.* In some extreme cases, legal action may need to be taken, and students can't initiate that themselves.

Gifted children are themselves not immune from being bullies. In the SENG Foundation-funded study, 28% of gifted students said they had bullied someone else, mainly through name-calling and teasing.[9]

Parents must act quickly if their child is bullying others, and consequences must be swift and sure. If a child is a cyberbully, do not hesitate to revoke computer and cell phone privileges, as well as access to any other means by which she can torment another student electronically. Cooperate with school officials who report any incidents in which your child is the bully.

Talk to the child to find out the reasons for his behavior. Some students begin to bully when they themselves are bullied. Others do it because they don't have an appreciation for the pain it causes others. Work with your child to devise ways he can stop himself if he feels the urge to intimidate someone else, and restore privileges as he moderates his behavior.

The social and emotional issues that gifted children face can be complex and sometimes heartbreaking to witness. However, true compassion for these children does not lie in coddling and pitying them. Compassion demands that adults equip children with practical strategies that will help prepare them to work effectively and to have fulfilling family lives and friendships. It is not rescuing them from every emotional bump and bruise the world hands them. It is standing beside them as they negotiate the challenges that make them stronger, more resilient human beings.

In summary

- Compassion for gifted children also includes high expectations and appropriate discipline.

- Gifted children can use their cognitive abilities to reflect on their social and emotional issues.

- The more highly gifted the child, the greater the chance that peer issues may become a concern.

- Being introverted is not the same as being lonely. Many introverted children are highly satisfied with a quieter, more contemplative life.

- Because they are "different," gifted children are sometimes the target of bullies, and they must be given the strategies to help them deal with cruelty and aggression.

Section IV

Special Issues in Motivation

Chapter 12
The Classroom that Works

Education for the future

American education is in need of an overhaul. *No Child Left Behind* and other educational reforms are attempts to make American students competitive with those in other countries, notably India and China. However, bringing students to minimum proficiency will not result in a competitive advantage and will not equip them for new jobs—the kinds of jobs that were unheard of as recently as five years ago.

To deal with planet-wide issues and the dizzying rate of change that will characterize the future, American students must be proficient not only in a particular content area, but also in learning how to learn. Tomorrow's problems will require multidisciplinary, creative, and sophisticated solutions. Students will have to be adept in applying concepts and principles from many different branches of knowledge.

For example, computational skills are essential to mathematics success, but learning mathematics is more than computation. Students must be able to reason mathematically and apply mathematics to problems and in situations that are unique to the times. Global warming and the possibility of catastrophic, international pandemics are not computational problems, but those who will be working on these worldwide concerns will have to be able to read and interpret data, analyze trends, make conjectures, extrapolate, predict, and devise potential solutions—all of which require a deep understanding of mathematical processes and are the types of higher-order thinking skills that come most naturally to gifted children and adults.

The hope for America lies in its most talented students, and greater emphasis should be placed on preparing exceptional students to lead innovation and change. Educational reform might better begin at the top of the intellectual spectrum than at the bottom because research clearly indicates that what's good for gifted students is good for every student. A rising tide lifts all boats, so by providing our best and brightest with what they need to fulfill their promise and potential, we are more likely to raise the level of learning for all. Classrooms that work should include the following.

Higher-level content and higher expectations

Gifted students—and indeed all students—respond to the challenges presented by advanced content and teachers who believe in the students' abilities. For example, Project Breakthrough, a demonstration program in South Carolina, trained teachers in three high-poverty, high-minority elementary schools in how to use high-end language arts and science units. Although the units were created by the Center for Gifted Education at the College of William of Mary, the South Carolina teachers used them with *all* of their students. During the three-year study, the teachers were forced to confront the low expectations they held for their disadvantaged students, and over the project's duration, they learned to increase the challenge of both content and instruction.[1]

The results showed that student achievement improved in the two schools that consistently reported testing data. In one school, the identification of gifted students increased dramatically, although the number of students identified was still below national norms.

This research supports earlier findings that using a rich, challenging curriculum leads to higher levels of learning and achievement and helps identify gifted children who might otherwise be overlooked. These types of curriculum units encourage children not only to list, describe, and identify facts and data, but also to summarize, interpret, analyze, modify, assess, and draw conclusions—all of which require greater abilities in abstract thinking, which is the kind of thinking in which gifted students excel.

Just as dramatic as the children's progress were the changes in the teachers who were trained in the new curriculum. They substantially altered their viewpoints about what children in poverty could accomplish, and they modified their teaching strategies to include greater rigor.

Although average-ability students clearly make gains when challenged by demanding curriculum, gifted students need this type of modification every day, from elementary school to college. Their minds require the stimulation of higher-order, beyond-the-facts thinking. Indeed, without opportunities to exercise their intellectual gifts in an atmosphere that promotes experimentation and growth, their motivation to learn in school is likely to dry up.

A constructivist environment

Little children teach themselves by observing and experiencing the world. Virtually without instruction, they learn to talk, walk, eat, run, spin, dance, sing, and master the challenges presented by their toys. Unafraid of making a mistake, many nowadays use a trial-and-error process to become computer literate before they ever enter elementary school.

In a constructivist classroom, teachers realize that as each child grows, her experience of the world is different from every other student's. Each student's school-based learning begins from a different starting point and integrates new information with what she already knows and believes. Because of these differences, constructivist teachers are more likely to lead students in various type of curricular explorations than to have them read a textbook and be tested on what they've absorbed.

For example, a study of immigration might involve not only the facts about how an immigrant becomes a citizen, but also the students' learning about their own families' arrivals in the United States. They might search for their relatives on the ship manifests now available online from Ellis Island. They might interview all of the students in their grade and create a graph detailing how many families came from specific countries to see if they can discern trends and patterns in immigration.

Open-ended, higher-level thinking are hallmarks of this kind of learning. Discussion and dialogue with both the teacher and other students are encouraged, and real-world applications are the norm. There are opportunities for individual and group work, as well as independent study.

A constructivist classroom is especially useful for gifted students because it accommodates their voracious curiosity and need to explore many facets of a topic. Immersion in learning projects that are relevant to them keeps their motivation high.

Self-pacing and student responsibility

With the explosion of knowledge in every discipline, the teacher's role can no longer be that of unquestioned expert and authority. The teacher's purpose should be to motivate and guide students in learning how to learn.

In a self-paced classroom, the teacher sets learning goals for the year but allows the students great freedom of choice in deciding how they will meet those goals—what materials they will use, what additional knowledge they need to understand important concepts, when and how they will practice their skills, whether they will work alone or together, and even when they will take tests.[2] After all, if they understand a concept in two days, why should they wait six weeks for the test? Self-pacing allows them to demonstrate mastery at the appropriate time and move ahead to new challenges. With the teacher's help and support, they can push into extended explorations of concepts and ideas that fire their intrinsic motivation and allow them to learn in depth.

Self-pacing puts a great deal of responsibility for learning onto the shoulders of the students themselves, and most gifted students thrive on the independence and autonomy. They may work harder than ever before because the amount of choice they have been given has unleashed their motivation in a way they haven't experienced before.

While self-pacing is essential for gifted students so they do not lose their motivation while others try to catch up, they sometimes must be provided with training in the practical skills of managing time, materials, and energy. Self-pacing requires that they be able to manage themselves, as well as the subject matter.

Paradoxically, gifted students' self-pacing does not always mean whizzing through the curriculum. Although their prior knowledge and understanding may allow them to master basic concepts quickly, their original work, which is characterized by more abstract thinking, may require a slower pace, and the teacher may need to help them structure their study and plan interim deadlines and final products.

Constant assessment and feedback

Whatever opinion parents and teachers might hold about testing and standards, the tests do set fairly specific guidelines about what students should know. Ongoing assessment takes three forms: *diagnostic*, which is usually a pretest to find out what the child knows and what he needs to learn; *formative*, which takes place concurrently with instruction; and *summative*, which is used to discover if the student has mastered important concepts and skills. This might be a pencil and paper test, but it might also be a demonstration, presentation, or project.

Unfortunately, the need to cram factual information into children's heads sometimes results in teachers spending enormous amounts of time on content and not much time assessing students' understanding.[3] That's a shame, because when a teacher carries out continual assessment, especially as the students learn new materials, she will naturally differentiate her instruction based on students' needs. Assessment will show which children are having specific difficulties, and the teacher can work to eliminate those deficiencies child by child, bringing each student the help he needs at the precise time he needs it. Good assessment supports learning. It is, in fact, part of instruction, not separate from it.

If the teacher discovers that several children are misunderstanding a particular concept, she may conduct a small group review at the ideal time to ensure students' understanding. Summative assessment is too late to figure out that children are perplexed. By then, they may have learned and practiced incorrectly for several weeks. More frequent informal assessment nips bad habits in the bud.

Useful formative assessment involves good feedback, and good feedback needs to make students think.[4] It should cause them to reflect on what they're doing right and wrong and why. Grades, stars, praise (or ridicule), and general evaluative comments ("Great!" or "Needs to be done again") don't provide any basis for reflection. The student simply feels judged and often stressed and threatened.

Good feedback is immediate and specific, consistent and accurate. It is descriptive, not critical.[5] The feedback may include not only what the student did, but also what he didn't do. It gives him information he can use to assess his own performance and improve it.

Excellent feedback is also positive and constructive. A mistake is viewed as a learning opportunity, not a character flaw. Masterful teachers help their students understand that constant success means only that the students aren't learning anything. Mistakes, on the other hand, demonstrate that the child is venturing beyond what she knows, and if she understands and corrects her mistakes, she has learned something new.

Gifted students, who often have unreasonably high expectations of themselves and take criticism too much to heart, flourish in a classroom in which the emphasis is on compassionate assessment, learning, and growth. Because of their ability to think about their own thinking (called *metacognition*), they are quick to understand and assimilate feedback. While other students may require several repetitions to grasp what they must do to improve, gifted children often correct their learning issues in one try and are immediately ready for new challenges. The teacher must be prepared to accommodate this rapid response by allowing the student to move ahead as quickly as necessary to reach the point of difficulty, which is where real learning will begin to take place again.

Continual assessment—which can involve a short test; a one-to-one demonstration with the teacher or another student; self-grading of homework; a "minute" paper, in which the student writes a minute-long response to a teacher-generated question about what he has learned ("What surprised me most today was..."); or other tech-niques—provides one unexpected benefit: a reduction in students' text anxiety. Students begin to view testing as a natural part of learning. When they are continually assessed and are the recipients of thoughtful, useful feedback, students discover that all types of assessments, including high-stakes tests, are opportunities for understanding and learning, not stress-ridden, do-or-die evaluations of their capabilities. Teachers who coach and guide, rather than instruct and test, turn out students with greater understanding and ability to excel.

An administration that supports gifted education

For gifted education to be truly effective, administration must want it to succeed. Far-sighted (and sometimes self-interested) administrators realize that gifted students' test scores can do much to raise the school's state "grade." For this reason, many gifted students are being better served in their talent areas than they were in the past. Although they may attend special classes in math or reading, their extended experiences are now viewed as part of the general curriculum.

In some too-rare cases, enlightened administrators are doing more than accommodating gifted students; they are giving the gifted program much higher priority. In one school, the principal has gone so far as to schedule gifted students' pull-out experiences first and wrap the rest of the school day around these classes. Other teachers have seen that the process works well, and there is little, if any, resistance to this type of scheduling.

In addition, this principal demonstrates a daily commitment to the needs of gifted students. She has regular conversations with her staff about how they can benefit from the knowledge of teachers in the gifted program. She makes important connections among teachers, parents, and students that highlight the importance of the program in her school. Therefore, everyone in the school, from the secretaries to the counselors to the classroom teachers, has come to feel a sense of ownership of the program. They have all discovered how to adjust the many options that exist for students who come to an Intervention Assistance Team.

This type of administrative leadership and support is invaluable. Without it, gifted programs are left to fend for themselves. Misunder-standings and "turf wars" are not uncommon, and the program is less effective than it should be.

An unexpected need

Teachers may have a difficult time summoning up energy and compassion for students if they do not live in a compassionate environment themselves. And today's schools are not always compassionate places for teachers to work.

Most teachers enter the profession because they care about young people and want to participate in their intellectual, social, and emotional growth. They believe that teaching is an art, that their immortality is found in their interactions with students, and that they make a difference every day. And they're right. Ask adults to list the five most influential people in their lives, and nearly every list will include at least one teacher.

The reality of schools today, however, gives little support to teachers' original ideals. Because of the overwhelming emphasis on content, methods, outcomes, and testing, teachers are becoming increasingly disconnected from their teaching missions and their visions of themselves as mentors and guides. They struggle daily with how to rekindle their own passion so they can pass it on to their students.

Inservice training for teachers is often a one-time-only content-driven presentation that shows them how to improve some minuscule aspect of pedagogy. The object of such training is usually to help them raise their students' test scores. However, what teachers really need is the opportunity to reflect, re-energize, and rekindle their sense of meaning. They should be provided with inservices that help them recapture their purpose and clarify their beliefs. Training should engage their hearts as well as their minds. When they have time and space to regard the purpose of their calling, they rediscover the motivation that drove them to become teachers. They become more vibrant, and that vibrancy infuses the classroom. Only when the teacher's soul is nurtured can he or she nurture the souls of students.

Parents who want the best education for their children should join together with teachers to demand that at least some teacher training be concerned with the whole person so that the teacher can attend to the whole child in the classroom. Remember, says Stanford University professor Eliot Eisner, Ed.D., "The more we stress only what we can measure in school, the more we need to remember that not everything that is measurable matters, and not everything that matters can be measured."[6]

A Quick Look: Reviving Enthusiasm

The following strategies may help teachers focus on their core values and bring about a new sense of purpose.

Journaling. A daily journal can help bring a new sense of clarity to a teacher who is exhausted and disillusioned. It invites the teacher to write the answers to such questions as: Why did I become a teacher? How have I grown? What do I need to attend to now to be a better teacher? What do I want my students to remember? What do I still love about going into the classroom every day? How can I do more of what I love?

Creating community. Putting together a small group of teachers who gather to listen to one another's stories and support each other's growth can be a powerful catalyst for renewal. Participants do not talk about methods or strategies, but about meaning and values and how these affect their interactions with parents, students, and other teachers.

Mentoring. New teachers must be mentored if they are not to burn out in their first years in the classroom. Rather than concentrating on pedagogical techniques, mentors need to help new teachers navigate the basics: How should I set up my classroom? How do I handle parents who may be angry or abusive? How do I deal with parents from other cultures? What is the first week really like?

Taking positive action. Bringing information about effective professional development programs to school boards, administrators, and foundations may result in diversion of training dollars to such programs. Teachers can also apply for grants for training.

Thoughts for teachers

In a classroom that works, the teacher comes to know her students through informal conversations, assessment, participation in a wide variety of school events, personal notes, and even homework assignments that invite the students to share their individual ideas, stories, and histories. She is creative in making herself available to students. If she is too busy to speak with them at a particular moment, she presents alternatives. She may ask the students to send her an e-mail, use a tape recorder to ask questions that she answers by the next day, or place questions or concerns in an envelope on her desk.

When a teacher knows the students and their stories, backgrounds, interests, strengths, and weaknesses, she can hook into those factors to motivate the child to learn in school. She realizes that there is no child who is incapable of learning and no child who cannot be reached. It takes hard work and sometimes a lot of tears—from the child, the parents, and often from the teacher herself—but she keeps trying. And she is often rewarded by a letter or a visit from the child many years later in which she learns of the impact that her persistence and dedication made in the child's life.

...[S]he left her signature upon us...[7]

Miss Diemer was such a teacher, and here's what one of her students had to say.

> "She never stopped being excited by learning, and her exhilaration made us want to learn, too, as much as we could and for our whole lives.

> "She loved being a teacher, but more important, she loved us—each and every one. She brought optimism and hope to each day. She challenged and revitalized our spirits.

> "She saw us as we were and as we could be. She insisted we be our best selves, but when we weren't, her gentle humor, her smile, and her tender concern led us back to the right path.

> "As we were in her heart, she took up residence in ours, and though she is gone now, she lives on in her students, and even in their children, as we try to impart to them all she taught to us.

> "For her, teaching was an art, a calling, and the world's most important work. She brought to us the wonder and excitement of learning so we could take her light out into the world, and that light will never go out."

In summary

- To fire gifted students' motivation, teachers must believe in the students' abilities to regulate their activities and pace their learning. Low expectations breed minimal performance.

- Hands-on, relevant explorations keep students' motivation alive.

- Continual assessment gives students necessary information and allows for more targeted instruction for each student.

- Administrative support is necessary to make gifted education work. Teachers and parents must continually advocate for programming for all gifted students.

- Teachers require self-care to keep their own motivation fresh.

Chapter 13

Motivating Every Student: Who's in the Classroom?

Just as languages and customs vary from culture to culture, so do motivational strategies. What may work with a gifted middle-class, white, English-speaking child born in the United States may be confusing or frightening to an immigrant child or even to a child born in this country but steeped in the traditions of a different culture. For example, in some countries and/or religious traditions:

- "No" is considered an impolite word, so the child may use euphemisms such as, "I'll try," or "That may be hard to do," when he actually means, "No, I can't." If the teacher doesn't understand this language convention, she may expect the child to finish an assignment, while the child believes that he has told the teacher he can't do it.

- The society is a rigid hierarchy, which will affect communication between teacher and child, as well as between parent and teacher.

- The concept of saving or losing face is paramount, so correction must be done very carefully to avoid humiliating the child. She may not be able to handle even the genial teasing teachers sometimes use to point out a mistake or ask for improvement.

- The head is considered sacred and should not be touched. A child from a culture that believes this can be mortified by a pat on the head.

Cultural gaffes can lead a child to believe that the teacher neither likes nor respects him, which causes undue stress, dries up motivation, and severely hampers the teacher-child-parent relationship. In addition, a motivational method that works for some children may backfire badly if used with a child who feels threatened by it.

Many of the strategies that we might use with gifted children today came from the early days of gifted education, and at that time, most students in the programs were in fact white and relatively well off. English was their native language. Today, we realize that gifted students abound in every culture and race. Nonetheless, identification of non-white students continues to lag because, says one educator, "Entrance into many top track programs…is subtly based on acquaintance with certain authors, certain ways of reasoning, and certain ways of behaving.… The result is that whole schools are full of African-American boys, for instance, who have not made it into these programs."[1]

Although identification of culturally and linguistically diverse students continues to be a concern, many educators are involved in removing the barriers to inclusion in gifted programs. They are supplementing required tests with biographical and autobiographical information, portfolio reviews, and performance assessment. For example, a biography of the student may indicate that though she has limited English proficiency, she is three years above grade level in reading and writing in her first language. That precocity is evidence of giftedness that would have been overlooked if only the child's test scores were taken into account. Casting a wider net results in a far bigger "catch" of talented students.

However, even if schools do a better job of recruiting students of color and linguistic minorities, some educators continue to voice concerns about retaining these students in the programs. Several factors may inhibit students' motivation to remain in advanced classes, and many of them are related to the atmosphere of the classroom and the attitude of the teacher.

The role of the teacher in any classroom, but especially in a multicultural setting, can hardly be overstated. Although native-born American students tend to view teachers as somewhat equal partners in the learning process, other cultures do not. In many countries, all elders are respected, and teachers are revered. What the teacher says and does can have a lasting effect on how these students view themselves and their capabilities.

The need for teacher diversity

The United States is becoming more a diverse nation with each passing day, with immigrants arriving primarily from Africa, Asia, and Latin America rather than Western Europe. The term "minority student" is losing validity, as children of color become the majority at many of the nation's elementary, middle, and high schools.

Nonetheless, American teachers are still predominantly young white females, and that can have implications for minorities' identification and retention in gifted programs. Of course, race alone does not qualify—or disqualify—any teacher from teaching any student, and for white children, the experience of learning from a teacher of a different race or culture can be eye-opening and mind-expanding. For minority students, having a teacher who truly understands the world in which they live can be a great motivator. When teachers and students have shared backgrounds, it's easier for teachers to make instruction relevant. The teacher has intimate knowledge of the vocabulary and examples that bring lesson content to life.[2] Many members of minority groups do not consider teaching when making career decisions. Colleges and universities should be in the forefront of reversing this trend. American classrooms need the brightest, most outstanding teachers of every race and ethnicity so students can find appropriate role models in their classrooms every day.

Because of the often significant cultural divide between students and teachers, some unintended and undesirable consequences can arise, including the following.

Racism

Some teachers may believe, however subconsciously, that children of color are not inherently as bright and capable as white students. Their unexamined attitudes about race may cause them to make erroneous and negative assumptions—that all Black children in their classes are disadvantaged or from one-parent homes, or that all of the Latino children are in the country illegally. In fact, many African-American children come from affluent, stable, two-parent families, and many Latino children, even those who speak heavily accented English, are multigenerational American citizens.

Some minority gifted students say that in their classes, white children are often asked to grapple with difficult questions, while African-American and Latino students deal with only simple issues. The students report that holding them to a lower standard makes them feel that their teachers have little confidence in their ability to learn, and if their teachers don't believe in them, why should the students believe in themselves? Their motivation to learn in school may go right down the drain.

Because of language deficiencies or cultural differences, immigrant children may require some accommodation in the way they learn and demonstrate mastery in their areas of expertise. Nonetheless, they can be as intellectually advanced as other gifted children, and they want the same thing the others do: to be challenged to the limits of their ability and to be held accountable for their learning.

If we expect all of our gifted students to achieve, we must provide all of them with the tough challenges that lead to meaningful learning, and we must make them responsible for their own achievement. All participants in the program should be expected to complete assignments, follow class rules, and do the best work of which they're capable. No exceptions.

A Quick Look: Does Race Matter?

Sharron is a gifted African-American woman who grew up when integration was a fact, but not always a reality. A success in every aspect of her education and her business life, she has this to say about African-American students and gifted education.

"In many ways, it's very tough for a Black child who's selected for a gifted program. There are several stumbling blocks he must avoid.

"First, these children often run up against someone who believes that Black kids just can't keep up. The majority community frequently has the mistaken belief that the only Black students who can succeed in such programming must be rich—the children of celebrities who can afford private schools and tutors—because the children can't possibly have the native intelligence to achieve at the same level as white students.

"Then there are children who have accepted this view—the kids who believe they got into the class on a fluke. They feel like imposters and may be terrified that they'll wash out.

"Finally, there's the community of the child's peers, the neighborhood kids who believe that achievement is somehow not for them and that any child who is curious and brilliant and wants to learn is "acting white." In my opinion, these are the kids who have forgotten where they come from. Although they may be the descendents of slaves, they are also the grandsons and granddaughters of African kings and queens. The underachievers don't go far enough back into their own history to claim their original heritage—the rich cultural tradition that existed before their ancestors were herded into slave ships.

"To motivate an African-American child to stay with gifted studies and to fight all the forces that militate against him, you have to deal with his racial identity first—to understand where he comes from. Don't hesitate to remind him that his forebears were part of a vibrant civilization that flourished before America was even a gleam in Columbus's eye. The child has something to live *up* to, and he needn't live *down* to the beliefs of his friends who don't know who they are.

"If you really want your minority students to stay in gifted programs, challenge them and don't back off. Don't accept excuses. Be the teacher who says, 'Oh, yes, you can. You have everything you need to succeed or you wouldn't be in this class.' Deep in their hearts, these kids know they're smart, and once they're motivated, they are also dogged in their desire to learn.

"Remember that you don't have to do it alone. Reach out to the community. African-American achievers will be happy to reinforce the teacher's work with the child. We have a history of mentoring students who want to achieve. But we have to know where they are. If parents, teachers, and the community work together, these children will learn to believe that they can make it—and they will make it."

Cultural illiteracy

In multicultural classrooms, there may be teachers who know little about the countries and cultures from which their students come. Lack of cultural knowledge can lead teachers, counselors, and others to base their assumptions about students' capabilities on non-cognitive qualities.

For example, in the United States and in many Latino cultures, communication includes a significant amount of eye contact. However, in certain Asian and African countries, it is considered disrespectful for children to stare into an adult's eyes while the adult is speaking. Therefore, the students will lower their eyes if the teacher is speaking directly to them. If a teacher misinterprets this sign of respect, he may believe that the student is, at best, shy and emotionally immature and, at worst, furtive and evasive.

In addition, many societies value and seek the wisdom of elders, especially teachers. Children brought up in these cultures are likely to want more guidance and be less self-directed in their studies than a typical American student would be. Once again, this quality does not reflect uncertainty, lack of initiative, or incompetence, but only deference to the teacher's greater experience and learning. It is a learning style preference and not a reason to believe that the child is not talented.

Americans think of themselves as family oriented, but in comparison to many other countries and regions of the world, we are only loosely connected with our families. In most cultures, the family is central, and extended families form a powerful support system for their members. The well-being of the entire family, village, or region comes before the needs of any one person.

It should not be surprising, then, that children from these cultures are not as individualistic as American students. These students are often more comfortable working together in small groups in which no particular student is singled out. This group consciousness is not a weakness; it's just a different way of seeing the world. However, if the teacher doesn't understand the student's background, she may view his reluctance to take center stage as a deficit. As the child assimilates, he may develop more independence, but he may always exhibit a preference for working in groups. It's part of who he is.

Sometimes as simple a thing as chair position can make a cultural difference. In most classrooms, children sit in rows while the teacher stands in front of the students. However, American Indian children may feel more comfortable in a semi-circle or circle because family and tribal groups often sit this way.

Motivating students from various countries and ethnicities requires a keen interest in the whole child and an understanding of the culture that produced her intellectual, emotional, and social dimensions. Teachers should make every effort to enter into the communities in which their students live and open their eyes to the myriad ways giftedness can be expressed in a multicultural world.

Boys and girls together

It comes as no surprise to teachers or parents that boys and girls are different, but just how different—and what these differences mean to their learning—was largely unexplored until the end of the last century. At that time, an explosion in brain-based research showed us that there was a scientific basis for many of the things we believed about gender differences.

Positron emission tomography (PET) and Magnetic Resonance Imaging (MRI) have allowed us to watch the brain work and to discover significant differences in the ways the two sexes learn. The research results by no means should be construed to mean that biology is destiny—that a woman can't be a scientist or a man must be strong and silent—because people are more than their brain waves. And biology doesn't exist in a vacuum. Biological factors are always tempered and shaped by environmental and social conditions.

One important fact that brain-based research has taught us is that the brain is always changing. It is plastic, adaptable, and constantly in flux, strengthening strong neural pathways and pruning others at various stages of children's development, and these ebbs and flows of activity are related to behavioral and intellectual changes.

Research has shown that most parts of the brain mature more quickly in girls than in boys, except the specific area that deals with mechanical reasoning, visual targeting, and spatial reasoning. This area matures as much as four to eight years earlier in boys.[3]

Girls' brains are characterized by greater activity in the areas that deal with communication—listening, talking, and remembering sensory details. Girls can sit still for longer periods, enhancing communication. In addition, girls produce more oxytocin, a chemical secreted by the pituitary gland that promotes bonding and empathy. Girls also have a larger, thicker corpus callosum, the strip of tissue that connects the two halves of the brain and allows the two hemispheres to talk with one another. This larger structure permits them to think more holistically and to multitask more effectively than males.

A female's brain is never truly at rest, because in its resting state, it is as active as the activated male brain.[4] The male brain requires a rest state to renew itself.[5] Boys may appear to "glaze over" during this period, not being particularly attentive to their surroundings. The female brain recharges itself without entering a rest state.

Not only do girls' and boys' brains mature at different rates, there are also differences in the amount of brain space given to various functions. Girls' brains have approximately twice as much space devoted to verbal and emotional concerns as boys' brains; boys have more space devoted to spatial and mechanical functions. In boys, the portion of the brain that deals with impulse control is smaller than in girls, so boys are more likely to make impulsive decisions and "act without thinking."[6]

The brain often works with sensory data: touch, taste, hearing, sight, and smell. In these areas, boys and girls are also different. Girls see and hear things that boys do not, while boys notice things that escape girls. Boys tend to notice an object's motion, while girls are more likely to be aware of its texture and color.[7]

Boys and girls often behave differently, too. The bases for the differing behaviors include brain development, environment, and personality. For example, when boys are emotionally upset, they often hold it in because they don't have the emotional vocabulary girls do. When emotionally charged information enters the boy's limbic system (the part of the brain that processes emotion), it tends to move downward to the brain stem, which controls the fight or flight response. Therefore, a boy may become aggressive (fight), or he may withdraw (flight). On the other hand, a girl's brain more likely moves the information upward to the thinking areas. She can then reflect on the situation, talk it over with others, and process it more fully.[8]

Even these few facts, which are only a fraction of what we've discovered about the brain, have interesting classroom implications. For example, a gifted girl whose brain doesn't require a resting period may be intensely bored by the lesson being taught, but because she is able to sit still and keep her eyes open, she looks tuned in, and the teacher may never know that she is unchallenged and frustrated.

A gifted boy, on the other hand, may make his boredom visible by fidgeting and acting out because he is less able to control his impulses. He may also fall asleep or at least mentally check out, especially if the teacher is lecturing. Boys tend to do better at viewing visual representations than listening to a fountain of words.

When planning classroom activities for mixed-sex classrooms, it's wise to include several different kinds of activities to keep children's brains active and involved. For girls, this may involve working in a variety of flexible groupings with lots of opportunity for conversation, journaling or other writing assignments, reading for content and also for enjoyment, and other tasks that involve the areas of the brain in which girls are naturally strong.

However, to enhance their spatial skills and help girls succeed in more abstract realms, it can be helpful to use manipulatives, puzzles, and three-dimensional models. If they are not already computer savvy, give them opportunities to become more adept. As the world becomes more wired, technology skills will be required in every aspect of adult lives.[9]

For gifted girls, self-paced computer programs allow them to move quickly through material they understand and repeat lessons that may be more abstract and difficult for them. Computers allow them considerable control over their learning and invite them to become more technologically competent.

For boys, make sure there's lots of room and opportunity for movement. Even if boys are not "hyperactive," they still like to move around more than girls do, and they use a lot of space, even when they're seated. Include some kinesthetic aspects in their learning activities. With boys, show, don't tell. Keep instructions short and to the point.

On the other side of the coin, build boys' reading and communication skills by inviting men to the classroom to read aloud or serve as reading mentors for boys.[10] Many men—from college students to retired businessmen—would welcome the opportunity to serve children in this capacity. Their presence is a powerful lesson in the importance of reading and developing expressive verbal skills. Boys, too, benefit from computer learning. Presentation programs can assist them in understanding how words can be used to reach and influence others.

Boys and girls not together

During early adolescence, boys and girls are probably as different from one another as they'll ever be. Hormonal surges affect everything from their sleep patterns to the function of their sexual organs. Their brains go through a period of great growth, which will be followed by a period of pruning in the areas that affect impulse control and regulation of emotions. When they hit the pruning period, they may be as emotional and irrational as toddlers. This fact is good news to moms and dads who may wonder what suddenly happened to their parenting skills!

In adolescence, girls often begin to suffer a dip in their self-confidence, and that dip may continue all the way through high school. Both gifted boys and girls may settle into an underachievement pattern, as their brain power begins to attract teasing and negative comments from peers. Some schools feel that the answer to these issues is to offer same-sex classes in core areas, while allowing boys and girls to socialize during other periods of the day.

Research results on the success of this program are mixed. In 2005, the United States Department of Education released a study that showed some slight positive effects on some measures of academic competence, but it did not show that such classes either helped or harmed achievement or socialization.[11] Nonetheless, some students like the sex-segregated classes. Girls like the freedom to be smart without boys making fun of them. Boys sometimes like the more intense competition of all-boy classrooms. However, boys also say that the competition can involve more bullying than is usual in mixed-sex classes.

The key to a successful single-sex classroom seems to be student choice and appropriate timing. If the students themselves choose the option, they are much happier with it than if they are forced into single-sex classes by parental or school board edict. In addition, the option seems to work better with younger middle schoolers. As students approach high school, they are less likely to want to remain in a single-sex environment.

What's important to remember is that most generalizations are riddled with exceptions. There are gifted girls who are talented in physics and chemistry and gifted boys who are brilliant writers. A gifted boy may be an excellent athlete or barely be able to find his way to the playing field. A gifted girl may be a highly creative artist and a cheerleader at the same time. A gifted boy may be sensitive and emotional, while a gifted girl may be tough and perseverant. All of these children are individuals, and it's counterproductive to try to pigeonhole them.

As adults, we need to watch, listen, and do the best we can to provide opportunities for learning that best meet our children's varied and particular interests, learning styles, and personalities. We must take the time to learn about and connect to each child in a different way. Provide opportunities for children to reflect and share their thoughts and feelings. Once you know how they think about the world and their place in it, you'll be more able to tailor motivational strategies that work.

Who's in the home school classroom?

Many gifted children and their parents opt out of public schooling, and for many children, it works beautifully. Both parents and children are highly motivated, and the home school offers many advantages that even the best public school would be hard-pressed to provide. It allows parents to truly differentiate—to meet the child precisely where he is and guide him as he studies an integrated curriculum that permits him to investigate, analyze, synthesize, and apply lessons and concepts in ways that are meaningful to him.

The school day can be as long or short as it needs to be, and learning can take place all year. The child can take part in community activities during times she would otherwise be in school, and these experiences can be as educational as anything she might experience within the confines of a classroom. The home school often provides exceptional opportunities for children to become happy, confident, lifelong learners.

However, just as public schooling is not for everyone, neither is home schooling. Lisa Rivero, author of *Creative Home Schooling: A Resource Guide for Smart Families*,[12] indicates that for home schooling to succeed, parents must be even more motivated than the child. It's the parents who must spend hours of time developing the philosophy that will guide the child's instruction—planning lessons, teaching, answering their child's questions, assessing the child's understanding of concepts, searching out community resources, finding mentors, looking for additional enrichment opportunities, analyzing curricula, and scaring up materials for creative projects. It's virtually a full-time job and surely impossible for parents who work outside the home. In addition, the combination of parent and teacher perspectives found in a public or private school may be useful. Even the best parent doesn't know everything about a child, and often another teacher can offer valuable insights and assistance.

To keep a child's motivation high, home schooling parents must adopt the strategies that good teachers have used for generations. In many cases, these strategies are easier to apply in the home school because there are fewer students than in the typical public school classroom:

- Have high but achievable expectations.

- Allow the child's interests and learning style to dictate at least some of the curriculum.

- Be flexible and adaptable.

- Reward the process as well as the product.

- Remove stress and threat from the learning environment.

- Play down competition. Play up the concept of "personal best" and achieving potential.

- Set the example. If parents want their children to learn, the parents must keep learning. If they want them to read, the parents must read. If they want them to exercise and eat properly, so must the parents. As both parent and teacher, the parents take on the obligation of primary model—squared.

Wherever and however the child learns, it's the adults who either fire the student's enthusiasm or quash it. There is no substitute for the combination of a loving, actively involved parent and a nurturing teacher who understands and values intellectual giftedness and the challenges it presents.

In summary

- In a multicultural world, teachers must have an appreciation for differences in culture that affect motivation.

- Different cultures display giftedness in different ways. Teachers must be accepting of all ways that giftedness shows itself.

- Gifted boys' and girls' brains are different in structure and mature at different rates. The two sexes may require different motivational techniques.

- Home schooled students are usually highly motivated and the rewards are great, but the work of home schooling is labor-intensive, and even the best-intentioned parents may find it tough going.

Chapter 14
Questions and Answers

Q. *My 10-year-old daughter doesn't want to try anything new. She has to be dragged kicking and screaming to any new activity. Then she usually likes it. What's this all about?*

A. If your daughter has to be dragged (I know you mean this figuratively), perhaps she hasn't had much input into the decision about whether she attends the activity. However, if she "doesn't want to try anything" yet finds that she enjoys the class or activity after she gets there, it may be that your daughter is not reacting to the new situation as much as she is to the transition from the familiar to the new.

Perhaps you could take her to the activity and let her observe before asking her to plunge in. She may respond well to observation and quiet communication before dealing with the stimulation of a whole new setting. Allow her to meet the leader, and let her know in advance what will be expected of her. That should lessen her apprehension.

In addition, you should speak with the activity leader and inform him or her of your child's hesitancy and of her special interests. If, after a period of familiarization, she doesn't want to continue, it would be wise to probe for reasons, and if they make sense to you, you might rethink her participation altogether. Every child does not have to do everything.

On the other hand, you may want to encourage further participation so that your daughter develops important life skills, including perseverance and making transitions from one activity to another.

Q. *I know my 12-year-old son is having some sort of peer issues at school, but I'm not sure what they are, and he doesn't want to talk about it. How can I get him to tell me what's going on?*

A. Boys are often resistant to talking about their feelings, but sometimes they'll become more open if you sit beside them and do an activity together. Build a model, do an art project, or bake a batch of brownies. If he doesn't want to sit down, stand beside him as you wash the car or trim a hedge.

It's important to sit or stand next to him so he doesn't feel threatened by a lot of eye contact. Don't plunge into talking about the issue that's troubling you. Just be with him as you work together. You can chat about what you're doing and work your way into some open-ended questions: "How do you think school is going this year?" or "Have you noticed anything about middle school that you didn't expect?"

Then just listen. The problem may come out. Or not. Persist, not in probing or questioning him too closely, but in setting up opportunities for him to speak in a way that's comfortable. There's something about involving a boy in a mechanical activity that makes it easier for him to reach down to his emotional core and become more willing to talk.

Q. *I know my child is gifted in language. He began reading when he was four, and he's been writing his own stories since he was a preschooler (often dictating them to me). He's in the second grade and was tested for inclusion in the gifted program. He didn't test well enough, but he could benefit so much from the program. What do I do?*

A. Call your son's classroom teacher and set up a conference to discuss his writing abilities. Those particular skills are unusual for a second-grade boy, and the teacher may not be aware of his special talents. Strategize with her about ways she can include his passion for writing in his classroom experience. He might be eligible for a single-subject acceleration in reading and writing, and that alone might be a sufficient accommodation for him.

Many school districts test for placement in gifted programming more than once in a child's academic career. You might find out if he could test again, or you could speak with the gifted coordinator about taking a more comprehensive look at his abilities. Show her a portfolio of his stories or other work that he's done at home. Talk with his first- and second-grade teachers to gain their assessment of his ability to keep up with the pace and rigor of the gifted program.

Remember that a child needn't be in a gifted program to extend his experience in an area he loves. Many libraries and literary centers have writing workshops for children of various ages. Check with your local librarian or bookstore. They will probably have information on these opportunities.

Keep encouraging your son yourself. Read and collect his stories. Take them to a copy shop and have them bound. He'll like it, and you'll have a permanent record both to show school officials and for you to enjoy.

Q. *I'm a teacher of the gifted, and for years, I've taught a multidisciplinary pull-out class. The kids study history, math, and language arts all related to a specific theme, and there's a culminating project at the end of each semester. This year, the theme is medieval history. Now my district wants to change the program to one in which kids are simply accelerated based on test scores in math or reading. This is nothing more than acceleration, which is good, but there's no attention to the social and emotional needs of the students. How do I attend to those in a classroom that's just speeded up? I'm so discouraged that I'm thinking about retiring.*

A. Change is hard, and it's evident that you're a dedicated teacher who cares about each student. However, a shift in classroom emphasis doesn't mean you have to shut off your compassion. In fact, most of these accelerated groups are relatively small. You may find that you can spend more time with each student and deal with social and emotional issues very effectively. When you have fewer students, you can learn in depth about their passions and tie your instruction to things that really interest them. You may be able to differentiate instruction more than ever before. And in a small group of like-minded students, you'll see friendships take off and students become generally happier. You may find that you have fewer social and emotional issues to deal with.

Q. *My child is brilliant, no question, but he missed the cutoff for the gifted program by two points. It was the achievement portion of the testing that dragged him down. Now he's been diagnosed with ADHD. Although I resisted it for a long time, I finally put him on medication, and the change is enormous. He's able to stay on task much better, and even his handwriting has improved. I think he would do much better on his achievement test this time because his ability to stay on task has improved so much. I also think he needs the challenge that our gifted program offers. But the school says he can't enter because of his previous test scores. What do I do now?*

A. Speak with the classroom teacher and building principal to see if they, too, have observed a significant change in your son's behavior. How is he doing day to day? Do they see an improvement in his work habits? Is he concentrating better and following directions more easily? If others concur that there's been a marked improvement in his ability to focus and complete learning tasks, you could ask for him to be retested. If that is not possible, you might consider having the testing done by an outside psychologist and sharing the results with the school.

There's no reason such a disability should keep your gifted son from participation in a program that will help him reach his potential.

Q. *My daughter, who is in the third grade, has been identified as highly gifted, but she does a miserable job on any kind of standardized test. She gets too nervous, sees too many possible answers, and makes careless mistakes. In our state, even if you have all A's from the first day of school, you have to pass a state test to go to fourth grade. I'm afraid she'll fail and that repeating third grade will kill any motivation to learn. Her school refuses any type of acceleration, and the gifted program hasn't done much for her. How do I help her learn to take tests?*

A. Many gifted students find these sorts of tests challenging, fun, and easy. They often make perfect scores on the ACT or SAT, seemingly without breaking a sweat. Sometimes, however, standardized tests are hard for gifted children because they see so many possibilities. Because they appreciate nuances of language, they may see ways in which even obviously incorrect responses could be right. They agonize over the choices and sometimes make a series of incorrect responses because they've misunderstood the initial question.

These students need little assistance with content, but they can benefit from strategies that will make the test-taking process less mystifying and allow them to show what they know. Here are some hints to share with gifted students whose test-taking isn't up to par:

- *Read the question all the way through.* Gifted students are often so eager to get to the answer that they don't read the entire question. Because they overlook one tiny piece of information, they may answer a whole series of questions incorrectly.

- *Be aware that on standardized, multiple-choice tests, everything needed to arrive at the correct answer is in the question itself.* On many types of tests, students must pull material from many sources and organize it into a coherent answer. This isn't the case with most standardized tests. The information is contained in the question, and choices must be made based on the material available. Don't over-reach.

- *Estimate the amount of time available for each question, and answer the easiest questions first.* If the test takes 60 minutes and there are 120 questions, the student has about 30 seconds for each one. But she can steal time by answering "sure thing" questions first and devoting the additional time to more difficult questions.

- *Decide if you should guess.* Many standardized tests do not count wrong answers, so your daughter may want to take some educated guesses. She won't lose points for a wrong answer, and if she gets it right, that's good.

- *Beware of questions that over-generalize.* Most answers that contain the words *always* or *never* are incorrect. However, there may be instances in which something really is always or never true. Don't leap to the conclusion that the answer must be wrong. Read the question thoroughly and think it through.

- *If you don't know the answer immediately, eliminate as many wrong answers as possible.* In most questions, there's usually at least one answer that's obviously incorrect. Eliminate it from consideration, and concentrate on the remaining answers. Keep up the process of elimination until you're left with a smaller number of possible responses. In a question with five possible answers, eliminating only two of them changes the odds of answering correctly from 20% to 60%

Sometimes, seeing the test as a puzzle to be solved or a game to be played changes the student's perspective. Once she has basic strategies in place, she can enjoy applying what she knows to "outsmart" the test.

Q. *What you said about introverts rings true for me. Our eight-year-old daughter, Jenna, is introverted, and if we praise her, she becomes really uncomfortable. How can we let her know we're proud of her without tying her up in knots?*

A. Kids believe that what they overhear is true, so one powerful technique for effective praise is called "referential speaking"—that is, referring to the child in a positive way when you know she will overhear what you say. Perhaps you're speaking on the phone with Jenna's grandmother while the child is in the next room. You could say, "I was so pleased today when Jenna finished her project on time. It looks as if she's really taking responsibility for managing her assignments." You can bet that Jenna heard you, feels proud of herself, and will continue to be responsible for her schoolwork.

Because this technique can be so powerful, make sure your praise is related to her efforts and acknowledges growth or progress, not perfection. If you say, "Jenna got her project done on time, and it's going to be the best one by far," your daughter may internalize that she is worthy of praise only when she is the best in the class. That's not the message you want to send.

Q. *My fourth-grade daughter has consistently scored higher in math than reading, yet she much prefers reading and has little confidence in her abilities in math. Should I continue to have her placed in accelerated math, even though she doesn't enjoy it?*

A. Your child obviously has a gift that she herself doesn't recognize. It would be a shame not to nurture that talent, especially when opportunities for those who are experts in math and science will continue to expand. When she is an adult, she might be sorry that she didn't learn to use her talents in math to their fullest.

You say that she doesn't enjoy math, but you don't mention if she actively resists the accelerated math class. It may be that she doesn't like the class because she is unsure of her abilities and wonders if she got in by mistake. Gifted girls often have feelings that they are imposters in a traditionally male-dominated program.

Talk with your daughter about the specific reasons she's not happy in the class. Perhaps the two of you could then sit down with the teacher to address your daughter's particular concerns.

On the other hand, if your daughter becomes more and more resistant to her placement in accelerated math and wants to pursue her passion in the language arts area, it's best to let her follow her own inclinations. She can continue with math in a less pressured environment, and without the stress of trying to measure up to others in a gifted class, she may discover that she really likes math after all. By the time she gets to high school, there will be many opportunities to take a variety of classes. By then, she may be more confident and ready to dig into math.

However, if that never happens, it's probably best to let her follow her passion rather than a talent area that doesn't make her happy. It would be terrible if she had the soul of a poet but felt that she had to choose a career in mathematics just because she was good at it. She could be unfulfilled and unhappy because she isn't being true to her real calling. Be patient and see what unfolds.

Q. *I have a gifted son who is now in middle school. Ever since third grade, I have watched him turn away from potential friendships with boys his own age. He says he has nothing in common with them, but I know he could find things if he tried. As a result, he wants to be with adults most of the time, and he's only 14.*

A. Of course you want your son to have age peers to pal around with, but it's important to assess how he feels about his situation. Is he lonely and wanting friends his own age, or is he a young man who is comfortable with himself and prefers the company of people he can talk to and who understand him? Has he been teased or bullied and thus been turned off wanting to be around kids he sees as immature and cruel? It's important to find out what underlies his indifference to potential friends.

Your son might be a good candidate for a summer workshop or institute for gifted students. There he would meet many people with whom he *would* have things in common. Be aware, however, that even those people might not be age peers. Some could be younger or older. They would at least be closer to his age, however.

Middle school is often a very hard period for young people, but as they enter high school, most begin to sort out peer issues more effectively. They are more mature, focused, and directed. Many find themselves in extracurricular activities such as band, choir, drama, or interest clubs, all of which expose them to age peers who have similar interests.

Q. *My daughter has taken ability tests in grades two, three, and five, and each time, her score has dropped. What's going on? I thought a person's IQ was for life.*

A. Remember that any test score is simply a reflection of how the student performed on a particular day under particular circumstances. In addition, children's brains are in a constant state of change.

Group ability tests are administered in different ways. For example, because not all children are fluent readers by second grade, the person administering the test may read the questions to the students. If your daughter is a good listener—and most girls are—she may do very well with this kind of arrangement.

By third grade, students are expected to read the test items themselves. If your daughter was not a strong reader, she might have made errors that affected her score. By fourth grade, high-stakes testing occurs in many states, and children can become very nervous. They focus on the outcome rather than on the test itself, and test anxiety can lower their scores.

If you'd like to get a more reliable reading, you might seek out a licensed psychologist to administer an individual ability test.

Q. *I'm a regular classroom teacher, and I ask all of my students, including the gifted ones, to explain the steps they took to solve a problem. Many times, my average-ability students do this much better than the gifted ones. If they're so smart, why can't they explain their thinking?*

A. They probably can explain their thinking. In fact, thinking about their thinking is one of the things gifted children do very well, and they're often quite articulate in explaining how they think. What you're really asking is why they can't give you a logical answer about how they solved a specific problem, and that's a different thing altogether.

Very often, gifted children can't describe specific steps because they didn't solve the problem in a step-by-step manner. They instead made an intuitive leap to the correct answer, and explaining an intuition is nearly impossible to do.

Children who can describe their thinking processes are usually auditory-sequential learners—that is, they learn by listening and they learn in sequence, piling fact upon fact, taking logical steps to arrive at a solution. Children who leap to solutions are usually visual-spatial thinkers who learn holistically. The answer comes all at once. They see it. They know it. And they can't explain it.

Some educators believe that it's unnecessary for students to show their work if the answers are correct and that we should let visual-spatial learners off the hook. To do so, however, isn't doing them a favor. Not teaching them this skill jeopardizes their ability to perform on standardized tests, many of which are necessary for high school graduation or college entrance.

Today's standardized tests, particularly in math, require that the student explain his answers. If he doesn't complete this portion of the test, his score will be lowered, sometimes dramatically. To excel, even visual-spatial learners must develop the ability to show their work to some degree.

In addition, those who learn holistically sometimes leap to the wrong conclusions. If the student can show her work, the teacher can more easily discover the exact place where she went astray rather than waste time making assumptions that may prove to be incorrect. Once reoriented, the student will make the same kind of rapid progress she originally exhibited, this time in the right direction.

Many students who resist this step do so because they don't write well and they don't enjoy the explanation section. These children need to understand that they do not need to do a page-long justification of their answers. They can explain themselves by using bullet points and very short responses.

Some students can grasp the process if the teacher presents the problems as a three-dimensional puzzle. Thinking of a math problem this way often allows a visual thinker to "see" the problem and visualize and explain the steps, just as he would explain how to put a puzzle together: first one piece and then another.

Some teachers believe that if a child answers all of the questions correctly but can't demonstrate how she arrived at her responses, she must have cheated or had her parents do her homework. This is a damaging assumption, and unless the teacher has incontrovertible proof, the accusation will destroy the relationship between the teacher and a very smart student who simply learns all in one gulp.

Oddly enough, children can sometimes show their work if they're allowed to begin at the answer and trace their steps backward to arrive at the question. You might suggest this "reverse engineering" process, but if it doesn't work, you'll need to work with the student to help him understand and carry out the process of explanation. Sometimes, though, if the stakes aren't particularly high and the answers are right, take the pressure off and accept the student's work as is.

Q. *My gifted son has basically checked out of the fourth grade. He doesn't pay attention, doesn't do his homework, and doesn't seem to care about anything related to school. The teachers have tried differentiating for him. They've asked him what he's interested in studying, but he doesn't seem to know. At home, however, he does math and logic puzzles in his head that even my husband and I have trouble understanding. What should we do?*

A. Sometimes finding a specific area in the curriculum that matches a child's interest will recapture him. Your son is telling you what he needs; speak with his teacher and see if the school is willing to consider a focused acceleration in this discipline.

Your son sounds as if he might be literally years ahead of other students in this subject. If you can find out where the ceiling of his ability is, you can work with school officials to give him the rigor he needs, possibly through a focused acceleration that involves several grade levels. You might have to have him tested in math to get a sense of his real abilities. Once he is happy and challenged in one area, he may be more amenable to the rest of his school experience. He sounds like a terribly frustrated boy who just can't take it anymore and has decided to go underground rather than act out his frustration.

Q. *Every day, my gifted—and very absent-minded—daughter forgets something important she needs at school: an assignment, a book, the project that's due today. I spend half my time in the car running things to her school, which is 15 miles away. It interrupts my day, and with the cost of gas, it's becoming expensive. What should I do?*

A. Gifted children often have so much going on in their heads that they can be forgetful. However, don't rescue your daughter in these situations. She needs to learn now that the world will not put a safety net under her and that she must take responsibility for those things that are under her control. This includes getting herself off to school with the assignments and materials that she needs to get through the day.

Help her devise a checklist of what she needs each day, and post the list on the door. Ask her to check each item off before she gets on the bus, and tell her that you will not be coming to school with the things she forgets to take with her. If she doesn't perform her checklist and finds herself at school without a required homework assignment or other item, stand fast when she calls and asks you to bring it "just this once." Unfortunately, she may need to endure the discomfort of natural consequences a couple of times before she realizes that you mean what you say.

Chapter 15

Parent to Parent: A Story of Hope

Suzanne Van Schaik is a fourth-grade teacher and the mother of four, including 13-year-old Michael, who is both gifted and learning disabled. Their story is typical of the trials and triumphs of rearing and tirelessly advocating for a twice-exceptional child—and for all gifted students—sometimes every day.

In Chapter 2, we stated that motivation is not a wish or a dream or a hope. It must include *movement* toward a goal. Suzanne and Michael have demonstrated such movement, and Suzanne has buttressed Michael in the times when he felt defeated and deflated. Although his motivation occasionally has flagged because of the difficulties he has faced, hers has not wavered.

Suzanne's interim goals have included making sure that Michael receives the academic rigor he requires for his giftedness and the accommodations he needs to work around his learning disability. The ultimate goal is for Michael to become independent and, as much as is appropriate, to advocate for himself.

Because for several years Michael was a student in the building in which Suzanne taught, she had a close look at what was happening to him in school. Her watchfulness and understanding of how schools work have helped her support his needs throughout his school career.

This story clearly shows the changeable nature of motivation and how a teacher's attitude can dampen it or set it ablaze. It is also a primer on the best way to create a strong parent-teacher partnership. Suzanne's professional, respectful approach is the one that is most likely to garner a positive response from teachers, but she also has been steadfast in refusing to accept second-best for her special gifted child. When the going got tough, Michael knew he could count on his mother to be in his corner and to champion his rights, even in the school system that employed her.

In this story of hope, and with Michael's permission, Suzanne shares both his story and her teaching and parenting strategies—and how Michael is doing today.

An easy start

Michael was the perfect infant and toddler. We could take him any-where. We'd go out to dinner, and he'd amuse himself and let the grown-ups talk. People often commented on our "well-behaved" child. Because he was my first child, I really didn't have any idea of how unusual that behavior was, or even how unusual *he* was.

He was, and still is, very small in stature but clearly had an outsized brain. I remember being floored at his two-year-old check-up when the doctor asked if he was putting together two- to three-word sentences. He'd passed that long ago and was already using eight- to 10-word complex sentences. I have video of him speaking at that age, and as I look back at my younger children at that age, I realize that they were nowhere near where he was verbally. It was amazing, really. Here was this little body with all these enormous words and intelligent thoughts pouring out of his mouth. It seemed as if any word he heard he could use. My twin sister always said, "Michael is an old soul trapped in a small body."

From the beginning, he was very attuned to my dad, his Papa. Dad was a genius and very musically gifted. Whenever we'd visit, Dad would play the piano or put on music like "The Hall of the Mountain King," and he would tell Michael jokes and teach him logic puzzles. They were really two peas in a pod.

Largely because of my dad's interest, I think, when Michael was two, he could already get a little "buzz" up on the trumpet. He also played around on the piano at Papa's house. He was crazy about show tunes, and we have a video of him singing "Man of La Mancha"—correctly—and the Ohio State Buckeye fight song. At the same age, he was furious when he found out we had gone to see *Phantom of the Opera* without him! He finally got to see it when he was 12.

If by chance Michael did need to be disciplined (he sailed past the terrible twos), he'd get a time-out, and then he and I would discuss why that had happened, as well as what he should have done. We could reason with him from the time he was 18 months old. Again, I had no idea how truly remarkable that was at the time. He had a very early sense of right and wrong.

Growing up with him was always entertaining and in some ways a challenge. He didn't sleep like small children sleep. He was not a napper, and he slept, at most, eight hours a night. He didn't want to miss any-thing, and when he was awake, he much preferred to hang around with adults and absorb everything going on around him.

From early childhood, he was set in his ways—very stubborn. And also very observant. On one of his toys, he had to have the right color ball on the right color ring. When he wasn't looking, we'd switch them around, but he always put them back the correct way.

When he was between two and three years old, he could put together a 20-piece puzzle in less than a minute. We'd take all the pieces away until there was an empty board. Then, as a game, we'd give the pieces back to him one at a time. He would place them exactly where they belonged, no matter which pieces we gave him and how far separated they were from one another. He knew right where each piece went as soon as he saw it.

Although Michael liked *Thomas the Tank Engine*™ and shows like that, he really loved to watch *Nova*™ and The History Channel®. Afterwards, he'd have to talk about what he'd seen, and if there was something he didn't understand, he asked questions, and more questions, and more questions! He wanted it clarified. I remember when we took him for his pre-kindergarten check-up, he wowed everybody in the office as he explained to the doctor and the nurse how black holes were formed. He'd watched a *Nova* show on it and just had to share how it all worked.

This performance came on the heels of the doctor walking in hearing Michael read aloud to me. The pediatrician looked at me with panic, knowing that I was a teacher, and asked if his daughter should be going to kindergarten because she couldn't read yet. Obviously, he now knows Michael very well and realizes that he is not the norm.

Off to school

When Michael was three, he used to watch the school bus pick up the neighborhood children. He would jump up and down, asking, "When is it my turn to go?" He was so excited when his turn finally came, but it was on the bus that he started to get a taste of the outside world. Because he was small for his age, he had to put up with bullying and teasing by fourth and fifth graders. They'd tell him he was a baby and belonged in preschool.

What was interesting was the way he reacted. The treatment he received actually made him more accepting of others and their differences. He would tell me what was happening on the bus, and we would talk about why the bigger kids felt they needed to tease him. We talked about how his strength was his brain; other kids' strengths might be their size or their muscles or their sports. Perhaps they might be jealous of his strength. I helped him understand that some kids don't handle others' strengths well and what he could do when he was teased.

He coped with it really beautifully. He was a little kindergartener who learned to ignore the bullies and feel sorry for them because they felt they needed to behave like that. And that was the end of it for him. To this day, he retains that empathy.

He was in kindergarten two and a half days a week, and the other days he was home with my husband, who worked out of the house. One day, my husband was working and gave Michael a logic problem to solve to keep him busy. He figured it would take a while for Michael to solve it and Dad could finally get some work done. But it didn't keep Michael occupied for very long, and the next day, he demonstrated it to the kindergarten class. The teacher said that, while she knew none of the kids had a clue what he was talking about, she thoroughly enjoyed listening to his "thinking."

I used to teach third grade and had boxes of supplies stored in the basement. One day Michael found a third-grade math Learning Adventures CD and put it in the computer so he could "work" like Daddy. He saw the multiplication sign on the screen and asked his dad what it was. And then he started doing multiplication.

A problem emerges

From kindergarten on, writing started to stand out as an issue. Developmentally and physically, it wasn't where it needed to be. Michael could read a lot, but he couldn't write well at all. His letter forms and spelling were pretty bad. Every year I asked his teachers if writing was something we should be concerned about. I saw it as a problem, but no one else seemed to think so. The older he got, the more I thought it was an issue, but everyone else said he was so bright that he'd never qualify for special help. In my gut, I knew we needed to do something.

First grade was a very difficult year for Michael. I knew that my son was a challenge and difficult to teach, and I shared that with his teacher. I told her I was there to support her in any way I could.

Right away, Michael did not understand why he had to read what everyone else was reading when he could already read chapter books. There were very few challenges for him in any area, and boredom became a big issue. Although he needed to learn to toe the line in school, I found it hard to criticize him for being bored. When he was disruptive, he was simply seeking challenges to motivate himself. However, he ended up being put on a behavior plan. I went along with it to support his teacher, although I disagreed with the need for it. Adequate challenge would have improved the behavior.

The one area where Michael needed the most help was spelling, but that was not part of the curriculum in his class that year. I spent time working with him at home to keep him motivated but also to encourage him to improve his behavior. It was a frustrating year for Michael and everyone else.

In first grade, he started piano lessons.

A roller coaster year

Second grade was a turning point for Michael. He had a very young, energetic teacher who challenged him in reading and math, but she encouraged and motivated him to try harder with his writing, and for once, he began to feel good about the stories he wrote. We still have his "books" at home. Unfortunately, his enthusiasm lasted only that one year.

His teacher was absent when he took the cognitive tests in the spring, and he's one of those kids whose scores fluctuate; they're all over the board. It depends on who he's with and how he's feeling. He had really bonded with that teacher. When she wasn't there, he didn't try nearly as hard as he would have if she'd been present. His score was 118. That's a good score, but it was much lower than anyone would have predicted. His teacher felt he was much brighter than his score showed.

That particular year, Michael's beloved Papa—my father—died of cancer. For his Papa's birthday in August, Michael had taught himself to play "Ode to Joy" on the piano, and it was the best and final gift my Dad ever received. He died in November at age 61. It was a devastating blow to my entire family.

Michael has always been private and keeps a lot to himself. At the funeral, he told me that he refused to cry and fought and fought to keep it in. He was able to hold it in until January. That month our cat died, and that was the final straw. Michael just broke down sobbing and told me how much he he missed his Papa—and then it came out that he was worried that I was going to die, too, because I was pregnant and he knew that women sometimes died in childbirth. You could have knocked me down with a feather. I had *no* idea those thoughts were stuck in his head.

That was really rough, but we got through it. But then in April, my mother died. However, Michael's sister was born in May. So while second grade was good in some ways, it was very challenging emotionally. I often think that the difficulties we were to face in the following years were a direct result of the emotional traumas that year.

Uncertainty and a dip in motivation

Michael and I were blessed in third grade. I knew that after the year we'd had in second grade, he needed someone who would love him, enjoy his sense of humor, and encourage him. I went to the guidance counselor and requested a specific teacher, something I'd never done before.

This teacher recommended that he be retested so he could join SOAR—our district's gifted program. She didn't feel that his scores reflected his intelligence. She said, "Suzanne, I don't think I've ever had a kid this bright. He needs to be in SOAR."

So Michael tested again, and this time his score was 138. He qualified for the program. But also at this time, his writing began to be a major stumbling block, to the point of Michael shutting down. He was discouraged and just didn't want to try any more. He was done.

By fourth grade, it was all his teacher could do to get him to write three sentences when the other kids were writing 10. She modified assignments and worked with him one-on-one, even though he wasn't on an IEP (Individual Education Plan). She pushed him.

Every year I had approached his teachers about writing, and that year, his teacher (one of my coworkers in the grade level) thought that his situation should be reviewed by the Intervention Assistance Team. She, too, was unsure whether he'd qualify for assistance. She said, "He stands out so much more than the other kids. You listen to him, you look at his math and his reading, and then there's his writing. There's something just not clicking with the writing."

Michael went through the whole evaluation process, and the discrepancy between writing and all his other abilities was enormous. He was finally placed on an IEP and started getting some additional help. At this point, though, all the years of his being small and a little unusual kicked in. He didn't want to be any more "different" than he already was. He didn't want to be pulled out of class for help, so most of the interventions were done in his regular classroom.

That year, he also added the violin to his musical repertoire.

Things get tougher...

In fifth grade, we were redistricted. Michael was moved to a new building, and that's where a lot of headaches really began. Because he was in a different school, I felt totally out of the loop about what was going on with him. Not that it was a cakewalk in the early grades, but six weeks into the school year, I had to call for a conference because Michael hadn't even *met* the intervention teacher. Six weeks had gone by with no intervention. No service. Nothing.

His classroom teacher was very defensive from the get-go, maybe because she was a third-year teacher and knew I'd been teaching for 16 or 17 years. I went in all nice and friendly, telling her (as I do all his teachers) that I was there to help and support her in any way I could. I know Michael is a challenge because he is two extremes: gifted and learning disabled. Because I know how hard it is for a teacher to deal with a confrontational parent—and one who's a teacher to boot—I tried to handle the situation with kid gloves, but I needed to stand up for his rights. An IEP is a legal document, and it needs to be followed. The teacher asked the principal, the guidance counselor, the SOAR teacher, and the intervention teacher to join the conference. I guess I made her a little nervous!

Later in the year, Michael grew very frustrated because it became evident to him that he was being graded on his writing in all subject areas, and that's when I started worrying about middle school. He was tested as reading independently at the upper middle school level and received an "S" (Satisfactory) in reading.

He had been very excited about a chapter book that he was writing (yes, writing!) as a book extension. It was a big project, and the fact that he was excited was huge progress. It ended up being about six typed pages. He got an "S" on it, which is probably the first one he'd ever gotten in writing. He and I were thrilled with his progress! But on his grade card, he got an "N" (Needs Improvement) in writing. You could almost see him deflate.

I met with his teacher again. I wasn't harsh with her, but I questioned the grade and told her how disappointed and hurt he was because he had worked so hard on what was, for him, a major writing project and had done well. She pulled out writing samples (on which he'd been given no accommodation) to justify the "N" grade.

Sensing that I wasn't getting anywhere, I backed off for the time being and asked about reading. She went on and on about what a great reader he was and about the insightful thoughts he shared in discussions. That being the case, I asked why he received an "S" instead of an "O" (Outstanding) in reading. His teacher pulled out Michael's six-page "chapter book" and said it was the reason for his "S" in reading. Although it was an extension from a reading assignment, it was really a writing grade. He was being graded in reading for his writing. It made no sense at all.

Writing was obviously a challenge for which Michael was on an IEP. Accommodations should have been made all year long but weren't. The teacher gave me all sorts of rationalizations, and it was a battle for the rest of the year.

This year he also took up the trumpet, so now he was playing piano, violin, and trumpet.

...and tougher

Then came middle school. The first big problem arose immediately. Michael was signed up for band and strings, but neither was on his schedule. I went to the guidance counselor, who told me they'd had to take away music because of the tutoring time required by his IEP.

I said, "This is what he loves most. You can't punish a kid for having a disability." Luckily the guidance counselor was understanding, but he still said that we had to work around the IEP. Band and strings happened to meet on alternate days, so we were able to do the same thing with the tutoring—we let him go to band one day and tutoring the next. That compromise meant that he had to give up strings.

In some ways, the tutor he had was a good match for Michael as he came into middle school. He was a man who was very positive and upbeat, and for getting into the middle school groove, it worked. But there was no assistance, no real learning with the writing; it was more like a study hall. So Michael's writing did not grow much at all.

A disheartening change

All of a sudden, Michael's greatest strength, math, became a sore point. In his favorite subject, he was continually getting poor grades because of his writing. In math! It was constant. His papers were covered with notes deducting points for incomplete explanations or other writing issues.

His IEP allowed for him to handle writing tasks orally in all of his other subjects—except for writing itself—because he couldn't pull the words from his head and get them onto the page. But he felt as if this teacher nitpicked everything.

Michael's fine-motor skills didn't allow him to do some things. On one assignment, his teacher had the students construct a bar graph on a half-sheet of graph paper. Michael used a whole sheet to give himself more space. It was nice and neat—for him. If he'd tried to cram it onto a half-sheet, he would have lost points for legibility. Instead of grading the content, his teacher took off points because he used a full sheet. And she would not bend. I always went in with a positive, non-confrontational attitude, but I wouldn't let up, and I know that every time I went into the building, she was thinking, "Oh, there *she* is again."

Finally, the gloves came off. I was respectful and professional, but I would not let this slide. Enough was enough. She was punishing my kid, and that was not okay. He hated math that year and was completely deflated. He and I struggled through together and supported each other.

It was becoming clear that every year there was one teacher who didn't understand him or his legal rights and made things very difficult. I had to be vigilant and assertive to make sure that his special needs were being met.

In seventh grade, the same scheduling issue came up again as once more, band was taken away. That was an easy fix. Michael and I went to the counselor, and I didn't have to say a word. "Hi, Suzanne. Let me guess. Band?" Michael played first trumpet first chair in seventh-grade band, first trumpet first chair in the sixth- to eighth-grade full orchestra, and first trumpet second chair in seventh- to eighth-grade jazz band. He was feeling great and was off to a good start.

Now it was the science teacher who became the issue. Science was another of his strengths, so I was surprised when failed a science test. When I went over it, I found that most of the points that were taken off were for writing issues: incomplete sentences and inadequate detail. I e-mailed the teacher and told her that a lot of what she had graded down was related to writing, for which Michael was on an IEP. I asked if she would speak with his tutor about the situation. She never responded.

An eye-opening conference

At conference time, I asked for a meeting of his whole team, and I e-mailed his SOAR teacher and his tutor. I told them what time the meeting was and that I assumed they had been notified. They hadn't been. They came only because *I* informed them of the conference.

I was so glad they were there because they really knew Michael. The SOAR teacher had had him for two years and knew his strengths and his challenges. The other teachers didn't have a clue about who he really was and what he needed.

I knew I had IEP issues to address but wanted to keep things light. His language arts teacher started off talking about Michael's lack of organization. I looked at Michael and chuckled a little, "That's nothing we haven't heard before, right?" He smiled. She went on to say that he never used his Franklin Speller, and I told her that he was able to go much faster on the computer. She responded that he could use the computer in the classroom anytime. Michael sat there completely shocked. No one had ever given him permission to use the computer before. Now he uses it a great deal.

Next, I brought up my concern that his science grade was being severely affected by writing. All of us at the conference knew about the test he had failed, but the science teacher then pulled out a new test on which he'd gotten a C+, and guess what, there was a full-page essay question with many points deducted. The SOAR teacher and I looked at each other because our suspicions were confirmed. He was being graded on his writing.

His tutor spoke up and said, "This is a perfect example of when he should come to me to give his answers orally." I wanted to hug her. That was what was called for on his IEP, but it wasn't being done. His teacher was ignoring it.

When the conference was winding down, Michel's SOAR teacher asked to see his science test (the C+) again. She flipped to the essay, looked at the tutor, and said, "Look at how much Michael's writing has improved! This is awesome, Michael!" What an affirmation—and at the perfect time.

I'm not unreasonable, and I know that Michael will have to live in the real world. What I want him to do is complete the writing part of his tests because he needs the practice, but then to be allowed to go to his tutor to clarify his answers orally.

It took three weeks of e-mails, but Michael finally was allowed to retake the test he failed, and by giving his answers orally, he got a B+. However, the second test, on which he received the C+, disappeared, and none of us ever saw it again. Obviously, he couldn't retake that one.

This year, his tutor has really worked hard with him on his writing, and she and the SOAR teacher have stood up for him time and again. My goal has been to get Michael to start standing up for himself. That's hard because it means going up to the front of the class in the middle of a test and saying it's time for him to go to his tutor. It means asking, "May I do this on the computer?" But he's beginning to do it, and that's terrific as far as I'm concerned.

After advocacy

Just recently, Michael had to do a big science project. Each child in the class was to create a magazine that explained mitosis. Michael did a PowerPoint® presentation, and then he printed it out and glued it together like a magazine. His motivation was out of the park. He ended up getting a better than perfect score, and the teacher wants to keep it as a sample. There is hope!

The teachers who have not understood are beginning to come around. They're starting to realize that fair doesn't always mean equal. Fair is doing what's right for the child, and in Michael's case, that's letting him work on the computer or do a presentation to show his knowledge or go to his tutor to explain his answers orally. That way he's being judged on what he knows, not on his writing ability or his handwriting. They're now starting to look at his giftedness, not just his disability, and that's critical. They have to deal with the whole child, not just part of him.

Because I'm a teacher, I know what IEPs are and what the laws are, but I think that even with IEP mandates, most teachers don't give themselves permission to change things for one student. Teachers need to know that accommodating the child is the right thing to do, whether the child is on an IEP or not.

I understand why they don't. Teachers are under so much pressure today to get everyone ready for testing that they honestly feel they can't "lower the standard" to help an individual child. But they need to. They need to let the child take the little steps that become big steps and eventually show the progress that's required.

It's sad that testing is everything, because the tests are being used the wrong way. Instead of a test score being a benchmark for extension or intervention, the scores are being used to measure teachers and children and schools.

Some final words

When Michael was younger, there were a couple of years that were sheer misery when it came to homework. If he had to write, he'd refuse. He'd just sit there and stare. He wouldn't pick up his pencil. Until he was identified as having a disability, I wondered if his reluctance was attitude or stubbornness, because there was plenty of both. We would get through as much homework as we could. Often I'd let him dictate, and I would write. To tell you the truth, sometimes I still do that. It's permitted by his IEP, and it keeps his frustration in check. Once the frustration hits in earnest, he shuts down completely.

I think things are definitely on the upswing now. Every year during the week before spring break, every seventh grader at Michael's school—about 250 of them—participates in a mental math challenge. Michael and two other kids from his class went to the finals this year, which included about 30 students.

As he was getting ready the morning of the finals, Michael said he'd e-mail me to let me know how he did. No e-mail came, so I figured he hadn't won and was disappointed. I hadn't really expected him to win, although I knew he had the ability to. But at lunch, I got a voicemail from my sister. She'd received a text message from her daughter, who goes to the same middle school Michael does. He had won the contest against the entire seventh grade. He was going to keep it a surprise, but the communication grapevine is just too fast these days.

There are many bright lights, but I think the best one is a poem Michael wrote this year. It was given to me at a conference, and I had to struggle to keep my tears back. There was so much passion in it that it made me think of my dad and the time they had spent together.

Michael, who has a writing disability, put this down on paper, and when I read it, I think, "*This* is my child. *This* is my son." There's so much more to my son than his disability. So much more. He is the picture of hope.

Michael's Poem

I am a seventh grade boy who dreams of music.
I wonder when I will get to play again.
I hear music like a poem.
I see the notes dancing.
I am a brass player with piano fingers.

I pretend that I'm always at a concert.
I feel the music pulse through my veins.
I touch the keys with intelligent thoughts.
I worry that my trumpet will break.
I cry to the dramatic music.
I am a keyboard.

I understand the music.
I say the chord's name.
I dream of the perfect improvise.
I try to stretch the farthest.
I hope to succeed.
I am a seventh grade boy whose dream is music.

Endnotes

Foreword

i   www.wcpss.net/news/2006-wechs/index2.html (Retrieved November 11, 2006).

ii www.edutopia.org (search Key Learning Community) (Retrieved April 6, 2006).

iii Gardner (1983) proposed the theory that it is inappropriate to think of intelligence as a single entity. He developed a strong case for "multiple intelligences," which may be independent of each other. Not every child who can be considered gifted shows high aptitude in traditional areas such in language or math—many children have specific talents in other areas that can benefit our world.

iv *Frequently asked questions about value-added analysis (gifted).* (2006). Retrieved April 14, 2006, from http://battelleforkids.org

Chapter 1

1   Names have been changed to protect identity, and some students are composites.

2   National Association for Gifted Children(1998).

3   National Association for Gifted Children (2004).

4   Self-Determination Theory (n.d.).

5   Black (2005).

6   Tomlinson (2002, p. 36).

7   Silverman (1998).

8   Sousa (2002, p. 11).

9   Gardner (1983).

10 Mathews (2004, p. A9).

11 Colangelo, Assouline, & Gross (2004, Vol. 1, p. 18).

12 Colangelo, Assouline, & Gross (2004).

13 *Dr. Michael Whitley: Motivating students to improve achievement* (2001, August 29). Retrieved November 30, 2006, from CNN.com chatroom

14 www.education.uiowa.edu/belinblank/talent-search/purpose.asp (Retrieved November 30, 2006).

Chapter 2

1   Austin (2000).
2   Huitt (2001).
3   www.psychrochester.edu/SDT/controversy.html (Retrieved January 30, 2005).
4   McCombs (1997).
5   Harms (1994).
6   Lepper (1988).
7   www.stophitting.com/disatschool/formCoalition.php (Retrieved November 30, 2006).
8   Jensen (1998).
9   Jensen (1998, p. 57).
10 Seligman (1995, p. 33).
11 Reis & McCoach (2000, p. 156).
12 Reis, Hébert, Diaz, Maxfield, & Ratley (1995).
13 Schultz (2000).
14 Evans (2004).
15 Rosenthal & Jacobson (1992).

Chapter 3

1   National Institute on Deafness and Other Communication Disorders (2002).
2   Center for Disease Control and Prevention. Retrieved December 1, 2006, from www.betterhealth.vic.gov.au/bhcb2/bhcarticles.nsf/pages/ Hearing_problems_in_children?OpenDocument
3   National Institute on Deafness and Other Communication Disorders (2006).
4   National Institutes of Health (2006).
5   Sousa (2002, p. 42).
6   Sousa (2002, p. 53).
7   Bright Solutions for Dyslexia, LLC (1998).
8   http://legacy.rmplc.co.uk/orgs.nellalex (Retrieved November 30, 2006).
9   Dyslexic children use nearly five times the brain area. (1999, October 4). Retrieved November 30, 2006, from www.washington.edu/ newsroom/news/1999 archive/10-99archive/k100499a.html
10 American Psychiatric Association (2000).
11 American Psychiatric Association (2000).
12 American Psychiatric Association (2000).
13 Webb, et al. (2005).
14 Webb, et al. (2005).
15 Lovecky (1991).

16 Csikszentmihalyi (1990) has pointed out that creative persons often become so involved in a task that they are unaware of time or surroundings.
17 Kaufmann, Kalbfleisch, & Castellanos (2000).
18 Moon (2001).
19 Neihart (2003).
20 Hartman (1996).
21 Moon (2001).

Chapter 4

1 Neihart (1999).
2 Whitmore (1980).
3 Murphy (2006).
4 Webb, et al. (2005, pp. 133–136).

Chapter 5

1 Benard (1995).
2 Neihart (2006).
3 Pellino (2001).
4 Academy of Achievement (2002).
5 Academy of Achievement (1999).
6 Academy of Achievement (1991).
7 Answers.com (2006).
8 Gross (2002).
9 Gross (2003).

Chapter 6

1 Baxter (2000).
2 *A Hypertext History of Instructional Design: The 1920s.* Retrieved December 1, 2006, from www.coe.uh.edu/courses/cuin6373/idhistory/individualized_instruction.html
3 Tomlinson (1995).
4 Kingore (2006).
5 Tomlinson (1995).
6 Slocumb & Payne (2002).
7 Matthews & Foster (2006).
8 Matthews & Foster (2006).
9 Aratani (2006).

Chapter 7

1   Csikszentmihalyi (2002a).
2   Csikszentmihalyi (1993).
3   Harms (1994).
4   Csikszentmihalyi (2002a).
5   Harms (1994).
6   Csikszentmihalyi (2002b).

Chapter 8

1   Rogers (1993).
2   Rogers (1993).
3   Rogers (2002).
4   Colangelo, Assouline, & Gross (2004).
5   Assouline, Colangelo, Lupkowski-Shoplik, Lipscomb, & Forstadt (2003).
6   Greenspon (2004).
7   http://inventors.about.com/b/a/151371.htm (Retrieved November 30, 2006).
8   Delisle (2003).
9   Halsted (2002, p. 108).
10 Bronfrenbrenner (1986).
11 Reis, Colbert, & Hébert (2005, p. 117).

Chapter 9

1   Betts & Kercher (1999, p. 12).
2   Aron (2002).
3   These techniques and others are described more fully in *A Parent's Guide to Gifted Children,* by Webb, Gore, Amend, & DeVries (2007).

Chapter 10

1   Winger (2005).
2   Tomlinson & McTighe (2006, p. 132).

Chapter 11

1   Seligman (2002).
2   Freedman (2002).
3   Hockman, McCormick, & Barnett (2005).
4   Silverman (2002).
5   Rimm (1988).
6   Peterson & Ray (2006).
7   Medaris (2006).

8 Peterson & Ray (2006).
9 Peterson & Ray (2006).

Chapter 12

1 Swanson (2006).
2 Vaughan (2005).
3 Wilcox (2006).
4 Leahy, Lyon, Thompson, & Wiliam (2005).
5 Wilcox, J. (2006).
6 Eisner (2006, p. 46).
7 Steinbeck (1955).

Chapter 13

1 Landsman (2004, p. 30).
2 Rodriguez (2000).
3 Ripley (2005, p. 55).
4 Gurian & Henley (2001).
5 Gurian & Stevens (2004).
6 Gurian & Stevens (2004).
7 Ripley (2005, p. 56).
8 Gurian & Henley (2001, p. 32).
9 Gurian & Stevens (2004).
10 Gurian & Stevens (2004).
11 Thiers (2006).
12 Rivero (2002).

Additional Resources for Parents and Teachers

Books

Assouline, S. G., Colangelo, N., Lupkowski-Shoplik, A., Lipscomb, J., & Forstadt, L. (2003). *Iowa acceleration scale* (2nd ed.). Scottsdale, AZ: Great Potential Press.

Davidson, J., Davidson, B., & Vanderkam, L. (2004). *Genius denied: How to stop wasting our brightest minds.* New York: Simon & Shuster.

Ford, D. Y., & Harris, J. J. (1999). *Multicultural gifted education.* New York: Teachers College Press.

Gurian, M., & Henley, P. (2001). *Boys and girls learn differently!: A guide for teachers and parents.* San Francisco: Jossey-Bass.

Halsted, J. W. (2002). *Some of my best friends are books: Guiding gifted readers from preschool to high school.* Scottsdale, AZ: Great Potential Press.

Isaacson, K., & Fisher, T. (2007). *Intelligent life in the classroom: Smart kids and their teachers.* Scottsdale, AZ: Great Potential Press.

Levine, M. (2002). *A mind at a time.* New York: Simon & Schuster.

Lovecky, D. (2004). *Different minds: Gifted children with ADD/ADHD, Asperger Syndrome, and other learning deficits.* New York: Jessica Kingsley.

Matthews, D. J., & Foster, J. F. (2005). *Being smart about gifted children: A guidebook for parents and educators.* Scottsdale, AZ: Great Potential Press.

Neihart, M., Reis, S. M., Robinson, N. M., & Moon, S. M. (Eds.). (2002). *The social and emotional development of gifted children: What do we know?* Waco, TX: Prufrock Press.

Rimm, S. B. (1995). *Why bright kids get poor grades: And what you can do about it.* New York: Crown.

Rivero, L. (2002). *Creative home schooling: A resource guide for smart families.* Scottsdale, AZ: Great Potential Press.

Rogers, K. B. (2002). *Re-forming gifted education: How parents and teachers can match the program to the child.* Scottsdale, AZ: Great Potential Press.

Ruf, D. A. (2005). *Losing our minds: Gifted children left behind.* Scottsdale, AZ: Great Potential Press.

Silverman, L. K. (2002). *Upside-down brilliance: The visual-spatial learner.* Denver, CO: DeLeon.

Strip, C. A., & Hirsch, G. (2000). *Helping gifted children soar: A practical resource for parents and teachers.* Scottsdale, AZ: Great Potential Press.

Tomlinson, C. A., & McTighe, J. (2006). *Integrating differentiated instruction and understanding by design.* Alexandria, VA: Association for Supervision and Curriculum Development.

Walker, S. Y. (2002). *The survival guide for parents of gifted kids: How to understand, live with, and stick up for your gifted child.* Minneapolis, MN: Free Spirit.

Webb, J. T., Amend, E. R., Webb, N. E., Goerss, J., Beljan, P., & Olenchak, F. R. (2005). *Misdiagnosis and dual diagnoses of gifted children and adults: ADHD, bipolar, OCD, Asperger's, depression, and other disorders.* Scottsdale, AZ: Great Potential Press.

Webb, J. T., Gore, J. L., Amend, E. R., & DeVries, A. R. (2007). *A parent's guide to gifted children.* Scottsdale, AZ: Great Potential Press.

Whitmore, J. R. (1980). *Giftedness, conflict and underachievement.* Boston: Allyn & Bacon.

Winner, E. (1996). *Gifted children: Myths and realities.* New York: Basic Books.

Websites

Belin-Blank Center for Gifted Education and Talent Development
www.education.uiowa.edu/belinblank

Center for Talent Development, Northwestern University
www.ctd.northwestern.edu

Duke University Talent Identification Program (TIP)
www.tip.duke.edu

Genius Denied
www.geniusdenied.com

Gifted Child Quarterly (scholarly journal)
www.nagc.org

Gifted Child Today (magazine for families and teachers); Journal for Education of the Gifted (scholarly journal)
www.prufrock.com

The Gifted Development Center
www.gifteddevelopment.com

Great Potential Press
www.giftedbooks.com

Hoagie's Gifted Education Page

www.hoagiesgifted.org

The Hollingworth Center for Highly Gifted Children

www.hollingworth.org

Johns Hopkins Center for Talented Youth (CTY)

www.jhu.edu/gifted

National Association for Gifted Children (also state affiliates)

www.nagc.org

Neag Center for Gifted Education and Talent Development

www.gifted.uconn.edu

Parenting for High Potential (magazine for parents); Teaching for High Potential (magazine for teachers)

www.nagc.org

Rocky Mountain Talent Search

www.du.edu/education/ces/rmts.html

The Roeper Review (scholarly journal)

www.roeperreview.org

Supporting Emotional Needs of the Gifted

www.sengifted.org

TAGFAM—Families of the Gifted and Talented

www.TAGFAM.org

UC Berkeley Academic Talent Development Program

www-atdp.berkeley.edu

References

Academy of Achievement. (1991, February 21). *Interview with Oprah Winfrey.* Retrieved November 30, 2006, from www.achievement.org/autodoc/page/win0int-1

Academy of Achievement. (1999, June 19). *Interview with Frank McCourt.* Retrieved November 30, 2006, from www.achievement.org/autodoc/page/mcc1int-1

Academy of Achievement. (2002, June 7). *Interview with Benjamin Carson, M.D.* Retrieved November 30, 2006, from www.achievement.org/autodoc/page/car1int-1

American Psychiatric Association. (2000). *Diagnostic and statistical manual of mental disorders* (4th ed., text rev.). Washington, DC: Author.

Answers.com. (2006). *Encyclopedia of children's health: Single-parent families.* Retrieved December 1, 2006, from www.answers.com/topic/single-parent-families

Aratani, L. (2006, February 22). "Gifted" label takes a vacation in diversity quest. *The Washington Post,* B1.

Aron, E. (2002). *The highly sensitive child.* New York: Broadway Books.

Assouline, S. G., Colangelo, N., Lupkowski-Shoplik, A., Lipscomb, J., & Forstadt, L. (2003). *Iowa acceleration scale* (2nd ed.). Scottsdale, AZ: Great Potential Press.

Austin, L. S. (2000). *What's holding you back? Eight critical choices for women's success.* New York: Basic Books.

Baxter, B. (2000). *Returning to the one-room schoolhouse.* Retrieved March 18, 2006, from http://ts.mivu.org/default.asp?show=article+id=1034

Benard, B. (1995). *Fostering resilience in children* (ERIC Digest No. ED 386327). Reston, VA: ERIC Clearinghouse on Elementary and Early Childhood Education.

Betts, G., & Kercher, J. (1999). *Autonomous learner model: Optimizing ability.* Greeley, CO: Alps.

Black, S. (2005, June). Test anxiety. *American School Board Journal, 192(6).*

Bright Solutions for Dyslexia, LLC. (1998). *What is dyslexia?* Retrieved December 1, 2006, from www.dys-add.com/define.html

Bronfrenbrenner, U. (1986). Ecology of the family as a context for human development: Research perspectives. *Developmental Psychology, 22,* 723-742.

Colangelo, N., Assouline, S. G., & Gross, M. U. M. (2004). A nation deceived: How schools hold back America's students. *The Templeton National Report on Acceleration* (Vols. 1 & 2). Iowa City, IA: Belin-Blank Center.

Colvin, R. L. (1999, January 25). Losing faith in the self-esteem movement. *Los Angeles Times.*

Csikszentmihalyi, M. (1990). *Flow: The psychology of optimal experience.* New York: Harper & Row.

Csikszentmihalyi, M. (2002a, April 11). *Mihaly Csikszentmihalyi on motivating people to learn.* Retrieved November 30, 2006, from www.edutopia.org/php/interview.php?id=Art_964&key=005

Csikszentmihalyi, M. (2002b). *Thoughts about education.* Retrieved December 10, 2005, from www.newhorizons.org/future/Creating_the_Future/crfut_csikszt.html

Csikszentmihalyi, M., Rathunde, K., & Whalen, S. (1993). *Talented teenagers: The roots of success and failure.* New York: Cambridge University Press.

Delisle, J. (2003). *Tips for parents: Risk-taking and risk-making. Understanding when less than perfection is more than acceptable.* Retrieved November 11, 2005, from www.geniusdenied.com/articles/Record.aspx?NavID=13_24&rid=11279

Eisner, E. (2006). The satisfactions of teaching. *Educational Leadership, 63(6),* 46.

Evans, R. P. (2004, November 5). *Opening remarks: Inspiring vistas, inspiring minds.* Paper presented at the 51st Annual Convention of the National Association for Gifted Children, Salt Lake City, UT.

Freedman, J. (2002). *An interview with Martin E. P. Seligman, Ph.D.* Retrieved May 6, 2006, from www.eqtoday.com/optimism/seligman.html

Gardner, H. (1983). *Frames of mind: The theory of multiple intelligences.* New York: Basic Books.

Greenspon, T. S. (2001). *Freeing our families from perfectionism.* Minneapolis, MN: Free Spirit.

Gross, M. U. M. (2002). Musings: Gifted children and the gift of friendship. *Understanding Our Gifted, 14(3),* 27-29.

Gross, M. U. M. (2003). *Gifted children and friendship: Comments and tips for parents.* Retrieved November 11, 2006, from www.gt-cybersource.org/Record.aspx?NavID=2_0&rid=12374

Gurian, M., & Henley, P. (2001). *Boys and girls learn differently!: A guide for teachers and parents.* San Francisco: Jossey-Bass.

Gurian, M., & Stevens, K. (2004). With boys and girls in mind. *Educational Leadership, 62(3),* 21-26.

Halsted, J. W. (2002). *Some of my best friends are books: Guiding gifted readers from preschool to high school.* Scottsdale, AZ: Great Potential Press.

Harms, W. (1994). *Enjoyment of learning crucial for students to excel.* Retrieved January 10, 2006, from http://chronicle.uchicago.edu/940203/teens.shtml

Hartman, T. (1996). *Beyond ADD: Hunting for reasons in the past and present.* Green Valley, CA: Underwood Books.

Hockman, K., McCormick, J., & Barnett, K. (2005). The important role of optimism in a motivational investigation of the education of gifted adolescents. *Gifted Child Quarterly, 49(2),* 108.

Huitt, W. (2001). Motivation to learn: An overview. *Educational Psychology Interactive.* http://chiron.Valdosta.edu/whuitt/col/motivation/motivate.html

Jensen, E. (1998). *Teaching with the brain in mind.* Alexandria, VA: Association for Supervision and Curriculum Development.

Kaufmann, F., Kalbfleisch, M. L., & Castellanos, F. X. (2000). *Attention deficit disorders and gifted students: What do we really know?* Storrs, CT: National Research Center on the Gifted and Talented, University of Connecticut.

Kingore, B. (2006, Winter). Tiered instruction: Beginning the process. *Teaching for High Potential,* 5-6.

Landsman, J. (2004). Confronting the racism of low expectations. *Educational Leadership, 62(3),* 28-32.

Leahy, S., Lyon, C., Thompson, M., & Wiliam, D. (2005). Classroom assessment minute by minute, day by day. *Educational Leadership, 63(3),* 19-24.

Lepper, M. (1988). Motivational considerations in the study of instruction. *Cognition and Instruction, 5(4),* 289-309.

Lovecky, D. (2004). *Different minds: Gifted children with ADD/ADHD, Asperger Syndrome, and other learning deficits.* New York: Jessica Kingsley.

Mathews, J. (2004, September 7). 21 years later: Multiple intelligences still debated. *The Washington Post,* p. A9.

Matthews, D. J., & Foster, J. F. (2006). Mystery to mastery: Shifting paradigms in gifted education. *Roeper Review, 28(2),* 64-69.

McCombs, B. (1997). *Understanding the keys to motivation to learn.* Retrieved May 15, 2006, from www.mcrel.org/PDFconversion/Noteworthy/Learners_Learning_Schooling/barbaram.asp

Medaris, M. (2006, April 6). *Study: Gifted children especially vulnerable to effects of bullying.* Retrieved May 1, 2006, from http://news.uns.purdue.edu/html4ever/2006/060406.Peterson.bullies.htm

Moon, S. M. (2001, June). Parenting gifted children with AD/HD. *Parenting for High Potential, 9,* 27-28.

Murphy, A. P. (2006, February 24). *Anorexia striking increasing number of boys: Symptoms similar to anorexic females.* Retrieved March 1, 2006, from http://abcnews.go.com/GMA/Health/story?id=1654439&page=2

National Association for Gifted Children. (1998). *Position statements of the National Association for Gifted Children.* Washington, DC: Author.

National Association for Gifted Children. (2004). *Who are the gifted?* Retrieved March 4, 2005, from www.nagc.org

National Institute on Deafness and Other Communication Disorders. (2002). Otitis media (ear infection) (NIH Publication No. 974216). Bethesda, MD: Author.

National Institute on Deafness and Other Communication Disorders. (2006, April 26). *How loud is too loud? Bookmark.* Retrieved December 1, 2006, from www.nidcd.nih.gov/health/wise

National Institutes of Health. (2006). *Dangerous decibels.* Retrieved November 22, 2006, from www.dangerousdecibels.org/hearingloss.cfm

Neihart, M. (1999). The impact of giftedness on psychological well-being: What does the empirical literature say? *Roeper Review, 22(1),* 10-17.

Neihart, M. (2003). *Gifted children with attention deficit disorder* (Report No. E649). Arlington, VA: ERIC Clearinghouse on Disabilities and Gifted Education.

Neihart, M. (2006, Winter). The difference is resilience: When trouble hits close to home. *Teaching for High Potential,* p. 1-2.

Pellino, K. M. (2001). *The effects of poverty on teaching and learning.* Retrieved November 11, 2006, from www.teach-nology.com/tutorials/teaching/poverty/print.htm

Peterson, J. S., & Ray, K. E. (2006, Spring). Bullying and the gifted: Victims, perpetrators, prevalence, and effects. *Gifted Child Quarterly 50(2),* 148-168.

Reis, S. M., Colbert, R. D., & Hébert, T. P. (2005, Winter). Understanding resilience in diverse, talented students in an urban high school. *Roeper Review, 27(2),* 110-120.

Reis, S. M., Hébert, T. P., Diaz, E. P., Maxfield, L. R., & Ratley, M. E. (1995). *Case studies of talented students who achieve and underachieve in an urban high school* (Research Monograph 95120). Storrs, CT: National Research Center for the Gifted and Talented, University of Connecticut.

Reis, S. M., & McCoach, D. B. (2000). The underachievement of gifted students: What do we know and where do we go? *Gifted Child Quarterly, 44(3),* 152-170.

Rimm, S. B. (1988). Popularity ends at grade twelve. *Gifted Child Today, (11)3,* 42-44.

Ripley, A. (2005, March 7). Who says a woman can't be Einstein? *Time,* 55-56.

Rivero, L. (2002). *Creative home schooling: A resource guide for smart families.* Scottsdale, AZ: Great Potential Press.

Rodriguez, V. J. (2000). Minority teacher shortage plagues region, nation. *Southwest Educational Development Laboratory, XII(2).*

Rogers, K. B. (1993). Grouping the gifted and talented: Questions and answers. *Roeper Review 16(1),* 8-12.

Rogers, K. B. (2002). *Re-forming gifted education: How parents and teachers can match the program to the child.* Scottsdale, AZ: Great Potential Press.

Rosenthal, R., & Jacobson, L. (1992). *Pygmalion in the classroom: Teacher expectation and pupils' intellectual development.* New York: Rinehart & Winston. (Original work published in 1968)

Schultz, R. (2000). *Flirting with underachievement.* Retrieved November 11, 2006, from www.gt-cybersource.org/Record.aspx?NavID=2_0&rid=11370

Self-Determination Theory. (n.d.). *The high stakes testing controversy.* Retrieved November 30, 2006, from www.psych.rochester.edu/sdt/cont_testing.html

Seligman, M. E. P. (1995). *The optimistic child.* New York: HarperPerennial.

Seligman, M. E. P. (2002). *Authentic happiness: Using the new positive psychology to realize your potential for lasting fulfillment.* New York: Free Press.

Silverman, L. K. (1998). *The false accusation of elitism.* Retrieved November 23, 2006, from http://gifteddevelopment.com/PDF_files/g10.pdf

Silverman, L. K. (2002). *Upside-down brilliance: The visual-spatial learner.* Denver, CO: DeLeon.

Slocumb, P. D., & Payne, R. K. (2002). Identifying and nurturing the gifted poor. *Principal: The New Diversity, 79(5),* 28-32.

Sousa, D. (2002). *How the gifted brain learns.* Thousand Oaks, CA: Corwin Press.

Steinbeck, J. (1955). *Captured fireflies.* Retrieved May 23, 2006, from http://portfolio.washington.edu/smcarson/portfolio

Swanson, J. D. (2006). Breaking through assumptions about low-income, minority gifted students. *Gifted Child Quarterly, 50(1),* 11-26.

Thiers, N. (2006). Do single-sex classes raise academic achievement? *Educational Leadership, 63(7),* 70.

Tomlinson, C. A. (2001). *How to differentiate instruction in mixed-ability classrooms* (2nd ed.). Alexandria, VA: Association for Supervision and Curriculum Development.

Tomlinson, C. A. (2002). Proficiency is not enough. *Education Week Quarterly, 22(10),* 36, 38.

Tomlinson, C. A., & McTighe, J. (2006). *Integrating differentiated instruction and understanding by design: Connecting kids and content.* Alexandria, VA: Association for Supervision and Curriculum Development.

Vaughan, A. L. (2005). The self-paced student. *Educational Leadership, 62(7),* 69-73.

Webb, J. T., Amend, E. R., Webb, N. E., Goerss, J., Beljan, P., & Olenchak, F. R. (2005). *Misdiagnosis and dual diagnoses of gifted children and adults: ADHD, bipolar, OCD, Asperger's, depression, and other disorders.* Scottsdale, AZ: Great Potential Press.

Webb, J. T., Gore, J. L., Amend, E. R., & DeVries, A. R. (2007). *A parent's guide to gifted children.* Scottsdale, AZ: Great Potential Press.

Whitmore, J. R. (1980). *Giftedness, conflict and underachievement.* Boston: Allyn & Bacon.

Wilcox, J. (2006). Less teaching, more assessing: Teacher feedback is key to student performance. *Education Update, 28(2),* 1-8.

Winger, T. (2005, November). Grading to communicate. *Educational Leadership, 63(3),* 61-66.

Index

Ability grouping 120

Ability tests 37, 59, 105

Acceleration xvi, 3-4, 17-18, 22, 106, 120-124, 132, 198, 200, 202, 205
  Advanced Placement (AP) courses 122, 125
  combined classes 121
  concurrent enrollment 121
  early entrance 3
  focused 205
  International Baccalaureate (IB) programs 122
Post-Secondary Enrollment Options (PSOE) 122
  single-subject 3-4, 17
  whole-grade 106, 121, 123

Achievers 40, 120, 189

Age peers 5, 63, 70, 92-93, 123, 160, 161-162, 202-203

Anxiety 11, 14, 25, 34, 62, 69, 74, 77, 80, 88, 123, 129, 143-144, 180, 203

Aron, Elaine 142, 224, 231

Assessment xix, 59, 68, 82, 123, 139-140, 154, 178-180, 182, 184, 186, 198
  diagnostic 100, 178
  formative 178
  summative 178-179

Attention Deficit /Hyperactivity Disorder (ADD/ADHD) 56, 58, 60-71
  identification 63-65, 68-70
  medication 62, 199

Attribution theory 26-28

Auditory processing disorders 53-56, 71

Autonomy 30, 57, 134, 140, 149, 178

Betts, George 134, 224, 231

Bibliotherapy 129

Boredom 8, 39, 64, 69, 91, 192, 210

Boys
  and communication styles 191-193

Brain
  and dyslexia 50, 57-59, 68-71
  differences by sex 44, 190-193, 196
  growth 193

Bullying
  by gifted children 171-172
  of gifted children 19, 35, 94, 136, 149-150, 169-172, 194, 209

Camps 21, 129, 161

Carson, Ben 87, 231

Challenge xv-xvi, 16, 20, 22, 24, 29-30, 34, 36, 40, 45, 64, 80, 95, 99, 113-117, 119-132, 143, 150, 153, 157, 159, 176-179, 189, 205, 210-211, 214, 216, 218

Charter schools 18

Commitment 45, 114-115, 149-158

Compacting 121

Compassion 19, 43, 45, 114, 118, 159-172, 181, 199

Compensation 59, 63, 65, 69

Competition xviii, 36-37, 109, 122, 129, 133, 136, 155-156, 194-195

Constructivism 43, 177

Control 26-28, 30, 41, 43, 45, 60, 63-64, 69, 78, 94, 114-117, 133-147, 150, 158-159, 163, 191-193, 206
Csikszentmihalyi, Mihalyi 32, 113, 115-116, 223-224, 232
Cultures 19, 167, 182, 185-187, 189-190, 196
Cyberbullying 169, 171

Defiance 37, 39, 50, 77, 100
Depression 24, 36, 49, 62, 74, 80-83, 88
Differentiation 4, 8, 9, 16, 18, 33, 39, 97, 100-103, 105-106, 110, 119-120, 132-133, 169, 178, 194, 199, 205
Diversity xi, xv, 98, 182, 186
Dual exceptionality ("Twice exceptional") 54, 64, 71, 207
Duke University Talent Identification Program 21, 228
Dyslexia 50, 56-59, 68-71

Eating disorders 78, 82
Eisner, Eliot 181, 225, 232
Elitism 14-15, 107, 110
Exercise 65, 75, 78, 135, 140, 143, 195
Existential depression 81, 83
Extrinsic motivation 30-34, 44, 163
Extroversion 164

Failure xii-xiii, 14, 24-26, 28-29, 36-38, 74-75, 77-79, 114-115, 123, 126-128, 131-132, 160
Fear
  of failure xiii, 74-75
  of success xiii, 79-80
Feedback 33, 44, 97, 103, 115-116, 154, 166-167, 178-180
Flow theory 113-117, 119, 150
Foster, Joanne 105, 223, 227, 233
Friendships 92-95, 119, 122, 129, 144-145, 160-162, 164, 168, 172, 199, 202

Gardner, Howard xvii, 15-16, 221, 232
Gender differences 44, 94, 190
Goal theory 26, 28-29, 44
Grades 151-156, 158

Halsted, Judith Wynn 129, 224, 227, 233
Hearing loss 51-53
  and noise 53
Highly Qualified Teachers 11
Home schooling 19-20, 194-196
Hyperfocus 63

Identification 7-8, 22, 60, 63-65, 105, 108, 110, 186-187
  ability testing 23, 105
  achievement testing xix, 23, 34, 105, 120, 199
  multi-factored 22
  traits 5-8, 50, 63, 78
Individual Education Plan (IEP) 212-218
Intellectual peers 64, 70, 81, 92, 119
Intensity 73-74, 114, 141
Intervention Assistance Team (IAT) 74, 105, 180, 212
Intrinsic motivation 30-37, 42, 44, 101, 113, 116, 119, 156, 163, 178
Introversion 5, 70, 93, 159, 164-166, 172, 201
Iowa Acceleration Scale 123, 237, 231
IQ 105, 107-108, 203

Jensen, Eric 35, 222, 233
Johns Hopkins University Center for Talented Youth 20-21, 229

Key Learning Community xvii, 221

Laziness 37
Learning disabilities 5, 9, 49, 53-54, 56-58, 66-71, 98, 207, 213

Learning skills 40, 67
Locus of control 26-27, 41, 116
Loneliness 161

Magnet schools xvi, 59, 131
Mastery vs. Mystery perspective
105-106
Matthews, Dona 105, 223, 227, 233
McCourt, Frank 67, 88, 231
Mentors xvi, 66, 87-88, 106, 130-132,
138, 146, 181-182, 189, 193, 195
Metacognition 179
Minorities xvi xix, 97, 105, 176,
186, 189
and recruitment 186
and retention 187
Mixed-ability classroom 16-17, 105,
119
Motivation
extrinsic 30-34, 44, 163
intrinsic 30-37, 42, 44, 101, 113,
116, 119, 156, 163, 178
Motivation theories
Attribution Theory 26-28
Goal Theory 26, 28-29, 44
Self-Determination Theory 26,
29-30
Multiple intelligences xvii

No Child Left Behind Act xv, 10,
12, 99, 153, 175
Northwestern University Midwest
Talent Search 21

One-room schoolhouse 97-98
Optimism 42, 109, 131, 163, 183
Over-commitment 80-81, 95, 141,
145

Passive-aggressive behavior 38, 77
Peer pressure 19, 168
Perfectionism 36, 75-83, 121, 124,
128-129, 141, 145, 155, 160
and parents 126-127, 132
and teachers 126-127, 132

Perseveration 63
Peterson, Jean Sunde 169, 225, 234
Poverty 85-88, 95
Praise 34, 36-37, 43, 77, 87, 125,
166, 179, 201
Priority-setting 139-141
Procrastination 78-79, 143
Proficiency testing 12, 98

Referential speaking 201
Resilience 37, 82, 85-89, 91, 128-131,
145
and "the one" 91
Richards, Todd 57
Rimm, Sylvia 168, 224, 227, 234
Rivero, Lisa 195, 225, 227, 234
Rosenthal, Robert 44, 222, 235
Rubrics 109, 153-154

Self-concept 36-37, 76, 85, 134
Self-determination theory 26, 29-30
Self-esteem movement 36
Self-pacing 20, 100, 177, 178
Seligman, Martin 36, 163, 222, 224,
232, 235
Sensitivity 8, 11, 35, 49, 67, 73-74, 78,
80-81, 83, 92, 108, 114, 128-129,
141-142, 164, 166, 194
School-based budgeting xviii, xix
Silverman, Linda Kreger 14, 221,
224, 228, 235
Single-parent families 89-90
Single-sex classrooms 193-194
Sleep 8, 82, 135, 137-138, 140, 143,
193, 208
Sousa, David 15, 221-222, 235
Standardized testing 6, 10-14, 200-201,
204
and students 200-201
and teachers 200-201
Step-families 88-89
Stress 141-145, 147
Stress management 143-145
Submersion 39-40

Suicide 82
Summer programs 21, 161

Talent searches 20-21
Teachers
  and cultural ignorance 185-186
  and parents as partners delete
  and racism 187-189
  and self-care 184
Teasing 70, 94, 136, 203, 209
Test-taking strategies 200-201
Threat 24, 35, 37, 90, 149, 154, 195
Time management 40-41, 65,
  138-139, 141, 147, 155, 165
Tomlinson, Carol 12, 221, 223-224,
  228, 235
Too-busy families 90-92
Transitions 165, 197

Underachievement xiii, 8, 20, 24,
  38-40, 45, 138, 193

University of Denver 21
University of Iowa Belin-Blank 20,
  228
  Exceptional Student Talent Search
  20

Value-added analysis xix
Virtual schools 18-19
Vision loss 49-51
Visual processing disorders 53-56
Visual-spatial learners 57, 204

Whitley, Michael 20, 221
William and Mary, College of 176
Winfrey, Oprah 88, 231

Year-round schools xviii

About the Authors

Carol Strip Whitney, Ph.D., is a Gifted Education Specialist with the Olentangy School District in Lewis Center, Ohio, and author of *Helping Gifted Children Soar*. She is also an instructor at The Ohio State University, where she teaches three graduate-level courses in cognition, learning styles, and creativity. With more than 30 years of daily classroom interaction with gifted children, a terminal degree in the subject area, and frequent teaching of other teachers, she has both a theoretical and an in-the-trenches perspective on issues related to gifted students.

Carol is a three-time presenter at the National Association for Gifted Children and a frequent presenter at Ohio Association for Gifted Children, who honored her as the Ohio Gifted Educator of the Year. She also received the Ashland Inc. Golden Apple Teacher Achievement Award.

Since the publication of her first book, she has twice served as a consultant to the Frederick (MD) County Public Schools' Office of Gifted and Talented Education on the social and emotional needs of gifted learners. She was also the keynote speaker for a meeting of the Los Angeles Unified School District, with an audience of 4,000 educators. She has led parent groups throughout the state of Ohio for many years and has appeared frequently on radio and television in local markets and in Boston and Palm Beach.

Carol has been published in *Roeper Review, Instructor,* and *Gifted Child Today* and was selected to teach and consult at the Governor's Summer Institute for the Gifted at Denison University in Granville, Ohio. She established successful gifted programs in two of Ohio's fastest-growing school districts and has consulted with many other communities as they researched and established gifted programming. She also has served on the board of the Ohio Association for Gifted Coordinators and received the Communications Award from the Educational Facilities Center in Chicago.

Carol earned her undergraduate and master's degrees at Western Michigan University and her Ph.D. in curriculum development at The Ohio State University.

Gretchen Hirsch is the author of *Womanhours: A 21-Day Time Management Plan that Works* (St. Martin's Press) and *Talking Your Way to the Top: Business English that Works* (Prometheus Books). She coauthored *Bud Wilkinson: An Intimate Portrait of an American Legend* (Sagamore Publishing) and *Helping Gifted Children Soar: A Practical Guide for Parents and Teachers* (Great Potential Press), which received the Glyph Award for the Best Education Book published in the state of Arizona in 2000.

President of Midwest Book Doctors, Gretchen produces award-winning business communications and Web content for clients in finance, insurance, healthcare, and education, and she provides editorial services for nonfiction writers. She speaks frequently at professional meetings and writers' conferences on issues ranging from grammar and usage to time management for communicators. Gretchen is currently a writer in the Office of University Communications at Ohio Wesleyan University.